DEADLY DOSES

A Writer's Guide to Poisons

by
Serita Deborah Stevens, R.N., B.S.N.
with
Anne Klarner

Writer's Digest Books

Cincinnati, Ohio

Other fine Writer's Digest Books are available from your local bookstore or direct from the publisher.

01   00   99   98   97   10   9   8   7   6

Library of Congress Cataloging-in-Publication Data

Stevens, Serita Deborah
    Deadly doses: a writer's guide to poisons/by Serita Deborah Stevens with Anne Klarner.
        p. cm.
    Includes bibliographical references.
    ISBN 0-89879-371-8
    1. Poisons—Popular works. 2. Poisons—Handbooks, manuals, etc. I. Klarner, Anne   II. Title.
RA1213.S74   1990   90-12227
615.9—dc20   CIP

Dedicated to:

Al and Frances Mendelson for encouraging me to attend nursing school even though I wanted to write

Gary Klarner for putting up with everything

Special Thanks to:
Anthony S. Manoguerra, Pharm D., Director, San Diego Regional Poison Center for his help in reading our material and his invaluable suggestions

and to:
Marina Stajic, Ph.d., whose expertise helped this to be a better book

to:
Mary Mullane, mycologist, for her work on the mushrooms chapter

to:
Barbara Evans, Poisonous Plants, the Deadly Deception, *Pictorial Histories for her assistance with the plant chapter*

to:
Rayanne Moore for her invaluable help

Special Acknowledgement to:
Joyce Madison, SoCal MWA Chapter President/Regional Vice-President 1987-88 for bringing us together and her assistance throughout the whole book

Contents

Introduction

*All things are poisons, for there is nothing without poisonous qualities.
It is only the dose which makes a thing poison.*
—Paracelsus, 1493-1541

Poisoning is a serious business. Once the preferred method of murder, homicidal poisoning has somewhat fallen in popularity because modern pathologists can detect almost any poison. Of course, the pathologist must know which poison to test for. There are, in fact, very few poisons that are ideal—odorless, colorless, tasteless, quick acting, and nontraceable. Many poisons meet one, two, even three of the criteria; many drugs have their own built-in clues for the detective.

Definition of Poison What is a poison? *Webster's New Collegiate Dictionary* defines poison as "a substance that through its chemical action usually kills, injures, or impairs an organism" or "a substance that inhibits the activity of another substance or the course of a reaction or process." Anything in a large enough dose can prove toxic. Our concern in this book is feasibly deadly doses.

If death by poison is involved, the writer owes the reader a respect for the reader's intelligence. This is why *Deadly Doses: A Writer's Guide to Poisons* was written. All too often, a writer loses credibility by creating a world very similar to the real one, then shattering it by using an incorrect fact. Poisons are a time-honored part of mystery fiction. Yet, too often a writer will have a victim swallow something and collapse, dying instantly, when in real life the poison would have taken at least twenty minutes to act. Or just as often, the victim's symptoms could not possibly have been caused by the substance given. Many readers would not know the difference, but those who do would find the story ruined because of it.

Until now, the writer has had trouble finding correct information about poisons. Agatha Christie had the advantage of working in a hospital pharmacy during World War I. Most other writers must ask questions where they can and go by what little information they have, or they struggle through materials written in medicalese, trying to make sense of such terms as *tachycardia, oliguria,* or *uremia.*

Deadly Doses is written in understandable English. All medical terms are in the glossary. Symptoms, forms, methods of administration, and reactions are cross-referenced, so writers who need a poison that will turn the victim yellow can turn to the symptoms appendix and find which poisons change a person's coloring.

Lethal Poisons This book deals with acute poisoning, as opposed to chronic poisoning. A chronic poisoning takes place when an antagonist slowly administers more and more of a given poison and eventually kills the victim. As this process can take years and does not guarantee death, this book focuses on more certain methods, except in a few cases where chronic poisoning could produce other symptoms helpful to a writer.

The majority of the poisons described are lethal immediately or in short periods of time. Some toxins, however, take more time to work. During that time, the killer must prevent the victim from seeking medical aid. Therefore, the quicker the better guided us.

Taste is an issue that is usually a problem. Most poisons have a bitter taste that needs to be hidden if the poison is to be swallowed. In real life, the old trick of slipping a barbiturate into a cocktail could not work unless the victim habitually gulped drinks or was a complete innocent with no idea of how a drink should taste. Admittedly, not all poisons taste bitter, but the people in the best position to know the tastes of many of these substances are no longer around to say what they are. It is best to assume, unless otherwise noted, that the poison in question has a bad taste.

The symptoms and toxicity ratings given in this book vary from person to person. This is because human beings are, as Shakespeare says, creatures of infinite variety. Alcoholics do not feel the effects of drinking as quickly as teetotalers do. An old lady with a bad heart can die from a dosage that would only cause a stomachache in her healthier daughter. When writing, it is best to avoid the exceptions to the rules, unless the exception is the whole point of the story. For the purposes of this handbook, it is assumed that the victim is a healthy specimen weighing approximately one hundred and fifty pounds.

It is possible that a preferred poison has been overlooked. Given the space limitations, some poisons simply could not be included. And many poisons lethal in large doses needed too much to kill. Others were not as poisonous as myth would have them. Tear gas, for example, has not been included, since the worst it can do is give the victim second-degree burns. Many household chemicals are not as toxic to adults as they are to young children.

The goal of this book is to give the average writer correct information on poisons. However, as writers' interests vary, so does their understanding of medicine and chemical science. Just as some doctors might be confused by legal briefs, so some lawyers might find necrosis and dyspnea foreign. The authors have assumed no medical expertise on the part of the reader. Check the glossary to find the definitions of all the medical terms used in this book.

Remember that in addition to providing correct information about poisons, this book can also be useful for story ideas. Poisonous chemicals are not to be taken lightly in real life, but the right poison can move the plot of a good story along nicely—and how nice it is to have correct facts!

Toxicology Rating Chart

The poisons in this book have been rated in terms of relative toxicity, with six (6) being supertoxic, requiring only a minuscule amount to cause death, and one (1) being practically nontoxic except in immense doses. Actual dosages do not seem to be an issue in current literature; therefore, a more specific rating system was deemed unnecessary. Few poisons in this book are rated one (1) or two (2), as they probably would not be useful to the mystery writer with a plot to advance.

Toxicity	Probable Oral Lethal Dose for 150 pound Human Being	
6 Supertoxic	less than 5 mg/kg	A taste (less than seven drops)
5 Extremely toxic	5-50 mg/kg	Between seven drops and one teaspoon
4 Very toxic	50-500 mg/kg	Between one teaspoon and one ounce
3 Moderately toxic	0.5-5 gm/kg	Between one ounce and one pint or pound
2 Slightly toxic	5-15 gm/kg	Between one pint and one quart
1 Almost nontoxic	above 15 gm/kg	More than one quart or 2.2 pounds

NOTE: The notations mg/kg and gm/kg can be confusing. They refer to milligrams (mg) or grams (gm) of basic substance to kilograms (kg) of host substance—in this specific case, milligrams or grams of poison required per kilogram of potential victim.

O N E

A SHORT HISTORY OF THE DREADED ART

Revolted by the odious crime of homicide, the chemist's aim is to perfect the means of establishing proof of poisoning so that the heinous crime will be brought to light and proved to the magistrate who must punish the criminal.

—Matthew J. B. Orfila
Traité de toxicologie (1814)

Man's first discovery of poisons probably came about by trial and error. While gathering different plants for food, foragers soon found some were deadly. Those who held knowledge of poisons were regarded with respect and fear; they might be venerated as tribal sorcerers or burned at the stake.

Though the first written accounts of homicidal poisoning come from the Roman Empire around the time of Christ, the early Sumerians, Indians, Chinese, Greeks, and Egyptians had already practiced the sophisticated art of poisoning for centuries.

In her search for the perfect suicidal poison, Cleopatra reportedly used her prisoners and slaves as guinea pigs. Her recorded reports indicate she was not satisfied with the effects of either henbane (*Hyoscyamus niger*) or belladonna (*Atropa belladonna*) since despite their rapid action, they produced too much pain. She was also further disappointed with *Strychnos nux-vomica*, from which strychnine was eventually extracted, because although the action was rapid, it produced convulsions that left facial features distorted at death. She finally selected the bite of the asp (small African cobra), whose venom produced a serene and prompt death.

There is an unlikely legend from the second century B.C. about the Greek king Mithradates VI who was in the habit of ingesting a little bit of every known poison so as to build immunity to them. In fact, since many poisons are fatal in minute doses, he would have quickly succumbed. However, many cultures have similar customs of consuming poison in small increased doses and so become immune to them—exactly what Dorothy L. Sayers had her villain in *Strong Poison* do. Alexander Dumas wrote about this subject also in *The Count of Monte Cristo*.

The use of poisons in trial-by-ordeal, on arrowheads, or as instruments of state by popes and princes of the Renaissance provided a fund of empirical knowledge that paved the way for the pharmacology of modern times. Such drugs as digitalis, ouabain, and atropine owe their existence to the scientific investigation of plant preparation used for killing animals and humans.

Poisoning in the Middle Ages

The Borgias of fifteenth-century Rome were a dynasty of poisoners who contributed greatly to the art. If someone said something that Cesare Borgia did not like, the speaker was apt to be invited to a party and would become quite ill afterwards. Experimenting with poisons involved trying them out on people with a complete disregard for life or death, and it was not always necessary to bring about death. Merely a warning often sufficed to quiet traitorous voices and offer a foretaste of what would happen if they did not behave.

The food during the era was so highly spiced that often it was impossible to taste alien flavors and one could easily take a poison without noticing; thus, most royalty employed the food taster who would eat a bite of each dish and wait. If nothing happened to him after a short period of time, the king would then consume his meal. However, that did little to sway the serious poisoner.

When Catherine de Médicis, the Italian princess, came to France to marry Henry Deux, she brought with her, as was customary, her train of attendants. Noted among these were the *parfumeurs* and astrologers. Royal use often secreted the making of poisons in the guise of these two occupations. And no sooner had Catherine arrived in France than mysterious illnesses and deaths began. Arsenic, the best-known poison of the time, formed the basis of the Borgias' *cantarella*.

Aqua toffana, or *aquetta di Napoli*, is another poison associated with the Médicis. Thought to be arsenic and cantharides, it was reportedly created by an Italian countess, Toffana. Four to six drops of this poison in water or wine was enough to deliver a painless death in a few hours. But there were other poisons of the time. Water hemlock, foxglove, henbane, and the prussic acid of the almond tree were all found in the Parisian woods and meadows. In France, the description *Italien* soon became synonymous with *Empoisonneur*.

Foremost among Catherine de Médicis' victims was the Dauphin Francois, who, having played an active game of tennis, asked for water. It was brought him by his *Italien* cupbearer. The dauphin died moments later and the cupbearer, under torture, admitted the poisoning. The next to die was the Cardinal of Lorraine, an old enemy of Catherine de Médici. His death came right after handling some money treated with a poison that penetrated his skin pores. A guess might be nicotine, just then discovered in the New World.

Another famous poison of that time was *venin de crapaud*. To obtain this, arsenic was fed to toads and other creatures. When they died, juices were distilled from their bodies.

In the early 1600s, notorious poisoner Antonio Exili toured the courts of Europe from the Vatican to Sweden and France to the Baltic countries, making his services welcome by some and feared by others. He boasted he could supply death in any form — lingering, quick, painful, or gentle as sleep. He even claimed he could foretell the hour, even a month ahead, when a healthy man would die.

La Voisin, a perfumer of Louis XIV's court, was well known for her sideline. Many royal relationships ended by her hand. Almost as famous was Christopher Glaser, a well-known Swiss chemist, who was noted for his antidotes to poison and soon became the favorite of many royals. His specialty was theriaca, a compound containing opium and numerous other drugs. Milk was another antidote he espoused, which royals then drank in large quantities for fear of someone slipping poison in their food. Unfortunately, a poisoner named Sainte-Croix seduced Glaser into the nefarious business of death, by showing him how much more money could be made by killing people than by curing them. Glaser committed suicide when it appeared likely he'd been found out.

Marie D'Aubray, Sainte-Croix's mistress, murdered her numerous family members to inherit the family fortune. Going in the guise of charity, she brought food and tested her poisons on the local hospital patients. Sainte-Croix himself died while looking for a poison that could kill with one sniff. He evidently found it but was unable to pass on the information.

Knowledge of many of the poisons used in the fifteenth, sixteenth, and seventeenth centuries, however, has disappeared with time.

Formal Study of Poison

Bernard Serturner isolated morphine from opium around 1805, but the formal study of poison began early in the ninteenth century when physiologist Claude Bernard researched the effects of curare, a vegetable poison used by South American Indians to poison their arrows. During the industrial revolution the findings of two scientists — Matthew J. B. Orfila and his colleague Francois-Vincent Raspail — were especially important. Orfila, considered the founder of modern toxicology, experimented with and cataloged poisons and their effects. His book *Traité des Poisons on Toxicologie General* was published in 1814. In 1829, Robert Christison published *Treatise on Poisons*.

Arsenic, the poisoner's favorite, was tracked down by James Marsh around 1836. It was Orfila, however, who applied the Marsh test to biological specimens, and it was his testimony as an expert witness that convicted Madame Lefarge in one of the world's most famous arsenic cases.

Marie Cappelle, a poor relation to the royal family, had married Charles Lefarge. The marriage was an unhappy one and when Charles fell ill in 1839, his wife attempted to nurse him. Despite or because of her ministrations, he became sicker. One of the servants saw Marie mixing a white powder into Charles's drink and when Charles died the next day, Marie was accused. She insisted that the fact that she had arsenic in the house to kill the rats had nothing to do with her husband's death. Two toxicologists claimed he could not have died from the arsenic, but Orfila showed there was substantial arsenic in the man's body. Marie was sentenced to life in prison and died in 1852 after writing her story.

By 1830, chemical analysis could detect most mineral compounds, but not organic poisons. In 1851, the Belgian chemist Jean Servais Stas was the first to discover a technique for extracting alkaloid poisons while investigating a homicide by nicotine. He was the first to isolate nicotine from postmortem tissue.

Use of poison as a favorite criminal weapon declined considerably when methods of detecting poisons improved and advances in medical care made it less likely the victim would die.

Modern Toxicology

With the beginning of the twentieth century, industry increased and so did the chemicals available for poisoning. Many drugs were produced by synthesis to replace or improve effects of the naturally occurring vegetable or animal substances.

The advent of synthetic drugs added to the problems of toxicologists. After World War II, barbiturate use became widespread, and the suicide rate increased. In 1954, the number of barbiturate suicides increased twelve times the number in 1938. During that time, people who had taken an overdose of barbiturates died at a rate of about fifteen to twenty-five per hundred, regardless of how quickly they received medical care. Today, the percentage of mortality, if the victim is hospitalized in time, is negligible.

In 1962, causes of death by poisoning in a worldwide survey listed 67 to 73 percent suicides, 30 percent accidents, and only .52 percent as homicides. Of course, one never knows how many of those suicides or accidents were really disguised homicides.

The National Clearing House for Poison Control Centers in the United States indicates that medicines for internal use are the most used for poisoning, followed by those for external use, cleaning fluids and other domestic products, pesticides or plant poisons, vegetable alkaloids, with gas and fumes being the least used to kill or commit suicide.

The Statistical Abstract of the United States-1988 indicates that carbon monoxide and gases still fall last in deaths by poison.

For several centuries people ignored the antidotes, concentrating only on the use of poisons for killing. Therefore, the use of antidotes is not as exact as it should be, and many superstitions have arisen regarding remedies. Once such myth is that milk is a universal antidote. The fact is that milk is not an antidote but a dilutant in many cases.

Salt water, once another common first-aid measure, has recently been shown to be dangerous. While intended to dilute and absorb poison in the stomach, large amounts of sodium chloride can bring on fatal heart attacks, especially in victims already weakened. Of course, since this information is relatively new, the killer trying to get rid of her maiden aunt could say she was only doing what she thought best.

No antidote should be attempted without medical supervision, since many supposed antidotes can cause more harm than the poison. For the purposes of this book, however, a dangerous antidote could become part of the murder plot.

M. J. B. Orfila, and others who researched the universal antidote, came to the idea that a universal antidote should be abandoned entirely. The use of any antidote depends on the type and amount of the drug taken, how it was administered, and the time delay between ingestion and medical treatment. In many cases, since each poison produces a variety of symptoms, all that can be done is to take care of these symptoms as they arise.

The science of toxicology is not static. New analytical methodologies, new antidotes, and new methods of treatment are being developed every day, and the network of poison and drug knowledge is expanding accordingly throughout the world. Forensic medicine and toxicology have always been closely linked, since toxicology deals with detection and identification of poison as well as with interpretation of their effects on the human body.

T W O

THE CLASSIC POISONS: ARSENIC, CYANIDE, AND STRYCHNINE

MARTHA: Well, dear, for a gallon of elderberry wine, I take one teaspoonful of arsenic, and add a half a teaspoonful of strychnine, and then just a pinch of cyanide.

—Joseph Kesselring
Arsenic and Old Lace

Arsenic, cyanide, and strychnine have been grouped into this chapter more because of their popularity than because of any relation they have to each other. Arsenic is a metal and acute poisoning affects the digestive system. Cyanide interferes with the use of oxygen by the body's cells. Strychnine is a stimulant that works on the central nervous system.

Arsenic

Arsenic is an element, which means it cannot be broken down further into different chemicals. It is found in the manufacture of opal glass, ceramics, enamels, paints, wallpapers, weed killers, insecticides, rodenticides, and pesticides as well as in textile printing, tanning, and taxidermy, thus making it one of the more accessible toxins.

Historically, arsenic was the murderer's most popular tool, primarily because it was found in so many common household items from wallpaper and paste to paints and pesticides. Nobody thought anything if you went into the pharmacy (chemists in Great Britain) to get rat poison. Of course, the Borgias and de Médicis had their own private supply.

Traces of arsenic are present in all human tissues. It is the twentieth most commonly encountered element of 103 known elements.

Name: Arsenic. *Other*: White arsenic, gray arsenic, metallic arsenic, arsenic trioxide, arsenous oxide, arsenic trihydride.

Toxicity: 5.

Form: Arsenic in its pure natural state is a gray metal. Most often it is found as arsenic trioxide — a white powder. In homicidal or suicidal cases, arsenic is generally swallowed. It can also be inhaled either as a dust or as arsine gas, with the gas producing somewhat different symptoms than the dust. Inhalation is generally a result of industrial exposure.

Effects and Symptoms: It is not completely certain, but most experts believe that arsenic interferes with the function of vital enzymes in the body. Side effects usually occur in chronic poisonings and include jaundiced skin. After longer periods of ingestion, the victim develops a rash that flakes away, called exfoliative dermatitis. Arsenic can be carcinogenic, causing skin cancer.

The best-known symptom of arsenic poisoning is severe gastric distress. In fact, before the poisoning could be diagnosed, Victorian physicians often called it "gastric fever." Other symptoms include burning esophageal pain, vomiting, and diarrhea with blood. The skin becomes cold and clammy to the touch, and the blood pressure falls so that the victim becomes dizzy and weak. Convulsions and coma are the final signs, and death usually comes from circulatory failure.

In cases where death is not immediate, the skin is jaundiced and the victim becomes restless and has headaches, dizzy spells, and an inability to void. Occasionally, there will be moments of paralysis. Because arsenic is an element and does not break down, it remains in the victim's hair, fingernails, and urine. In the case of immediate death, however, the pathologist will find only an inflamed stomach and possibly some arsenic in the digestive tract. Red blood cells are destroyed in the veins, and the body may look somewhat yellow and take on the appearance of someone who's been very sick.

If death is delayed by several days, arsenic will show up in the liver and kidney.

Chronic arsenic poisoning causes the victim to experience burning pains in the hands and feet, numbing sensation throughout the body, localized swelling and skin irritations, hair loss, cirrhosis of the liver, nausea, vomiting, cramps, weight loss, visual impairment, and finally cardiac failure.

Reaction Time: Symptoms begin as early as one-half hour after ingestion. In acute conditions, death may occur in a few hours or take as long as twenty-four hours.

Antidotes and Treatments: In acute arsenic poisoning, the first measure a physician will take is to pump the stomach (gastric lavage). Then the victim will probably be given dimercaprol for two to three days to bind the arsenic, and after that penicillamine until the arsenic level in the urine goes down. In the meantime, the physician will also treat dehydration, shock, pulmonary edema, anuria, and liver damage. In severe cases, the victim may be put on a kidney dialysis machine after the dimercaprol therapy to remove the dimercaprol and the arsenic. Milk is often used since it acts as a demulcent and a "binder" for arsenic and other heavy metals.

Case Histories: Although scientists have found ways to detect arsenic in autopsy specimens, murderers still use this poison.

Modern forensic tests on samples of Napoleon's hair saved over the years have found arsenic. While Napoleon did believe he was being poisoned, in addition to rumors of the same, it is also a fact that arsenic was a common ingredient in the dyes used in wallpapers of the time. Vapors from this wallpaper could account for the traces in the samples.

In the 1970s, a man was admitted to a hospital complaining of weight loss, severe gastric problems, hair loss, numbness, and skin rashes. Test upon test was done, all proving negative. The physicians were at a loss as to what was wrong with this patient. At the nursing desk, one physician overheard several nursing students talking about the case. One, who read a lot of mysteries, jokingly said, "Maybe he's being poisoned with arsenic." The physician stared at her a moment, shrugged, and wrote the order to test the patient's arsenic levels. All were shocked when the tests came back positive. Only then was it discovered the patient's wife had been giving him poison in his morning coffee. No wonder he thought he was drinking espresso!

In the early eighteenth century, a Frenchman with a penchant for beautiful, rich wives decided to "pleasure" his women before killing them, much as in snuff movies today. Using a thin goatskin sheath on his penis to protect himself, he placed a lethal dose of arsenic on the sheath. The poison absorbed in the women's vaginas during sexual intercourse, and they died shortly thereafter. Only his carelessness, and the fact that so many of his wives had met ill fate, made the authorities suspicious. He was found guilty and hanged.

Among other famous cases is Mary Ann Cotton, a thrice-married forty-year-old nurse who, in 1871, was considered Britain's greatest mass murderer. She was accused of fifteen deaths, though twenty-one people close to her died in twenty years. Among them were all her children, the children of her three husbands, two of her lovers, and several neighbors. The children all suffered from "gastric fever," and suspicion arose when the physician refused to issue a death certificate. All the exhumed bodies showed arsenic. Cotton's defense argued the children had been poisoned accidentally by arsenic contained in the green floral wallpaper used in their home. But her purchase of soft soap and arsenic—to be used, she said, for cleaning bedsteads and killing bedbugs—proved fatal to her case. Mary Ann Cotton was found guilty and sentenced to death.

There are numerous other cases in history, but among our favorite literary cases is *Strong Poison* by Dorothy Sayers. White arsenic was slipped to the victim in an omelette prepared at the table by the killer. The book stands out because it also uses arsenic tolerance as the key to its solution.

Notes: Arsenic's primary symptoms of stomach distress are the same as for any number of stomach disorders that are usually lumped together under the catch-all diagnosis of gastroenteritis.

In cases of chronic poisoning, arsenic can cause conjunctivitis. Humans can develop a tolerance for the poison, such as the case of the arsenic eaters throughout the centuries who made a practice of having arsenic daily. One of the tests of the Hell Fire Club of Regency and Victorian England was to see how much arsenic and other poisons one could consume without being affected.

Cyanide

Hydrocyanic acid and its sodium and potassium salts, like arsenic, have many industrial uses. Hydrocyanic acid acts quite rapidly and occurs naturally in a large variety of seeds and pits, including those of the *Prunus* genus, such as the peach, apricot, apple, wild cherry, plum, or jetberry bush. Many other plants have cyanogenetic glycosides, which take longer to react but will have a similar effect. In addition to containing cyanogenetic glycosides, apricot pits are used to make Laetrile, an anticancer drug.

Hydrogen cyanide has many uses, such as a fumigant, insecticide, rodenticide, electroplating solution, and metal polish.

Name: Cyanide. *Other*: Potassium cyanide, sodium cyanide, and hydrogen cyanide are the most common forms of cyanide. Prussic acid is hydrogen cyanide or hydrocyanic acid.

Toxicity: 6.

Form: Potassium cyanide and sodium cyanide are white solids bearing a faint bitter-almond odor. Hydrogen cyanide is a gas. Cyanide, in its various forms, can be swallowed, inhaled, or absorbed through the skin. It is generally released from its host compound by acids, such as the hydrochloric acid found in the stomach. The poison in the seeds is released only if the seeds are chewed.

Effects and Symptoms: Cyanide interferes with the enzymes controlling the oxidative process, preventing the body's red blood cells from absorbing oxygen. Cyanide action has been called "internal asphyxia."

Swallowing or smelling a toxic dose of cyanide as a gas or a salt can cause immediate unconsciousness, convulsions, and death within one to fifteen minutes or longer. If an amount near the lethal dose is absorbed through the skin, inhaled, or swallowed the symptoms noted will be rapid respiration, a gasping for breath, dizziness, flushing, headache, nausea, vomiting, rapid pulse, and a drop in blood pressure causing fainting. Convulsions precede death within four hours except in the case of sodium nitroprusside. Here death can be delayed as long as twelve hours after ingestion.

The famous bitter-almond odor can be a clue and may be noticeable at autopsy, but not everyone is capable of smelling it. The victim's blood may appear cherry red, as in carbon monoxide poisoning, and the corpse may have skin pinker than normal.

Reaction Time: Usually immediate or nearly so. With a sufficient amount, death may occur in as little as one to fifteen minutes. In gaseous forms, death can be instantaneous.

Antidotes and Treatments: If a victim is going to be saved, it must be done within the first half-hour after the poison is given.

Amyl nitrite is administered first. If the cyanide is ingested, the stomach is pumped. In both inhalation and ingestion cases, the victim is given artificial respiration with 100 percent oxygen. Afterward, an intravenous injection of sodium nitrite is given followed by an injection of sodium thiosulfate. Dicobalt edetate (a.k.a. Kelocyanor), most toxic of all the antidotes, can be used, but only when cyanide poisoning is clearly evident, and only outside of the United States, as it is not available here.

All cyanide antidotes are poisonous themselves. They must be used carefully, and as such could be useful in a plot with a murderous doctor wishing to deflect suspicion by first poisoning the victim, then killing him with the cure. However, the antidotes are not as toxic when counteracting the cyanide.

Victims who live four hours will probably recover.

Case Histories: Lizzie Borden, who is said to have killed her parents with an axe, was also suspected of using prussic acid, a form of cyanide, on them prior to their dismemberment. Police found traces of the poison in the sugar bowl.

In another incident, Roland B. Molineux, a New York City factory worker, joined the famed Knickerbocker Athletic Club in 1868. He sought the attentions of an attractive young woman who was interested in another young man. When that young man died mysteriously, it was said he had taken a poison he had received in the mail. The young woman married Molineux. Weeks later, Molineux quarreled with a weight lifter who bested him at the club. The following week, the weight lifter received a bottle of Bromo Seltzer in the mail.

When his landlady complained of a headache, the weight lifter gave her some of the medication. She complained of a bitter taste, went into convulsions, and died. The Bromo had contained mercury cyanide, which was later traced back to a purchase Molineux had made for his factory. The factory worker was at first found guilty and then acquitted on appeal in 1902.

Rasputin, the mad Russian monk, reportedly consumed a normally lethal dose of cyanide served him by would-be assassins. No one could understand why he survived the attempt, and, in frustration, he was shot and finally drowned. It was conjectured later that a lack of sufficient hydrochloric acid in the monk's stomach prevented a fatal reaction.

During World War II, the Nazis used hydrogen cyanide in their gas chambers. The same gas has also been used to execute criminals and is the prescribed means of death in California and ten other states.

Spy stories abound with the secret cyanide pellets. The Allies in World War II supposedly made a special bullet with a cyanide tip to insure the deaths of Nazi attackers.

One interesting case of cyanide poisoning involves Richard Brinkley, a midwestern carpenter who, in 1969, befriended a seventy-seven-year-old widow. He forged a will leaving all her money to him and obtained her signature by obscuring the papers' contents and telling her he was collecting signatures for a political cause. In much the same way, he obtained signatures of two witnesses. When the woman died days later, Brinkley produced the will, which the widow's granddaughter contested.

Brinkley brought a cyanide-laced bottle of drink as a gift for one of the witnesses, but the witness's landlord and his wife and daughter saw the bottle and decided to sample it. Only the daughter survived and Brinkley was hanged at Wandsworth Prison.

In Chicago several people died in 1983 when they took cyanide-laced capsules of Extra-Strength Tylenol. With help from the Tylenol company, the Chicago police proved that the capsules had been tampered with. The killer was never found, but Tylenol and other pain reliever manufacturers no longer make capsules. Personal product packaging is now almost tamper-proof.

Agatha Christie frequently did her victims in with poisons, and cyanide was one of her favorites. *Endless Night* featured two cyanide poisonings disguised as riding accidents. The second victim was found almost immediately after her poisoning while the bitter-almond scent still lingered, and thus gave the murder away. Emily Brent from *Ten Little Indians* was injected with cyanide after being knocked unconscious with chloral hydrate in her coffee. Tea hid the cyanide in *A Pocket Full of Rye*. In *Remembered Death*, a supposed suicide took place in which the victim drank cyanide-laced champagne.

In Isaac Asimov's *Whiff of Death*, the fictional killer used potassium cyanide gas. The potential victim, an unlikable student chemist, was alone in his lab. The killer had previously mixed chemicals, knowing the student would check the experiment and wouldn't ask for help. Even though the room was open, the poisonous vapor was released in an area covered with a metal hood and fan specially designed to contain poisonous gases created by experiments. When the student leaned over to check the chemical process, he inhaled the gas and died.

In *Sudden Death*, William Kienzle killed off an obnoxious football player by combining DMSO, a chemical that opens the skin's pores, with cyanide and putting it in the player's shampoo bottle.

Notes: Apricot kernels, widely available in health food stores, have been associated with cyanide poisoning. One man was poisoned after eating forty-eight kernels roasted at 300 degrees for ten minutes. Laetrile, made from apricot kernels, has also caused fatal cyanide poisoning.

Some cyanogenetic plants include mahogany, Christmas berry, cherry laurel, choke-cherry, pin cherry, wild black cherry, flax, yellow pine-flax, velvet-grass, Johnson-grass, Sudan-grass, arrow-grass, and small arrowgrass.

Strychnine

While strychnine is not the fastest-acting poison, it is certainly one of the most startling. The drama of a victim jackknifing back and forth in agony while in the final throes of strychnine poisoning may account for its popularity in literature and film. Strychnine, however, is not that popular for real-life homicides.

The convulsive effects were first documented in 1818, and the poison was later developed for medicinal purposes as a stimulant. Presently it's used primarily as a rodent poison. It can also be found as a component of various tonics and cathartic pills used to cure nausea.

Name: Strychnine. *Other*: Dog button, mole-nots, mole death.

Toxicity: 6.

Form: Strychnine is a colorless, crystalline powder with a bitter taste. The substance is usually swallowed but can poison by skin or eye contact. It can also be inhaled as a dust.

The substance occurs naturally in some seeds and plants, in particular the dog button plant, *Strychnos nux-vomica*, which grows in India and other tropical places such as Hawaii. The fruits resemble a mandarin or Chinese orange in shape and color and are borne abundantly in March. The seeds resemble gray-velvet covered buttons as large as nickels. The fruits are attractive-looking, and many people are tempted to eat them despite their somewhat bitter taste.

The entire tree contains strychnine but the seeds contain the greatest concentration. The blossoms have an odor resembling curry powder and are a potential cause of poisoning since they might easily be eaten by a child or even added to food as a condiment.

Effects and Symptoms: Strychnine attacks the central nervous system and causes exaggerated reflex effects, which results in all the muscles contracting at the same time. The strychnine victim dies from asphyxiation or sheer exhaustion from the convulsions.

Symptoms start with the victim's neck and face becoming stiff. Arms and legs spasm next. The spasms become increasingly worse, until the victim is almost continuously in an arched-back position with the head and feet on the floor or other surface. The slightest sound or movement will generate spasms. Rigor mortis sets in immediately upon death, leaving the body in the convulsed position with eyes wide open and extreme facial grimace.

The symptoms of strychnine poisoning are almost the same as those of tetanus or lockjaw.

Reaction Time: Ten to twenty minutes approximately, longer if given on a full stomach.

Antidotes and Treatments: The stomach can be pumped and activated charcoal administered if the victim is caught before the symptoms start. This is also done after the spasms have been brought under control. The convulsions can be controlled by slow intravenous administering of succinylcholine, which is dangerous itself, or Valium. While spasms are occurring, the victim needs to be kept quiet since any loud noise or sudden light will cause the intensity of the spasms to increase.

Case Histories: As with the other two poisons in this chapter, strychnine poisoning has numerous case histories.

Dr. Thomas Neill Cream, a Chicago physician, was typical of most murderers, thinking he would never be caught. Having poisoned the husband of his current mistress, Cream then wrote a letter to the district attorney suggesting the body be exhumed. He seemed to take pride in his accomplishment and was sent to prison.

Upon release in 1891, Cream headed to London. There he frequented Lambeth Palace Road where several prostitutes plied their trade. One by one, he gave them pills containing strychnine. Four young women died and, as before, Cream put an ad in the papers for information leading to the arrest of the "Lambeth poisoner." Despite this, Scotland Yard picked him up.

Prostitute Louisa Harvey related how Cream had stayed the night with her and offered her pills for her acne. He had insisted she swallow them there, but Louisa had managed to palm the pills and had dropped them into a pot. A chemist identified Cream as having bought the pills. Cornered, Cream gave a lecture to the jury, speaking eloquently of the poisoner's trade. The jury found him guilty in twelve minutes, and he was hanged on November 15, 1892.

In 1924, Jean-Pierre Vaquier, a vain forty-five-year-old Frenchman, poisoned his lover's husband with strychnine-laced "bromo-salts." After meeting with Mary Jones, his mistress, to plot her husband's demise, Vaquier followed her to London and there went to a chemist's shop. He purchased twenty grams of perchloride of mercury and twelve grams of strychnine, saying they were for wireless experiments and signed the poison book, which all chemists were required to keep.

Joining his lover and her husband at a party at their London hotel, Vaquier noted the husband drinking heavily. When Mr. Jones needed some Bromo Seltzer, Vaquier offered him the bottle kept behind the counter with a lethal dose. "My God! They are bitter!" Mr. Jones said. Within a short time, Jones had died in agony, and postmortem examination found strychnine. Mary and Jean-Pierre tried to wash out the bottle, but traces still remained. Vaquier was identified by the chemist and hanged in August of 1924.

During the same time period, Californian Eva Rablen poisoned her deaf husband, Carroll. Fun loving and a good dancer, Eva often went to the local parties and Carroll would go along reluctantly since he could neither hear the music nor dance. One April night, Carroll decided to stay in the car, finding it too much to watch his wife dancing with others.

At midnight, Eva came out, bringing her husband coffee and refreshments. Seconds later, he was writhing in agony. His cries brought several parties to his aid. Before dying, he complained of the bitter taste of the coffee. Eva was accused of poisoning Carroll for the insurance, and a thorough search of the dance hall located a bottle of strychnine with the address of a local pharmacy. The label had Eva's name on it. The coffee cup showed traces of the strychnine, and Carroll's stomach contents proved murder beyond a doubt. Pleading guilty, Eva was given life-imprisonment.

The Mysterious Affair at Styles, Agatha Christie's first novel, was a strychnine killing of the lady of the house. The killer hid the bitter

taste of the poison by putting it in the lady's evening hot chocolate. Strychnine does in Mr. Appleton of *The Mysterious Mr. Quinn*.
Notes: Doses less than necessary to cause acute poisoning will show no symptoms. South American missionaries reputedly take minute doses of strychnine to rid themselves of intestinal worms.

T H R E E

HOUSEHOLD POISONS

The house was blessedly silent as Geri headed up toward the bathroom,
ready to begin her cleaning. She wouldn't have to pick Kim up from
nursery school for several hours yet. At the tub she stared down at the
mess her daughter had made and, taking out the ammonia, she began
to scrub. No effect. Well, maybe bleach was needed. The strong odor
assailed her in a moment, dizziness had struck. Surprised, Geri sank
down on the toilet seat, not understanding what was happening. She
was still unconscious when her husband found her several hours later.

> — adapted from
> Northwestern Memorial
> Hospital Emergency
> Room Record, 1973
> Chicago, Illinois

Given the huge number of chemicals in the home, it's surprising that relatively few are lethal. Because they can do severe damage, however, and many will kill small children, these potential poisons should be stored carefully.

In pre-1970 households, lethal products abounded, so characters in a novel set in this time or before would have access to stronger detergents and poisons. One of the many changes made is in the type of gas found in the home. Illuminating gas used in gaslamps around the house in the 1890s and as late as the 1950s in some remote areas would kill quickly because many of them contained carbon monoxide. Nothing in use today is quite as lethal. According to the gas company, since methods of manufacturing the gas have changed, putting a victim's head in the stove à la poetess Sylvia Plath will cause illness but might not kill because the gas today is not the same as coal gas used in the 1920s through 1960s. However, all gases eventually suffocate the person because they replace oxygen. Therefore, the gas kills (despite what the gas company would have you believe) even though it might take a great deal longer than in past days, and the room must be sealed.

Although a common poison cited by medical references, carbon monoxide is not technically a household poison. For the purposes of this book, however, carbon monoxide poisoning is being listed here since many instances of death due to carbon monoxide suffocation occur in sealed garages with the car engine running. (*Also see industrials.*)

There are several other interesting household items accessible to the mystery writer. Many will recall the Twenty Mule Team Borax commercials. Borax, a laundry agent, contains boric acid, which will be discussed further in the industrial section. Boric acid, also found in the medicine chest as an antiseptic, is often used for eye injuries in diluted amounts.

Those who go camping can find propane fuel useful. Not deadly enough to kill, a good snort or contact with exposed skin can affect the central nervous system, causing dizziness, disorientation, irritability, and frostbite — and can act as a good red herring. Most campers who accidentally spill it on themselves are wise to wash it off quickly. If gotten into the eyes, it can burn. Clothing or cloth, wet from the propane, which is rather foul smelling, is a flammability hazard. Our hero can spray the villain with it to stop him. If that doesn't work, light a match. Propane is also found in industry for refrigerant and aerosol propellant.

Foods are not commonly found on poison lists — unless one happens to be allergic to them. While food allergies are seldom so severe as to send someone into anaphylactic shock, they can do so. In fact, there is one recent case of a woman whose body could not tolerate caffeine. She'd asked for decaffinated coffee at the restaurant but the waiter had mixed up the containers, and after three cups of supposed decaffinated coffee, she found her throat closing off as she fought for breath. Luckily a physician at the next table kept her alive with an emergency tracheotomy until the paramedics arrived.

People not allergic to caffeine (which occurs in more than just coffee and soft drinks) but who have not had it for some time, will find even a small dose as a shock to the system. For a time, coffee enemas were popular among health enthusiasts, and many a student takes pill after pill of No-Doz to stay awake for studying. Overdosing on caffeine causes restlessness, epigastric pain, nausea, vomiting, gastric irritation, palpitations, fever, tachycardia, headache, hyperventilation, convulsions, and even in extreme cases, respiratory failure. Caffeine withdrawal, as those who have tried to get off this nasty poison know, causes headaches. More about caffeine can be found in the drug section.

Food poisoning can be an interesting weapon, although inducing it can't always be guaranteed. Bacterial food poisonings, such as salmonella, are only fatal in 1 percent of the cases. Botulism, on the other hand, kills 50 percent of its victims.

Botulism

Botulism poisoning gave home canning a bad name. It's easy to prevent and to kill since boiling at 100 degrees C for one minute renders this poison harmless. Meat, fish, and vegetables that have been insufficiently heated and improperly canned usually invite the tasteless and odorless growth of botulinus toxin. Babies can get botulism from honey, even if it is processed, which is why honey is not a recommended food until after the age of two. (Honey can be deadly to adults, especially if bees have pollinated on oleander or rhododendron, but that's in the plant chapter.)

Name: Botulism. *Scientific Name: Clostridium botulinum.*

Toxicity: 6.

Form: The botulism bacillus is eaten with the contaminated food. It's a gram-positive anaerobic bacillus, which means it grows without oxygen. As a spore, it is invisible to the eye.

Effects and Symptoms: Botulism causes muscle paralysis by keeping the nerve impulses from getting to the brain. It also affects the other organs in the body, especially those of the autonomic nervous system.

Double vision, muscular paralysis, nausea, and vomiting. Symptoms are often delayed twelve to twenty-four hours. An autopsy shows congestion and hemorrhages in all of the organs and especially in the central nervous system. The liver and kidneys also degenerate. The corpse looks as if the victim had been very ill.

Reaction Time: This varies according to source and victim but can start around eight hours after eating the contaminated food; death occurs as late as eight days.

Antidotes and Treatments: There is a type ABE botulinus antitoxin that can be given, except in a few cases. The physician might also try to remove the toxin by pushing sodium bicarbonate or activated charcoal via a gastric tube that goes directly into the stomach. The charcoal absorbs the poisons, but in this case it works only if the patient hasn't yet developed symptoms. If symptoms have started, the stomach should be pumped. The patient might also be put on a respirator to alleviate breathing problems.

Case Histories: In *A Pint of Murder* by Alisa Craig, an improperly canned jar of food was used to murder the victim.

A TV episode of *Murder, She Wrote* had a poisoned jar of preserves at the victim's table. The killer, in this case, ate a small amount also so as to allay suspicion and make it look as if the restaurant was at fault.

Alkaline Corrosives and Inorganic Salts

Sodium hydroxide, potassium hydroxide, sodium phosphates, and sodium carbonate are all corrosive chemicals found in many cleaning products. Acids are generally thought of as being the principal corrosives; but alkalies, the chemical opposites of acids, can be just as vicious. As with many weak acids, such as vitamin C (ascorbic acid) that aren't at all corrosive on or in the human body, there are many weak alkalies that people use on their skins daily, such as facial soap.

Batteries also contain alkalies, and small watch batteries, when swallowed, can do impressive damage to the esophagus and upper gastrointestinal tract.

Even though there are several chemicals involved here, they are grouped together because they have the same effects and are treated the same way.

Name: While there are all sorts of alkalies, those focused on here are potassium hydroxide, sodium hydroxide (better known as lye), sodium phosphates, and sodium carbonate.

Toxicity: 6. Alkalies are so corrosive, even a suicide would be hard pressed to be successful since one taste would likely give the victim a third-degree burn on the mouth and esophagus. Many people, accustomed to their five o'clock martini, however, will down a drink without even checking it. Since very little poison is needed to actually cut into the tissue and cause damage if a large gulp is swallowed, the esophagus and stomach could quickly be perforated, bringing about eventual death.

Form: Because penetration through the skin is painful and slow, ingestion causes what fatalities there are.

Potassium hydroxide is found in cuticle remover and in some small batteries. In addition to benign soaps, sodium hydroxide is found in aquarium products, drain cleaners, and other small batteries. Drano is one product that combines several alkalies. Sodium phosphates help give cleansers, or abrasive cleaners, their punch. Dye removers remove dye with sodium carbonate, which is also found in dishwasher soap.

Furniture polish once contained alkalies but now does not.

Effects and Symptoms: These chemicals team up with the proteins and the fats in the body to turn firm healthy tissue into soft, decayed (necrotic) tissue. The chemical penetrates deeply upon contact and liquifies the tissue.

Severe pain immediately follows ingestion, then vomiting and diarrhea, at which time collapse occurs, and the victim may die. Survivors show blood-tinged vomit. The first twenty-four hours may show apparent improvement which will last from two to four days, then a sudden onset of stomach pain, boardlike abdominal rigidity, a rapid fall in blood pressure, dizziness, headache, blurred vision, and fainting occurs. These last symptoms indicate stomach or esophagus perforation.

Death, usually by the third day, is painful. Necrotic (dead) tissue is shed in strips through vomiting.

An autopsy finds gelatinous, dead areas wherever the alkali went. Not a pretty sight.

Reaction Time: Alkalies cause an immediate reaction upon contact. Death, if it's to occur, may take several days.

Antidotes and Treatments: The alkali is first diluted with water or milk. Vomiting is not induced since it brings up the poison and causes more injury. As soon as possible, the physician will put a specially equipped tube down the victim's throat to examine the injuries.

Afterward, antibiotics may be given to patients with fever or other sign of perforation, and surgery may be needed to repair damaged tissues.

Case Histories: In the movie *Throw Mama from the Train*, the character Owen Lifts (played by Danny DeVito) tries to kill his mother (Anne Ramsey) by adding lye to her soft drink, but then chickens out and knocks the cup away.

Notes: Even when a victim survives ingestion of an alkali, the esophagus can constrict weeks or months later, making swallowing very difficult.

Label instructions on Drano clearly read: Do not mix with ammonia, toilet bowl cleaners, household cleaners, or other drain cleaners. Mixture may release hazardous gases or cause violent eruption from drain. (Wouldn't that be a great sight to write about?) If gases are released, leave the area immediately. (Need more be said?)

Most people believe that alkalies neutralize acids and to some extent, they do. According to one source, however, it's important to have a professional administering the neutralizing dose since too much of the "cure" can cause more damage than anticipated.

A detective may be thrown off (momentarily, of course, since all detectives get the villain in the end) by the killer setting up a "murder attempt" on himself using cleanser (alkali) in his lemonade (acid).

Ammonia

Real ammonia is a gas at room temperature. Colorless and strongly alkaline, it has a characteristic odor. The ammonia commonly used for dry cleaning is actually hydroxide solution. The cleaner is a frequent source of poisoning around households. The gas has a number of industrial uses, including as a refrigerant, pesticide, dye, plastic, and fertilizer. Other sources of occupational exposure include the silvering of mirrors, glue-making, and tanning of leather.

Name: Ammonia. *Other*: Ammonium hydroxide.

Toxicity: 4½.

Form: Ammonia is an ordinary gas that is inhaled. Ammonium hydroxide is a solution that is ingested.

Effects and Symptoms: Both gas and liquid damage cells with caustic action and very painfully irritate mucous membranes.

If swallowed, extreme pain in the mouth, chest, and abdomen; coughing; vomiting; and shocklike collapse occur. The stomach and esophagus may perforate later, which increases the abdominal pain, fever, and rigidity. After twelve to twenty-four hours, lung irritation and fluid retention in the lungs occur. If inhaled in high concentrations, the lips and eyelids swell, there is temporary blindness, restlessness, tightness in the chest, foaming at the mouth, reddish skin color, and the victim suffers rapid but weak pulse. Autopsy findings are those of alkali poisoning in ingestion cases; in inhalation cases, there will be pulmonary edema, irritation, and pneumonia.

Reaction Time: Immediate.

Antidotes and Treatments: The physician dilutes the poison. In an inhalation case, the victim is removed from the contaminated area and kept in bed.

Case Histories: In 1972, one depressed man tried to kill himself by locking the poorly ventilated bathroom door and mixing the chemicals ammonia and bleach together. He soon lost consciousness but was found in time and appeared to have suffered no permanent ill-effects from his attempted suicide.

Notes: Ammonia becomes an extremely toxic gas when combined with strong oxidizers, calcium, gold, mercury, silver, or bleaches. This is the product people have been warned about—mixing chlorine bleach with ammonia creates chlorine gas causing unconsciousness, especially if the area is small and unventilated. The victim would need to be in the fumes for over an hour for the effects to be severe. Because of the length of time needed to kill, a short duration can be used either as a warning to "get off the case" or as a red herring.

Chlorine gas, which results, is treated as an acid. (See industrial poisons for more information.)

Bromates

Not as common nowadays, bromates were found primarily in the neutralizer solutions of cold permanent waves popular from the 1940s to 1970s. Someone working in a beauty supply house might still have access to this chemical.

Bromate becomes poisonous in the stomach, where the hydrochloric acid there turns the potassium bromate into hydrogen bromate, which is an irritating acid.

Name: Bromate, or more specifically, potassium bromate.

Toxicity: 5.

Form: It is usually found as 3 percent of a solution with water. To be poisonous, bromate must be taken orally.

Effects and Symptoms: When ingested, bromates have a corrosive action on the tissues. Vomiting, collapse, diarrhea, abdominal pain, oliguria or anuria, lethargy, deafness, coma, convulsions, low blood pressure, and fast pulse occur. Tiny, pinprick red spots can appear on the skin as a later reaction. These will remain on the corpse, and an autopsy will also show damaged kidneys.

Reaction Time: Within five to twenty minutes.

Antidotes and Treatments: Stomach pumping or an enema is the basic emergency procedure, with solutions containing sodium bicarbonate or sodium thiosulfate. Sodium thiosulfate is also given intravenously as an antidote.

Cationic Detergents

Cationic detergents are found mainly in dishwasher soap and fabric softeners. The other major use is as an antibacterial disinfectant on skin, surgical instruments, cooking equipment, sickroom supplies, and diapers.

Many cationic detergents are found in solutions, which means they are usually too diluted to be lethal in a reasonable dose. Creativity comes in when the fictional killer must slip a cup or more of fabric softener past that rich, but annoying victim. As always, the elderly, the infirm, or the very young are the most susceptible to these compounds. A villain may work for a diaper service, or some other cleaning company, and might have access to stronger solutions used to disinfect diapers.

Name: Benzethonium chloride, benzalkonium chloride, methylbenzethonium chloride, cetylpyridinium chloride are just a few cationic detergents.

Toxicity: 4.

Form: Cationic detergents are found in solutions or creams. Benzethonium chloride and benzalkonium chloride are both antiseptics. Cationic detergents are usually swallowed but can be absorbed through the skin after the poison has undergone prolonged heating. A fatal bath or Jacuzzi could be prepared for the killer's rich uncle.

Effects and Symptoms: The body's cells readily absorb the detergents, which in turn interfere with the cells' functions. Cationic detergents will also injure mucous membranes.

Nausea, vomiting, corrosive damage to the esophagus, collapse, low blood pressure, convulsions, coma, and death occur. Symptoms are the same whether ingested or absorbed.

An autopsy shows nothing characteristic of cationic detergents.

Reaction Time: The first symptoms take ten minutes to an hour. Death occurs in one to four hours.

Antidotes and Treatments: First, an airway is established and respiration is maintained as convulsions are treated. Because the esophagus is often injured, gastric lavage and forced vomiting are not advised. Milk or activated charcoal is administered. Ordinary soap is a good antidote for whatever cationic detergents have not been absorbed into the body, but there is no antidote once the detergent has been absorbed.

Isopropanol

Found in the home as rubbing alcohol and in aftershave lotions and window cleaners, this brother of ethyl alcohol is twice as toxic. While all alcoholic beverages are generally not considered lethal, they can be. Isopropanol is twice as deadly.

Name: Isopropanol. *Other*: Isopropyl alcohol, rubbing alcohol.

Toxicity: 5.

Form: Always a liquid at room temperature, isopropanol evaporates very easily to a gas. It can be swallowed, inhaled as a vapor, or absorbed through the skin.

Effects and Symptoms: Isopropanol depresses the central nervous system, leading to coma. Similar to being very drunk, isopropanol poisoning causes much more persistent and severe nausea, vomiting, abdominal pain, depressed respiration, vomiting of blood (hematemesis), diminished urination, and excessive sweating. The autopsy may show hemorrhaging in the trachea and bronchial tubes; and pneumonia, swelling, and hemorrhaging in the chest cavity.

About 15 percent or more of the amount ingested becomes acetone in the body.

Reaction Time: Ten minutes to a half-hour, although the contents of the stomach would dictate. Just as with drinking alcohol, food in the stomach slows the reaction time.

Antidotes and Treatments: Artificial respiration may be necessary. Stomach pumping is also useful, even if treatment has been delayed. A glucose (sugar) solution is usually given intravenously while maintaining blood pressure with other drugs.

Notes: The residual effects of isopropanol poisoning last two to four times longer than those of the average alcoholic drink.

Physicians once prescribed alcohol sponge baths to reduce high fevers, but it was discovered that besides removing the fever, it sometimes produced a coma. Of course, an elderly housekeeper or grandmother who hasn't caught up with modern medical practices might not know this and might do it by accident or on purpose. The coma itself can be a good red herring. While a coma alone won't kill anyone, unconscious people can die by swallowing their own vomit or choking on their tongues. For that reason, nursing and medical students are always taught to keep unconscious patients lying on their side.

Since the effects of isopropanol are so similar to those of being drunk, it can make hiding the poison among the liquor a good way for a villain to spring a trap, especially if the bystanders have no reason to suspect that the victim's stupor is not from ethanol (drinkable — or ethyl — alcohol).

Methanol

Ethyl alcohol's country cousin, methanol or methyl alcohol, has myriad industrial uses but is as easily found in perfumes, antifreeze, paint removers, and as a solvent in shellac and varnish. Considerably more toxic than booze, probably because it metabolizes into formaldehyde in the body, a victim could become truly pickled. The body also takes its time excreting methanol, about one-fifth as fast as it does ethanol.

Name: Methanol. *Other*: Methyl alcohol, wood alcohol.

Toxicity: 5. (The toxic dose varies by individual metabolism of alcohols.)

Form: As with other alcohols, methanol is a liquid at room temperature and evaporates quickly. Methanol can be swallowed, inhaled as a vapor, or absorbed through the skin.

Effects and Symptoms: Methanol damages the liver, kidneys, and heart. In addition, the lungs take on fluid and develop pneumonia, the brain swells, and irreversible blindness can occur.

Fatigue, headache, nausea, vertigo, back pain, severe abdominal pain, blurred vision, dizziness, vomiting, and blindness are caused by the formaldehyde, which adversely affects the optic nerve. Pupils are generally dilated and nonreactive. Finally, rapid and shallow respiration, cyanosis, coma, rapidly falling blood pressure, and death occur from respiratory failure. An autopsy will show massive organ damage, particularly in the eyes.

Reaction Time: A prominent feature of methanol poisoning is the latent period of twelve to forty-eight hours before signs and symptoms appear. This is due to the slow metabolism of methanol to its toxic metabolites.

Antidotes and Treatments: Ethanol (100 proof) is given to slow the metabolizing of the methanol. If the victim has been found within two hours after ingestion, syrup of ipecac is given to encourage vomiting — or the stomach is pumped. Ethanol is given either orally or intravenously for the next four days until the methanol is excreted. Kidney dialysis is used to remove methanol from the blood.

Notes: In some parts of the United States, deep in the woods, people still make moonshine — illegal or raw whiskey. Methanol is distilled from fermented wood, much as ethyl alcohol is distilled from fermented grain. It wouldn't be hard to accidentally make up a bad batch of moonshine by mixing wood shavings in the mash (fermented grain), which has frequently happened. Wood alcohol poisoning is a definite hazard.

Naphthalene

Naphthalene has several industrial uses but is better known as mothballs or moth flakes. The familiar mothball smell comes from naphthalene.

Name: Naphthalene. *Other*: Mothballs, moth flakes.

Toxicity: 4 (except in the special case mentioned below).

Form: A white crystalline solid, naphthalene will usually be ingested.

Effects and Symptoms: Naphthalene destroys red blood cells by clumping them together and forcing the hemoglobins out, then causing kidney damage. The first symptoms are nausea, vomiting, headache, diarrhea, oliguria, hematuria, anemia, fever, jaundice, and pain while urinating. With more serious poisoning, excitement, coma, and convulsions.

Reaction Time: Rapid — five to twenty mintues, depending on whether the poison is inhaled or ingested.

Antidotes and Treatments: The stomach is pumped. Convulsions are treated. Sodium bicarbonate is given as well as fluids with furosemide to stop further injury to the kidneys. With severe central nervous system problems, blood transfusions are administered.

Notes: Some people have a hereditary deficiency of glucose-6-phosphate dehydrogenase that can make them more susceptible to naphthalene poisoning. This occurs most frequently in people of Mediterranean descent and is very rare. The same deficiency also makes these people sensitive to aspirin, so there's a good likelihood they will know they have the trait unless perhaps they were adopted and have never taken an aspirin. This could be a good clue or a good red herring.

Petroleum Distillates

Kerosene, gasoline, and paint thinner are three of the most common products distilled from petroleum oil. Petroleum jelly is another, but it is about as nontoxic as a compound can be. While people have survived fairly large doses of the toxic distillates, some have died from minuscule amounts, although this is unlikely.

Name: Kerosene. *Other*: Paint thinner, gasoline, naphtha, solvent distillates.

Toxicity: 4.

Form: All petroleum distillates are liquids. While inhalation of fumes is possible in some cases, ingestion is much more common.

People who pump their own gasoline at self-service stations notice warning signs that indicate gasoline can be harmful or fatal if swallowed or the fumes breathed for any length of time and can cause fetal defects. While getting someone to swallow gasoline is highly unlikely, especially since the odor is so strong, the noxious fumes could possibly be pumped into a closed room, rendering the victim unconscious for a red herring/warning effect.

Effects and Symptoms: Petroleum distillates dissolve fat; but before taking them for a reducing diet, remember they also change the way the nerves work, causing depression, coma, and occasionally convulsions.

If an extremely large dose of gasoline is ingested and retained, weakness, dizziness, slow and shallow respiration, unconsciousness, and convulsions occur. Smaller doses cause nausea, vomiting, and coughing and spitting up blood. Chest irritation often becomes pulmonary edema and bronchial pneumonia.

Reaction Time: Between five and twenty minutes.

Antidotes and Treatments: Most important is to keep the victim from inhaling or choking on vomit. The physician will try to remove the poison by pumping the stomach with a special tube to prevent aspiration. When the patient vomits, the head should be kept lower than the hips so that nothing goes into the lungs. Oxygen may also be necessary if the breathing is slowed.

Case Histories: In *The Palace Guard* by Charlotte McLeod, a guard in an art museum was found dead after the liquor in his private bottle had been substituted with paint thinner. The villain is far more likely to have positive results with the external explosives formed by some petroleum distillates than by traditional poisoning.

Notes: Petroleum distillates can cause mild heart attacks after either ingestion or inhalation. They also cause reddened and calloused skin.

Potassium Permanganate

Potassium permanganate is used by aquariums and hospitals as a disinfectant and as an oxidizing agent. It has a reputation of producing abortions when placed in the vagina, but the amount needed to cause an abortion will also kill the victim.

Name: Potassium permanganate.

Toxicity: 5.

Form: Potassium permanganate is a violet crystal compound that dissolves in water. Might make a nice gift of bath salts for an intended victim.

Potassium permanganate is usually swallowed but can also be absorbed through mucous membranes, usually the vagina. In fact, many drugs mixed in a petroleum base are given as vaginal suppositories; so if your victim is treating a yeast infection or is taking progesterone for PMS, the killer can substitute the poison dose. This would, however, be a lot of work since the suppository must be properly shaped and of the right consistency. The killer could also prepare a sitz bath or could administer the drug during sex, as the arsenic lover-killer did in the historical chapter.

Effects and Symptoms: Potassium permanganate destroys mucous membrane cells with the same caustic action as alkalies. The main symptom of potassium permanganate poisoning is corrosion. Swallowing will cause brown discoloration and swelling of the mucous membranes in the mouth and throat, coughing, swelling of the larynx, decayed tissue in mucous membranes, a slow pulse, and shock with a drop in blood pressure. If death is not immediate, jaundice and shutdown of the liver and kidneys may occur. Topical application of potassium permanganate to the vagina or urethra will cause severe burning, hemorrhages, and collapse of the blood vessels. The vaginal wall may be perforated, which will cause peritonitis with fever and abdominal pain. The telltale brown stain will also appear. An autopsy will show decayed tissue, hemorrhage, and corrosion in the mucous membranes where the potassium permanganate came in contact. The liver and kidney will also show damage.

Reaction Time: Within five to ten minutes.

Antidotes and Treatments: Washing the affected areas with water is the first emergency step. The victim is treated for shock. The physician will also look into the throat with a laryngoscope to determine damage, and any perforations will be surgically repaired.

1,1,1–Trichloroethane

This heavy-duty cleaner is a degreaser for machine and airplane engines. Found in paint removers, it has similar uses to carbon tetrachloride and is used in craft materials.

Name: 1,1,1–Trichloroethane. *Other*: Methyl Chloroform.

Toxicity: 5.

Form: 1,1,1–Trichloroethane is a colorless liquid that smells like chloroform and evaporates readily. It can be swallowed or its fumes can be inhaled. Irritating and dangerous gases of phosgene, hydrochloric acid, and dichloroacetylene form when 1,1,1–trichloroethane is mixed with such metals as aluminum, magnesium powders, sodium, or potassium. Contact with ultraviolet radiation does the same.

Effects and Symptoms: 1,1,1–Trichloroethane depresses the central nervous system, similar to anesthesia.

Symptoms include headache, dizziness, nausea, fainting, unconsciousness, respiratory depression, skipped heartbeats, and a drop in blood pressure.

An autopsy does not reveal anything particularly significant, except some small hemorrhages in the lungs and brain in severe inhalation cases.

Reaction Time: Five minutes when inhaled; twenty to thirty minutes when ingested.

Antidotes and Treatments: If ingested, the stomach is pumped;

if inhaled, the victim is removed to fresh air and given artificial respiration.

Turpentine

There are few garages that don't have some turpentine stored away. A volatile oil, turpentine is a mixture of hydrocarbons, ethers, alcohols, esters, and ketones. This venerable old paint remover is a plant derivative from the sapwood of pines, firs, and other cone-bearing trees. A natural product, it also has several medical applications as a skin irritant. Like other irritants, it's rarely lethal, simply because it's too painful to swallow or breathe enough for a fatal dose, even for a determined suicide. This can be used as a villain's sympathy-getting ploy or as a red herring for making it appear life has been threatened.

Name: Turpentine.

Toxicity: 5.

Form: Turpentine, as are all volatile oils, is a liquid that evaporates easily at room temperature. Turpentine can be inhaled or swallowed. There is a characteristic odor.

Effects and Symptoms: Turpentine irritates the skin and any other tissues it comes in contact with. Locally, turpentine will cause an immediate reddening of skin. Coughing, chest pain, and respiratory distress as initial reactions indicate it has been taken into the lungs. Swallowing causes abdominal burning, nausea, vomiting, diarrhea, painful urination, blood in the urine, unconsciousness, shallow respiration, and convulsions. The pulse is weak and rapid. Breathing the fumes causes dizziness, rapid shallow breathing, fast heartbeat, irritation of the bronchial tubes, and unconsciousness or convulsions. Kidney shutdown, pulmonary edema (water on the lungs), and bronchial pneumonia can also develop. Should the victim survive, this may complicate recovery.

An autopsy shows damage to the kidneys and intense congestion and swelling in the lungs, brain, and stomach linings.

Reaction Time: As an irritant, turpentine works within seconds. If ingested, within minutes.

Antidotes and Treatments: Vomiting should be avoided since if it's reswallowed, it can go into the lungs and cause pneumonia and other problems. Artificial respiration is sometimes necessary. Gastric lavage is often done, then milk is given to soothe the stomach.

Topical application is treated by a thorough scrubbing of the area with soap and water.

Miscellaneous Household Hazards

Sodium (Na), as in sodium chloride (NaCl) or table salt, is the bane of those with high blood pressure. It disrupts the acid balance in the blood, which can bring on heart attack. A certain amount of sodium is necessary for life, but some people are more sensitive to it than others. Many foods (like celery) are naturally loaded with sodium. After baking a nice celery-and-cheese casserole in tomato sauce for an aggravating and hypertensive relative, a fictional villainous cook could proclaim innocently, "But I didn't know they had sodium!"

In real life, while the patients on a low-sodium diet should know they shouldn't eat the casserole, many such patients are not adequately instructed in safe dietary habits when discharged. Some salt-cured hams don't taste as if they contained as much salt as they actually do. Kidney patients drinking Coca-Cola, which has much more sodium than Pepsi, can put themselves in a life-threatening situation. MSG (Monosodium glutamate), found in Chinese foods and preservatives, is loaded with sodium, and many people have such allergic reactions as headaches, increased blood pressure, nausea, vomiting, and diarrhea. But since each body reacts differently, what might cause one person to have high blood pressure and a stroke, might just cause a slight headache and dizziness in another, or swelling of the hands. Too much sodium is known as hypernatremia.

An excessive intake of **water** or other fluids can also be dangerous. Drinking massive amounts of water—perhaps while on a health kick or a water fast—can cause sodium depletion and death from a heart attack.

Loss of sodium (hyponatremia) can cause lightheadedness, dizziness, blurred vision, inability to balance correctly, profuse sweating, palpitations, difficulty breathing, and heart failure. Staying out in the sun too long causes sunstroke and depletion of sodium. Salt tablets are often suggested for people who will be crossing the desert or working out in the sun all day.

Sodium bicarbonate (baking soda) can be lethal to heart patients if enough is swallowed. Of course, a fatal dose would be about a cup or more. Mixed with sterile water and injected, much less sodium bicarb is needed for a lethal dose — although it would still involve a good-sized syringe. While sodium bicarb is used in hospitals to save patients going into respiratory acidosis (heart attack), an overdose could swing the body into alkalosis, which would prove just as fatal.

Potassium (K), on the opposite end of the scale from sodium, balances the body the other way. Excessive potassium (hyperkalemia) causes the heart to dilate and become flaccid and slows the heart rate. Other symptoms are nausea; diarrhea; muscle weakness; numbness of hands, feet, tongue, and face; as well as apprehension. Large quantities weaken the heart, causing an abnormal rhythm, and cardiac arrest occurs.

Too little potassium (hypokalemia) can cause respiratory alkalosis, resulting in cardiac failure. Too much potassium causes acidosis, which can be just as fatal. People who take diuretics (water pills) often have potassium prescribed to balance the water loss. [K-Lyte, one brand of potassium, comes mixed in an orange-flavored tablet that foams with water. Potassium also comes in capsule or pill form as well as an orange- or cherry-flavored liquid. As with all drugs, the elderly and the infirm are most susceptible to overdoses. Hidden potassium often causes heart problems that can quickly lead to death.] The symptoms of potassium depletion and sodium overdose are the same.

Calcium (Ca) is another element that is crucial to proper heart and bodily function. Excess calcium works opposite from excess potassium causing the heart to go into spastic contractions. A lack of calcium causes flaccidity of the heart and other muscles similar to excessive potassium. Calcium deficit (hypocalemia) involves such symptoms as tingling of fingers, muscular cramps, hyperactive reflexes, convulsions, and spasms of the hands and larynx. This is why calcium pills are given for nightly leg cramps and calming the nerves.

Other **medications** found commonly in the home are aspirin, Tylenol, and such prescription drugs as Tylenol with codeine (in varying strengths) and 222s (a Canadian over-the-counter mixture of aspirin, acetaminophen, and one-quarter grain codeine). The medicine chest can also contain iodine, which causes vomiting when ingested (discussed in industrials), and many households with kids have syrup of ipecac available to induce vomiting should a poison be taken (see the plant chapter).

Most medicine chests contain **hydrogen peroxide**, an antiseptic/

acid. This often burns on contact and bleaches the skin. A colorless, unstable liquid with a bitter taste, hydrogen peroxide is quite corrosive. Highly concentrated solutions cause blistering burns and severe eye injuries on contact, and inhalation may cause lung problems ranging from bronchitis to pulmonary edema.

Health faddists used hydrogen peroxide in colonics (enemas of the intestines) until they realized it caused gas embolism and gangrene of the intestine. More than one person died this way, convinced the colonic was curing their many ills.

Besides being used in hospitals and for other health-care needs, hydrogen peroxide is used in connection with liquor and wine agers, dyes, electroplaters, fat refiners, photographic-film developers, printers, veterinarians, and water treaters. Commercially, it's sold in concentrations of 3 to 90 percent. If ingested, a quantity of water should be swallowed immediately and vomiting induced.

While many patients are supposedly given dietary information regarding the medications they are on, wine and cheese can be deadly to those on certain antidepressants known as monamine oxidase inhibitors (MAO inhibitors).

Laxatives and **purgatives** are among other items found in the medicine cabinet. While these will not kill immediately, the resultant diarrhea or vomiting, if severe enough, can cause dehydration and thirst. If the victim does not know to seek medical help, the problem can lead to death. The flavored laxative can be used to make a "delicious" chocolate cake for a chocolate lover. The victim's hemorrhoids might appreciate it, but the victim won't. If nothing worse, the patient might think the symptoms are stomach flu instead of poisoning and not seek medical help.

The warning on a bag of barbecue charcoal clearly states that to breathe the fumes of the burning briquettes in a closed room can be fatal. One family recently burned their hibachi indoors in an attempt to heat their room. They became extremely ill from the carbon monoxide fumes released by the burning briquettes.

Insect repellants for human use sometimes contain N,N–diethyltoluamide. To cause harm from ingestion, a great deal would need to be consumed. While poisonings are rare, eye irritation can occur if sprayed into the face. In the movie *Extremities*, a fictional heroine, running for her life, grabbed a can of insect repellant and sprayed it in the villain's eyes to temporarily blind him. (See chapter 8 for information on stronger insecticides, and look for other household items that are treated in different sections of this book.)

Fluorocarbons are used as a refrigerant and as a propellant in aerosol cans. When they were first developed, chemical industries were ecstatic—at last there was a family of chemicals that were neither toxic nor polluting. Unfortunately, it has been discovered recently that fluorocarbons have a negative effect on the atmosphere's ozone layer.

The manufacture of aerosol cans is slowing down, which is not only good for the ozone, but also for young kids who sniff the aerosol to get high. Youngsters spray the fluorocarbon into a plastic or paper bag and then breathe it in deeply. The result could be initial hyperactivity followed by sudden death.

F   O   U   R

POISONOUS PLANTS

Someone at the picnic had really given Thea an oleander branch. With three notches in it . . . to let the deadly sap escape? . . . And she skewered her frankfurter on it?

— Lucille Kallen
The Piano Bird

Around the year 1800, more than 90 percent of poisoning cases were caused by poisons of vegetable origin. Now, with the increase of medical, industrial, and agricultural poisons, vegetable substances account for a mere 7 percent of the total. Of course, many medicines today are synthetic re-creations of plants.

Note that unless a specific location is mentioned, the plants can be found virtually anywhere. Of course, it's also possible to find exotic poisonous plants in greenhouses, if they are not found naturally in the landscape where you've set your mystery.

Many plants are poisonous. They may cause itching, dermatitis, or vomiting; but not all are fatal. Many references conflicted regarding actual toxicity.

This chapter is the longest since plants are the most accessible poison to the average poisoner. In an effort to categorize, the plants have been divided into groups of:

Quickly fatal, like oleander.

Plants that can be mistaken for edible, like hemlock, and those where the animals eat the plant and then we eat the animals, as in laurel; plants that are edible in small quantities like nutmeg, or that have certain edible parts, like rhubarb; and plants that are edible only certain times of the year.

Plants used for medicinal purposes or that cause abortions, like ergot.

Flowering plants, like rhododendron or azalea.

Other miscellaneous plant poisons.

If your villain plans to do a victim in with plants, the taste must be disguised in a credible way: salads are popular, as are casseroles. Remember that some plant poisons lose their lethality when cooked.

The categories of *location* and *deadly parts* have been substituted for *form* in this chapter. Unless otherwise mentioned, antidotes and treatments for plant toxins consist of gastric lavage (stomach pumping) and treatment of individual symptoms as they occur.

Quickly Fatal

Name: Barbados nut. *Scientific Name: Jatropha curcas. Other:* Physic nut, purge nut, curcas bean, kukui haole (Hawaii).
Toxicity: 6.
Location: It is found in Africa, Mexico, Central America, Asia, and South America. Within the United States, it's found in southern Florida and Hawaii.

The barbados nut is a small spreading shade tree about fifteen feet high. It has thick branches and copious, sticky yellow sap. The flowers are small, greenish-yellow, and hairy.
Deadly Parts: All. (The American Medical Association lists only the raw seeds.) The poison is jatrophin (curcin), a violent purgative.
Effects and Symptoms: Difficulty breathing, sore throat, bloating, dizziness, vomiting, diarrhea, drowsiness, dysuria, and leg cramps.
Reaction Time: Fifteen to twenty minutes.
Antidotes and Treatments: Gastric lavage is often done unless vomiting has been extensive. It's treated much as castor bean poisoning is treated.
Notes: The threat of this nut lies in the very pleasant taste of the seeds, since anyone who tastes one will instinctively eat more of them.

The seed contains 55 percent (or more) of "Hell oil." More potent than castor oil, it was formerly given as a purge but has long since been abandoned even in veterinary practice. In the tropics, the nut is still used for soap- and candle-making and the seeds are taken as a folk remedy, even though they are dangerous.

Physic nuts are ground up and mixed with palm oil as a rat poison in Africa.

The poison inhibits protein synthesis in intestinal wall cells resulting in death. Poisonings in children living in tropical countries are frequent, some with fatal results.

Name: Belladonna. *Scientific Name: Atropa belladonna. Other:* English nightshade, black nightshade, nightshade, banewort, deadly nightshade, dwale, sleeping nightshade, belladonna lily, Barbados lily, cape belladonna, lirio, naked lady lily, azuncena de Mejico (found near the U.S.-Mexican border).

Toxicity: 6.

Location: Introduced as a drug plant from central and southern Eurasia, nightshade is occasionally found in waste places of the eastern United States. A native of Europe, it's often found as an ornamental plant in the United States.

Deadly Parts: All parts, especially roots, leaves, and berries. The medical alkaloids atropine, scopolamine, hyoscyamine, hyoscine, and belladonna come from this plant. They work by paralyzing the parasympathetic nervous system, blocking the action at the nerve endings. Atropine and various synthetic substances also stimulate the central nervous system. Atropine is eliminated almost entirely by the kidneys, which must be working normally to process the drug.

Fruits are purple-black berries; flowers (June through September) are dull, pale purple-blue.

Effects and Symptoms: Dilated pupils; blurred vision; increased heart rate; hot, dry, red skin; dry mouth; disorientation; hallucinations; impaired vision; loud heart beats audible at several feet; aggressive behavior; rapid pulse; rapid respiration; urinary retention; fever; convulsions; coma; and death.

Reaction Time: Several hours to several days.

Antidotes and Treatments: Gastric lavage with 4 percent tannic acid solution and vomiting. There is likely to be a very dry mouth sensation and visual disturbances, so pilocarpine or physostigmine are given.

Notes: The name *belladonna* comes from the Italian, meaning "beautiful woman." During the Renaissance, women applied an extract of the plant to their eyes to dilate their pupils and give a wide and beautiful appearance.

Rabbits often eat deadly nightshade and pass the effect on to anyone who might eat them.

A powder made from the leaves and roots of belladonna is used to treat asthma, colic, and hyperacidity.

Name: Curare. *Scientific Name: Strychnos toxifera* of the family Loganiaceae, or *Chondodendron tomentosum* of the family Menispermaceae. *Other:* Succinylcholine, tubocurarine, pavulon, moonseed.

Toxicity: 6.

Location: It is found in Central America and northern South America.

Deadly Parts: All of the plant is fatal, not just the sap from which curare is made. Curare is harmless when swallowed, however.

Effects and Symptoms: Injection or intravenous administration causes paralysis of muscles starting with the eyelids and face. Then there is inability to swallow or lift the head, and then the poison continues to the diaphragm within seconds of injection. The pulse drops dramatically. Paralysis of the lungs occurs next. Death is due to respiratory failure. During the death throes, the victim turns blue. Labs give a diagnosis of inflamed liver. Spectrograph in the lab would pick up the amount of drug in the tissues.

Reaction Time: Almost immediate.

Antidotes and Treatments: None. It works too fast.

Case Histories: In fiction, curare is the favorite drug of medical killers.

In the 1960s, a real-life case was written up in *Final Treatment: The File on Dr. X* by Matthew L. Lifflander. It described the use of curare by New York Dr. X to kill many of his patients. Becoming "god," Dr. X decided life and death by what he judged of his potential victims' contribution to society. Dr. X went from hospital to hospital, making his choices, until, like most killers, he became careless. The drug was discovered in his locker. Dr. X. was acquitted and never admitted to his deeds.

In Carter Dickson's *Red Widow Murders*, Detective Sir Henry Merrivale has a locked-room case, in which a man dies even though no one appears to have entered and the postmortem examination shows curare in his system. The question is how the villain got the drug into his victim's blood stream. The stumped detective searches the body for a puncture wound and realizes the victim had had a gum lanced that day. The culprit had mixed the drug in a flask of whiskey to kill the victim's pain. When the victim drank, the drug entered through the cut on his gums. Of course, to actually have killed him the victim would need to have drunk several swallows, and curare has a bitter taste.

Notes: Curare is sold under different trade names by numerous drug companies.

The drug mimics the effects of heart failure. It's used medically when the lungs are being worked on, as it stops normal breathing and enables the patient to be put on a respirator. Most physicians also use it as a muscle relaxant before surgery because it reduces the amount of anesthesia needed.

The drug is also used to relieve spastic paralysis, for treating fractures or dislocations, and as an anticonvulsant treatment for tetanus.

Used by South American Indians, the Orinocos, to paralyze animals and enemies, curare is now widely found as a drug in the States. A poison similar to curare called **urali** is used in Guyana by the Macusi tribe. Peruvian tribes call it woorar, ourari, urari, or urirarey. Most call it "flying death" because it is used to tip arrows and darts. Crude curare is a resinous, aromatic, dark sticky mess from a climbing vine.

Name: Hemlock. *Scientific Name: Conium maculatum. Other:* Poison hemlock, lesser hemlock, deadly hemlock, poison parsley, muskrat weed.

Toxicity: 6.

Location: Poison hemlock is native to Europe and Asia, but has become naturalized in the United States and is common on the waysides and in waste places around farm buildings, especially in the eastern United States and on the Pacific Coast.

Deadly Parts: All—especially the fruits at flowering time. The poisonous leaves can be made into a fatal salad. Hemlock contains coniine, which paralyzes the muscles much like curare. The root is said to be nearly harmless in spring, but deadly afterward, especially during the first year of growth.

Effects and Symptoms: Gradual weakening of muscle power. The pulse is rapid and weak. There is quite a bit of pain in the muscles as they deteriorate and die. The sight is often lost, but the mind remains clear until death, which comes from paralysis of the lungs. This differs from water hemlock, which causes convulsions.

Reaction Time: First symptoms start in a half-hour, but it takes several hours for death.

Antidotes and Treatments: Gastric lavage works only if done *immediately* after ingestion.

Case Histories: Plato says Socrates drained the cup and walked about until his legs felt heavy. He lay down and, after a while, the drug had numbed his whole body, creeping up until it reached the heart.

Lia Metera in *Hidden Agenda* killed her lawyer victim with a delicious salad of hemlock.

Notes: Quail often eat poison hemlock seeds. They are immune, but the flesh of one quail that has eaten hemlock seeds can paralyze a man. Diarrhea and vomiting as well as paralysis appear three hours or longer after eating.

The variety known as American Musquash root, whose symptoms are the same, is a tuber often confused with its edible counterpart, horseradish.

Name: Jimsonweed. *Scientific Name: Datura stramonium. Other:* Devil's trumpet, stinkweed, thorn apple, mad apple.

Toxicity: 6.

Location: It is usually found in warm climates. While not native to Britain, it can now be found in southern England, growing in gardens.

The funnel-shaped flowers are white or purple. The entire plant has an unpleasant odor. The fruit, appearing in autumn, is prickly, ovoid or globular, and contains numerous wrinkled black seeds.

Deadly Parts: The whole plant is toxic. The poison, hyoscyamine, occurs especially in the roots, leaves, and seeds. The plant also contains hyoscine and atropine. The juices and wilted leaves are particularly poisonous.

Effects and Symptoms: Headache, vertigo, extreme thirst, dry burning sensation of skin, dilated pupils, blurred vision, loss of sight, involuntary motion, mania, delirium, drowsiness, weak pulse, convulsions, and coma can end in death.

Reaction Time: Several hours.

Antidotes and Treatments: Treatment is symptomatic. A purgative such as magnesium sulphate may be used, and sedatives such as Valium are effective for convulsions.

Case Histories: Jimsonweed was originally called Jamestown weed because the soldiers sent in 1666 to quell "Bacon's Rebellion" in Jamestown, Virginia, ate the berries of this plant when food ran out. Mass poisoning resulted. Another man was poisoned after he drank an herbal tea brewed from the leaves.

Jonathan Kellerman's *Over the Edge* uses jimsonweed as a mysterious agent to cause the mental collapse of one of his characters. **Notes:** There are several species of *Datura*; all are poisonous. The fragrance varies between pleasant and unpleasant, depending on the season, with the sweeter smell found during growing season.

All species contain belladonna alkaloids. Accidental poisoning is most often caused by the seeds. "This plant is responsible for more poisonings than any other plant," writes Barbara Evans in *Poisonous Plants, the Deadly Deception.* Rubbing the eyes after handling the leaves can cause dilation of pupils. Both adults and children have been fatally poisoned by tea brewed from leaves or seeds of this plant.

In the past this plant was used in various medicinal preparations, especially for asthma. The smoke from the burning leaves would be inhaled. Medicinal and culinary use of the plant often resulted in poisoning.

Name: Lily of the Valley. *Scientific Name: Convallaria majalis.*
Toxicity: 6.
Location: The lily is found in western North America, northern Rocky Mountain states, Pacific Coast, Midwest, and Canada. This spring-flowering plant is also native to Britain, especially in the eastern parts.

The white bell-shaped flowers are well known. The plant occasionally bears orange-red, fleshy berries.
Deadly Parts: All parts are toxic, especially the leaves, and even the water in which the cut flowers are kept. The poison is a glycoside called convallatoxin, which is similar to digitalis.
Effects and Symptoms: Symptoms include hot flushes, tense irritability, headache, hallucinations, red skin patches, cold clammy skin, dilated pupils, vomiting, stomach pains, nausea, excess salivation, slow heartbeat, sometimes leading to coma and death from heart failure.
Reaction Time: Immediate.
Antidotes and Treatments: Stomach lavage is recommended as well as cardiac depressants like quinidine to control cardiac rhythm. The treatment is similar to digitalis poisoning.

Notes: The plant is often mistaken for wild garlic and made into a soup.

Name: Monkshood. *Scientific Name: Aconitum napellus, A. columbianum,* or *A. vulparia. Other:* Wolfbane, aconite; western monkshood (*A. columbianum*); yellow monkshood (*A. lutescens*); wild monkshood (*A. uncinatum*).

Toxicity: 6.

Location: Monkshood is found throughout the Northern Hemisphere's Temperate Zone. Western monkshood is found at higher altitudes in the northern Rocky Mountain and Pacific Coast states. The yellow is native from Idaho to New Mexico, and the wild monkshood can be found from Pennsylvania to Georgia.

Deadly Parts: The whole plant is poisonous, especially the leaves and roots, which contain aconitine and aconine.

Effects and Symptoms: The drug can be ingested or absorbed through the skin. The first signs appear almost immediately: burning and tingling; numbness in the tongue, throat, and face; followed by nausea, vomiting, blurred vision, prickling of skin, paralysis of the respiratory system, dimness of vision, low blood pressure, slow and weak pulse, chest pain, giddiness, sweating, and convulsions. As anesthesia gradually spreads over the entire body, with subnormal temperatures and a pronounced feeling of cold, it's as if there's ice water in the veins. At the end, severe pain occurs, associated with the paralysis of facial muscles. Breathing is at first rapid, then slow, and finally there is respiratory arrest. Slow paralysis of the heart muscle causes death. Consciousness often continues until the end. Some victims complain of yellow-green vision and tinnitus.

Reaction Time: Symptoms start rapidly. Death occurs in ten minutes to a few hours.

Antidotes and Treatments: There is no specific antidote. Gastric lavage and oxygen to help breathing as well as drugs needed to stimulate the heart may be used.

Case Histories: In one case, cardiac failure occurred due to excessive application of aconite liniment.

In the south of France, during World War I, young soldiers, put on a survival exercise and required to live for several days on what they could find in the surrounding countryside, ate aconite roots. Several died.

A dentist, wishing to be rid of his father-in-law, placed monkshood into the filling he made, killing the older man.

In 1882, Dr. George Lamson, an English physician, made use of this little-known vegetable poison to kill his brother-in-law and help his wife inherit. He placed the poison in a Dundee cake, which he served. When his brother-in-law complained of a headache, Lamson offered some prepared sugar pills (empty capsules with sugar in them). The brother-in-law suspected trickery and refused the sugar pills but ate the cake. Then Lamson left, saying he had to catch a train. The brother-in-law became ill within ten minutes. He died that night.

At his arrest and trial, Lamson brazenly admitted he had fooled his brother-in-law. The poison had been on the pre-cut pieces of cake and not in the capsules. Lamson was executed in April of that same year.

Notes: Monkshood causes poisoning when the leaves are eaten in a salad or when the root is mistaken for a radish. If a less than fatal amount is eaten, recovery occurs within twenty-four hours.

The tuberous root of aconite is carefully collected early in October when the root matures. The Indians of Napal and Bhutan believe evil spirits are present in the aconite plants. Roots are dug up carefully and spread out in the sun to dry. The man in charge of the drying operation ties a cloth around his head, covering his nose, to prevent inhalation of the roots' fumes. These fumes cause giddiness and heaviness in the head. The process of drying takes three to four days. When sufficiently dried, the roots are taken to commercial markets for sale. Aconite roots are sold in the bazaars of Calcutta and elsewhere.

Name: Oleander. *Scientific Name: Nerium oleander. Other:* Jericho rose.

Toxicity: 6.

Location: A native of Asia, it has been introduced as an ornamental shrub in southern United States. In the northern United States, it's grown as a house plant. An evergreen summer favorite, it favors such temperate climates as Greece, India, Italy, and California, but it can grow almost anywhere. In Italy, it's used as a funeral plant.

More or less fragrant, the evergreen shrub has narrow leaves; milky sap; and white, pink, or red blossoms.

Deadly Parts: All parts, including the nectar of the flower, are poisonous, as well as smoke from the burning plant and the water in which the flowers are placed. Using the twigs for skewered meat or for children's whistles may result in serious poisoning. The poison contains cardiac glycosides, oldendrin, and nerioside.

Effects and Symptoms: A cardiac stimulator, the drug causes sweating, vomiting, bloody diarrhea, unconsciousness, respiratory paralysis, and death. See digitalis.

Reaction Time: Immediate.

Antidotes and Treatments: Prompt vomiting is encouraged. Atropine is used cautiously. Gastric lavage is recommended as well as cardiac depressants like quinidine to control cardiac rhythm. The treatment is similar to digitalis poisoning.

Case Histories: Oleander is a favorite of many authors, including Lucille Kallen, who skewered hot dogs with oleander branches in *The Piano Bird.*

Notes: In Europe, oleander is used as a rat poison. When bees use oleander pollen for their honey, the honey may be poisonous. Oleander is a popular poison in Bengal and Madras, India.

Extracts of the plant have been used in India to treat leprosy, as an abortifacient, and as a means of suicide. In Sanskrit the plant's name means "Horse Killer"; in Arabic and Italian, "Ass Killer." Goats, however, are immune.

Yellow oleander (*Thevetia peruviana*) works in the same way but has a milky sap. Its seeds are very poisonous and contain digitalislike glycoside. It is just as deadly as *Nerium oleander.*

Name: Paternoster pea. *Scientific Name: Abrus precatorius. Other:* Jequirity bean, lucky bean, prayer bean, love bean, rosary pea, precatory bean, crab's eyes, bead vine, red bead vine, mienie-mienie Indian bean, black-eyed Susan, wild licorice, Seminole bead, weather plant, Indian licorice.

Toxicity: 6.

Location: The pea is a climbing plant common in Africa and Asia. It's also found in Florida, Hawaii, Guam, Central America, southern Europe, as well as India.

Deadly Parts: Abrin, one of nature's most toxic substances, is the poison. Abric acid, which contains a tetanic glycoside, is in the seeds.

Effects and Symptoms: The drug inhibits the digestive process, so autopsy may show undigested food. In the tropics, it's used as an arrow poison and is released by heat. Diarrhea, nausea, vomiting, tachycardia, convulsions, diffuse hemorrhages, coma, and death from heart failure. Ulcers are found in the mouth.

Reaction Time: Action takes from several hours to three days.

Antidotes and Treatments: There is a long latent period associated with this poisoning, and the plant should be removed as quickly as possible. Convulsions and vasomotor collapse are treated as they occur. A high carbohydrate diet is given to minimize liver damage.

Case Histories: In 1976, a young man died five days after suicidally ingesting a lethal dose of beans, which he purposely ground up in his blender.

Notes: Each seed has an impermeable envelope, so the poison is not released unless chewed. This fact was often used in trials by ordeal in the Middle Ages, when a favored contestant was privately tipped off beforehand to swallow without chewing.

These beads are used in rosaries, bracelets, necklaces, leis, and sometimes children's toys.

Name: Rhododendron. *Scientific Name: Rhododendron ponticum.* *Other:* Azalea (*R. arborescens*).

Toxicity: 6.

Location: It is found everywhere. Rhododendrons are evergreen shrubs often forming dense growths in Canada and in the United States, and are found in the Appalachians and West Coast. They are the state flower of West Virginia and Washington, and are common in Britain.

Azaleas are native deciduous shrubs of the United States, introduced from Asia and cultivated extensively for the showy flowers. They're also very popular in the British Isles.

Rhododendrons are bell-shaped and usually odorless. Azalea flowers, on the other hand, are funnel-shaped, somewhat two-lipped, and often fragrant. The latter are part of the evergreen family.

Deadly Parts: All are poisonous and contain carbohydrate andromedotoxin. They have the same poison as mountain laurel (*Kalmia* family).

Effects and Symptoms: The victim can experience nausea, irritation, drooling, vomiting, increased tear formation, paralysis, slowing of pulse, lowering of blood pressure, diarrhea, seizure, coma, and death.

Reaction Time: About six hours after ingestion.

Notes: Children have been poisoned by sucking nectar from the blossoms or by making tea. The Greeks found that honey from bees that have fed on azaleas, rhododendrons, oleander, or dwarf laurel is poisonous. A honey cake, anyone?

Name: Savin. *Scientific Name: Juniperus sabina. Other:* Savin oil.

Toxicity: 6.

Location: This shrub grows everywhere.

Deadly Parts: The entire plant is toxic.

Effects and Symptoms: In small doses, it enhances water loss and encourages menstruation to start. At high doses, it causes convulsions. On the skin, the oil causes blisters and sometimes decay. When swallowed, the irritant causes gastroenteritis with hemorrhages and vomiting of greenish masses with an etherlike odor. Polyuria may occur with bloody urine, followed by oliguria and anuria, convulsive coma, and acute kidney problems.

Reaction Time: Death from respiratory arrest in ten hours or several days.

Antidotes and Treatments: Milk is given to allay gastric irritation and then stomach lavage and vomiting is needed to remove the material. Fluids are encouraged, if kidney function is normal. Other symptoms are treated as they occur.

Notes: This plant tastes bitter. Savin oil is the drug version and is used to combat overdose of cardiac medications like digitalis.

In ancient times, savin was used to cause abortions. The amount needed to abort, however, was usually fatal for the mother.

Name: Star of Bethlehem. *Scientific Name: Ornithogalum umbellatum. Other:* Dove's dung (biblical name), summer snowflake, nap at noon.

Toxicity: 6.

Location: It's found in warm climates, especially the Middle East. White starlike flowers are found on a high, leafless, slender bulb-produced stem.

Deadly Parts: All parts are poisonous, especially the bulb, which contains the same poisons as lily of the valley: convallatoxin and convalloside, and glycosides similar to digitalis.

Effects and Symptoms: Shortness of breath, respiratory distress, and death can occur.

Reaction Time: Immediate.

Antidotes and Treatments: Gastric lavage and symptomatic treatment.

Notes: Bulbs can be used in meal and mixed into flour, but they do have a bitter aftertaste.

Name: Tanghin. *Scientific Name: Tanghinia venenifera. Other:* Ordeal bean of Madagascar.

Toxicity: 6.

Location: This is found mainly in Madagascar and sparsely found in Hawaii. This beautiful, fragrant plant has star-shaped flowers and milky, sticky sap.

Deadly Parts: The seeds are notoriously poisonous, containing tanghin, a cardiac glycoside, which causes digitalislike activity.

Effects and Symptoms: Digitalislike.

Reaction Time: Immediate.

Antidotes and Treatments: As digitalis.

Notes: The seeds have a long history as an ordeal poison for judgments of all kinds of crimes from murder, conspiracy, and witch doctory, to stealing and settling debts. Forced to drink a draft or be killed by a soldier's spear, the accused was judged innocent by the ruling regime if he swallowed only a gulp and promptly vomited. If afraid, he would sip slowly and die almost immediately. Guilt, of course, was predetermined, since death was related to the strength of the extract. The judge could decide how he wanted the trial to go. Such ordeals became infamous, and the French, who colonized Madagascar, destroyed all the tanghin trees they could find.

Name: English yew. *Scientific Name: Taxus baccata. Other:* Pacific or western yew (*T. brevifolia*), American yew or ground hemlock (*T. canadensis*); Japanese yew (*T. cuspidata*).

Toxicity: 6.

Location: Yew trees are found throughout the Northern Hemisphere.

Deadly Parts: All but the red fruit of the plant is toxic, especially the wood bark, leaves, and seeds. The poison is taxine.

Effects and Symptoms: Nausea, vomiting, diarrhea, severe gastroenteritis, giddiness, abdominal pain, dilated pupils, weakness, pale skin, convulsions, shock, coma, and death due to cardiac failure. The poison can be detected only in gastric contents.

Reaction Time: Within one hour.

Case Histories: Before treating his girlfriend with a tea made from *Taxus* needles to assist with her abortion, a young man ingested the yew tea himself to test its effects. Within an hour, he was hallucinating. Three hours later, he was deeply comatose. When admitted to the hospital, his skin was covered with cold sweat. His face, neck, and entire thorax were cyanotic, but the rest of his body was pale. His pupils were dilated and reactionless. Despite emergency measures, he died shortly thereafter.

Notes: In earlier days, pregnant women wanting an abortion took this and often overdosed without realising it. Survival after poisoning is rare.

Mistaken for Edible or Eaten by Mistake

Name: Baneberry. *Scientific Name: Actaea alba* (white), *A. rubra* (red), and *A. spicata* (black). *Other*: Cohos, doll's eyes, herb-Christopher, necklaceweed, snakeberry, black baneberry, western baneberry, European baneberry.

Toxicity: 5.

Location: Baneberry is native to woods of eastern North America. Western baneberry can be found in the forests from the Rocky Mountains to the Pacific Coast. There is also a European version similar to the American.

The plants grow to three feet tall in richly wooded areas. The leaves are large and spreading with sharp-toothed margins. The underside is hairy along the veins, and the plants have small white or bluish flowers. The shiny berries are found especially in summer and autumn.

Deadly Parts: The AMA poison plant handbook lists all parts as being poisonous, but other references indicate only the berries and roots. The rootstock is a violent purgative, and the plant as a whole also acts on the heart.

Effects and Symptoms: Ingested, a small dose is enough to produce burning in the stomach, dizziness, and increased pulse. Increased amounts lead to nausea, vomiting, bloody diarrhea, convulsions, and shock. These symptoms are similar to those of digitalis. Prolonged contact with the plant produces skin rashes.

Reaction Time: Several hours to days. Forty-eight hours is average, but symptoms have started as early as thirty minutes.

Antidotes and Treatments: Gastric lavage should be instituted at once. Milk, egg white, or other demulcents are then added to nullify the poison. Often the electrolytes and fluids of the body are depleted, kidney failure may occur, and death may follow if the problem is not cared for immediately.

Case Histories: In 1972, one English family was poisoned after they made a pie out of the berries they had gathered. All but the mother died as a result of the fatal pie.

In another case, the victim stated: "At first there was a most extraordinary pyrotechnic display of blue objects of all sizes and tints, circular with irregular edges; as one became interested in the spots a heavy weight was lowered on the top of the head and remained there, while sharp pains shot through the temples.

"Then suddenly the mind became confused and there was a total disability to recollect anything distinctly or arrange ideas with any coherency. On an attempt to talk, wrong names were given to objects, and although at the same time the mind knew mistakes were made in speech, the words seemed to utter themselves independently.

"For a few minutes there was great dizziness, the body seeming to swing off into space, while the blue spots changed to dancing sparks of fire."

Notes: The black berries are often confused with blueberries in mountain forests.

Name: Castor bean. *Scientific Name: Ricinus communis. Other:* Gourd (biblical name), African coffee tree, castor-oil plant, palma Christi, koli (Hawaii).

Toxicity: 6. Even two beans, well chewed, can be fatal.

Location: The product of the castor-oil plant, the castor bean is grown in Africa and India for both ornamental and commercial use; it is now found in North America and most tropical regions and is grown for ornamental purposes.

Deadly Parts: The beans are poisonous, and six to eight beans can be fatal. If swallowed whole, however, poisoning is unlikely because the hard seed coat prevents rapid absorption. The poison is ricin, one of the most toxic substances known.

Effects and Symptoms: Burning in mouth, nausea, vomiting, cramps, drowsiness, cyanosis, stupor, circulatory collapse, blood in urine, convulsions, coma, and death; the toxic agent causes hemolysis (breaking up) of red blood cells even at extreme dilution, severe hemorrhaging results. It can also induce labor in pregnant women. Autopsy shows vomit and stool contain blood.

Reaction Time: Several hours or days. Death may occur up to twelve days after ingestion. The first symptoms may take anywhere from two hours to two days.

Antidotes and Treatments: Gastric lavage should be done, and bismuth subcarbonate or magnesium trisilicate is sometimes given to protect the stomach. The diarrhea can cause electrolyte depletion, which must be treated.

Case Histories: There is a much publicized case of homicidal poisoning by ricin. A Bulgarian broadcaster died as a result of a small, perforated metallic sphere containing the poison that had been forcibly inserted into his leg.

Ricin was used to kill writer and playwright Georgy Markov in *Murder and Detection* by David Peat.

Notes: Sometimes mingled with linseed to make press cakes, this mixture will poison anyone who eats it unless it is heated first to destroy the ricin.

Name: Corn cockle. *Scientific Name: Agrostemma githago. Other:* Purple cockle.

Toxicity: 4.

Location: Native to Europe but brought to North America, this noxious weed is found in wheat and corn fields. It's sometimes cultivated as an ornamental annual. Because of the difficulty in screening the seeds from the wheat, it is particularly common in wheat fields.

This winter annual weed is tall, silky, and grayish. A few varieties are grown as ornamentals. Petals are purplish-pink and single flowers are pink. The many black seeds, each covered with a pitted surface, are a source of poisoning.

Deadly Parts: The whole plant is poisonous, but the seeds are even more so, especially if accidentally ground up with cereal. The poisons are githagin and saponin glycosides.

Effects and Symptoms: Rawness of throat, nausea, acute gastroenteritis, fever, giddiness, headache, delirium, severe stomach pains, weakness, slow breathing, sharp pains in spine, coma, death from respiratory arrest.

Reaction Time: One-half hour to one hour after ingestion.

Antidotes and Treatments: Gastric lavage and symptomatic treatment.

Notes: In former times, this caused bread poisoning. Poison from the tuber of *Cyclamen europaeum* takes a similar course.

Name: Daphne. *Scientific Name: Daphne mezereum. Other:* Spurge olive, dwarf bay, lebruary daphne, flax olive, spurge flax, wild pepper, spurge laurel, wood laurel, copse laurel (*D. laureola*).

Toxicity: 5.

Location: Native of Eurasia, it is distributed throughout the British Isles as well as the northeastern United States and eastern Canada. Introduced from Europe, it is widely planted as an ornamental. In the spring, fragrant lilac-purple, rosy-purple, or white flowers grow in stalkless clusters of three and bloom before the leaves appear.

Deadly Parts: All parts are poisonous, but the fruit is especially deadly. The berries of *D. mezereum* are bright red and those of *D. laureola* are green at first, then bluish, then finally black when fully ripe. The poisons are daphnetoxin and mezerein. The juice from the berries or sap from the bark may be absorbed in sufficient quantity through abraded skin to produce systemic reactions. Heating or cooking will not diminish toxicity.

Effects and Symptoms: Severe burning of lips, mouth, and throat; stomatitis; abdominal pain; vomiting; bloody diarrhea; weakness; convulsions; kidney damage; coma; and death.

Reaction Time: Forty-five minutes to several hours.

Antidotes and Treatments: Gastric lavage should be instituted with caution, since damage may have been done to the mucous membranes. Often the victims go into shock due to fluid loss, which is treated as it occurs.

Case Histories: One case of poisoning in the 1870s occurred in Toronto, Canada, when a woman presented a fatal pie to her former husband. He didn't eat it, but his current wife did and died.

Notes: The poison is not destroyed even after the leaves and fruit wither. Eating only a few berries can be fatal to a child. It is one of the oldest plants recognized as poisonous.

Name: Death camas. *Scientific Name: Zygadenus venenosus. Other:* Alkali grass, black snake root, soap plant, poison sego, water lily, wild onion, squirrel food, hog's potato.

Toxicity: 4.

Location: Part of the lily family, it is found in most of North America, except for the extreme southeast, as well as in Hawaii, Canada, and Alaska.

Leaves are long, narrow, and grasslike, gathered around a stem base. At the top, the stem has a branched cluster of greenish-white to yellow-white flowers. The onionlike bulb has a dark-colored coat but lacks the onion odor.

Deadly Parts: The fresh leaves, stems, bulbs, and flowers are poisonous, but the seeds are particularly so. Poisons contained are zygadenine, zygacine, and veratrine.

Effects and Symptoms: Increased salivation, weakness shown by staggering or complete prostration, difficult breathing, coma, followed by death.

Reaction Time: At least one hour.

Antidotes and Treatments: There is no satisfactory antidote. Gastric lavage is recommended if spontaneous vomiting doesn't occur. Other symptoms are treated as they happen.

Case Histories: There are two cases in recent literature of poisoning from this plant. A two-year-old boy ate the flowers and shortly thereafter vomited, became drowsy, and then went into a coma. His respiration became slow and irregular, and his blood pressure dropped dangerously. His pupils became unequally dilated, but he recovered after several days.

The second case also concerned a child who ate some bulbs that had been roasted on a bonfire. Within an hour, he staggered and vomited before losing consciousness.

Notes: It is often mistaken for an onion since it has an onionlike bulb, but there is no onion odor.

Plants retain their poison properties after being dried. This is mainly a cattle poison, but it can kill humans, too.

Name: Fool's parsley. *Scientific Name: Aethusa cynapium. Other:* Dog parsley, "wild parsley," fool's cicely.

Toxicity: 4.

Location: An annual herb, hollow, with thin grooves and ridges, it was introduced from Europe and is found in fields and waste places in northeastern United States and eastern Canada. It looks very much like poison hemlock, but the purple spotting is absent.

Deadly Parts: The whole plant. The active poisons are cynapine, which is similar to coniine (hemlock) and cicutoxin.

Effects and Symptoms: Symptoms are similar to hemlock poisoning.

Reaction Time: Several hours to several days.

Antidotes and Treatments: Gastric lavage and symptomatic treatment.

Notes: Humans have died after eating leaves or roots mistaken for parsley, anise, or radishes.

Name: Meadow saffron. *Scientific Name: Colchicum autumnale. Other:* Autumn crocus, fall crocus, naked ladies.

Toxicity: 5.

Location: Primarily found throughout Eurasia, it is often found in damp meadows and woodsy areas of England and Wales as well as some parts of Scotland.

Deadly Parts: All parts are toxic, especially the bulb.

Effects and Symptoms: Burning in the throat, intense thirst, vomiting, difficulty swallowing, watery or bloody diarrhea, abdominal pain, no urine, cardiovascular collapse, delirium, sensory disturbances, convulsions, muscle weakness, and respiratory failure. Some symptoms are similar to arsenic poisoning. Sudden death may occur after rapid intravenous administration of a small amount of colchicine. In chronic poisoning, hair will start to fall out in ten to fourteen days. Lab findings include blood and protein in urine. Colchicine is also eliminated in feces. Fatalities occur in 50 percent of those poisoned.

Reaction Time: Two to six hours. Death may take as long as two to three days to occur. The patient is fully conscious until the end.

Antidotes and Treatments: Besides gastric lavage, activated charcoal is used. Atropine and hypotensive drugs can combat other symptoms.

Notes: The crocuslike plant is often mistaken for an onion. Tincture of colchicine is made from the seeds. The plant was used as an abortifacient in past times and now the drug, colchicine is used for rheumatism and gout.

The drug can be dissolved in milk. Goats, immune to the poison, eat autumn crocus, and their milk can have the same poison.

Name: Mountain laurel. *Scientific Name: Kalmia latifolia. Other:* Calico bush, poison laurel, ivy bush, mountain ivy; sheep laurel, lambkill, narrow-leaved laurel, calfkill (*K. augustifolia*); hook heller, swamp laurel, alpine laurel, pale laurel (*K. microphylla* or *K. polifolia*).

Toxicity: 5.

Location: Poisonous laurels can be found throughout North America in moist areas.

Deadly Parts: The leaves, twigs, flowers, and pollen are poisonous. The fruit is a many-seeded capsule. The pollen sometimes results in bees making a very bitter, poisonous honey, so astringent to the taste that it is unlikely that one would ingest enough raw honey to be harmful. A cooked honey cake, however, could mask the taste. Poison here is andromedotoxins.

Effects and Symptoms: Severe gastrointestinal distress; watering of eyes, nose, and mouth. Breathing becomes difficult, and heartbeat is slower. Kidney failure can happen. There is depression, convulsions, and paralysis. Coma and death come as quickly as twelve hours.

Reaction Time: Symptoms usually start in six hours but may take from several hours to days before death occurs.

Antidotes and Treatments: Gastric lavage and symptomatic treatment.

Notes: North American hazel hens eat laurel (*K. latifolia*) making their flesh deadly.

Name: Pokeweed. *Scientific Name: Phytolacca americana. Other:* Poke, inkberry, pokeberry, pigeonberry, American nightshade.

Toxicity: 4.

Location: This large shrub grows to eight feet tall, with white drooping flowers and black juicy berries. A native weed throughout the eastern United States and southern Canada, it's common to open fields, along fences and roadsides, in waste places, and can be found occasionally on the West Coast and in Hawaii, as well as Europe and southern Africa. While not native to Britain, it was introduced from the Americas and is now commonly found in gardens there. It is also a problem in New Zealand, where it threatens the cattle.

Deadly Parts: All parts, especially the rootstock and leaves, are poisonous. The seeds are almost as poisonous as the roots. Some poison is found in the stems, with less in the fruit. Poisons are phytolaccine, saponins, and glycoproteins. A small child can be fatally poisoned by eating two to three uncooked berries.

Effects and Symptoms: Severe stomach cramps, nausea, persistent vomiting, diarrhea, slowed and difficult breathing, weakness, spasms, severe convulsions, and death.

Reaction Time: A violent but slow-acting emetic, symptoms begin about two hours after ingestion.

Antidotes and Treatments: Gastric lavage and symptomatic treatment.

Notes: Young tender leaves and stems are sometimes eaten as cooked greens and are edible only if cooked twice in two different pots of water. The long fleshy root resembles a horseradish; the young shoot resembles asparagus.

The plant is used extensively in preparation of certain drugs and as a household remedy for skin diseases and rheumatism.

Name: Privet. *Scientific Name: Ligustrum vulgare. Other:* Prim, lovage, hedge plant, Japanese privet.

Toxicity: 5.

Location: Native to northern Europe, it is now found almost everywhere, especially in parks and gardens as hedges. A deciduous hedge or shrub plant, it grows up to fifteen feet high.

Deadly Parts: The entire plant is poisonous, especially the blackish berries. The poison is ligustrin.

Effects and Symptoms: Severe gastroenteritis, frequent vomiting, watery stools, abdominal colic, collapse, kidney damage, and fall of blood pressure all culminate in death.

Reaction Time: A lethal dose can cause death in two hours.

Antidotes and Treatments: Gastric lavage and symptomatic treatment.

Notes: Most cases of human poisoning come from eating of the ripe berries. Privet can also cause skin rashes. In one case, a boy working on a privet hedge developed a severe skin reaction.

Name: Water hemlock. *Scientific name: Cicuta maculata, C. californica, C. douglasii, C. vagans, C. bolanderi, C. curtissii. Other:* Beaver poison, spotted water hemlock, cowbane, spotted cowbane, California water hemlock, gray hemlock, Douglas water hemlock, Oregon water hemlock, tuber water hemlock, lesser hemlock poison, American musquash root, locoweed.

Toxicity: 6. The toxicity varies with the season and age of the plant. The younger plants have more poison.

Location: Water hemlock (*C. maculata*) is found in eastern North America and west to the Great Plains; California water hemlock (*C. californica, C. bolanderi*) is found in middle western California; Douglas water hemlock (*C. douglasii*) is found along the Pacific Coast states and British Columbia; tuber water hemlock or Oregon water hemlock (*C. vagans*) is found in the Pacific Northwest; western hemlock (*C. occidentalis*) is in the Rocky Mountain states west to the Pacific Coast; bulbous water hemlock (*C. bulbifera*) is in the northern United States.

Cicuta grows primarily in wet or swampy ground, frequently along streams or in swales in pastures. In such places, the plant becomes greener before the rest of the pasture. The plant is also found in seepage areas, in marshes, and in roadside ditches throughout the eastern United States and Canada. Other species of *Cicuta* occur in various areas over the entire United States, Alaska, and Hawaii.

Deadly Parts: The whole plant contains poison, but the root and rootstocks have the most. *Cicuta* contains a resinlike substance, cicutoxin, which is brown and sticky. The poison is soluble in alcohol, chloroform, ether, and diluted alkalies.

A perennial herb with jointed stems and purple spots, it grows to eight feet tall. The flowers are small and white. When the root-stock is split, drops of yellowish aromatic oil appear, which gives the plant a peculiar odor.

Effects and Symptoms: Restlessness and feelings of anxiety, pain in the stomach, nausea, violent vomiting, diarrhea, dilated pupils, labored breathing, sometimes frothing at the mouth, weak and rapid pulse, and violent convulsions terminated by death. Respiratory failure is the cause of death.

Reaction Time: Twenty minutes to an hour or more for death.

Antidotes and Treatments: Emetics and cathartics are necessary to get rid of the poison. Intermuscular injections of morphine are sometimes used to control convulsions. Short-acting barbiturates are also used to control convulsions.

If seizures have occurred, or appear imminent, gastric lavage should not be attempted without the aid of an anesthesiologist.

Notes: *Cicuta* contains the most violent poison available in plant form in the States. Numerous poisonings have been reported from the plant being mistaken for parsnips, artichokes, or other roots. Most cases of poisoning occur in the early spring when the plant is first growing. Children have been poisoned by making peashooters and whistles from the hollow stems.

Cows have been poisoned by water contaminated with the juice of the crushed plants, although quite a bit is needed, since the poison is not as soluble in cold water.

Edible in Small Quantities, Certain Parts Edible, or Edible Certain Times of the Year

Name: Akee. *Scientific Name: Blighia sapida. Other:* Aki, ackee, arbre, fricasse (Haiti), vegetal (Cuba, Puerto Rico).

Toxicity: 5. There is a mortality rate of 40 to 80 percent.

Location: The stiff-branched tree is native to western Africa. Akee is also found in Cuba, Jamaica, Puerto Rico, Haiti, Florida, and Hawaii. It is a native of western Africa and cultivated in the West Indies.

Deadly Parts: The unopened, unripe fruit and cotyledons of the tropical plant cause several deaths each year. The ripe, fully opened fruit is fine to eat. But the rancid spoiled aril is just as poisonous as the unripe one. The fruit capsule and seeds are toxic, as is the water in which the fruit is cooked.

Effects and Symptoms: The poison causes hypoglycemia. Nausea and vomiting begin two hours after ingestion. The victim then appears symptom-free for several hours before convulsions, low blood sugar, fall of blood pressure, coma, and death occur. Convulsions occur in 85 percent of fatal cases.

Reaction Time: The latent period of six hours to more than a day usually occurs between ingestion and sudden onset of symptoms. Death can occur twenty-four hours after eating.

Antidotes and Treatments: Besides gastric lavage and symptomatic support, intravenous glucose is important because of the severe hypoglycemia.

Notes: An autopsy will usually find hemorrhages in the brain.

It was named for Captain W. Bligh, commander of the *Bounty*.

Name: Cassava. *Scientific Name: Manihot esculenta, Crantz/Manihot utilissima. Other:* Bitter cassava, tapioca yuca, juca, sweet potato plant, manioc tapioca, mandioc.

Toxicity: 5.

Location: Cultivated in tropical America, including Florida and southern United States, it is a native of Brazil.

Deadly Parts: There is no danger if used normally. The greatest danger occurs when the plant is improperly prepared by those unfamiliar with the correct way to cook the plant. The raw root or peelings from the tubers have high concentrations of prussic acid sufficient to cause death from cyanide poisoning.

The roots are the primary source of poison, but the leaves contain variable amounts. The poison amygdalin breaks down into hydrocyanic acid, which can cause cyanide poisoning.

Effects and Symptoms: Severe gastroenteritis, including nausea and vomiting; respiratory distress; twitching; staggering; convulsions; coma; and death.

Reaction Time: The AMA lists "some hours"; *Plants That Poison* lists death within minutes.

Antidotes and Treatments: Gastric lavage and symptomatic treatment.

Notes: The tuberous plant yields the starch for cassava-meal and tapioca, but the plant must be heated and the poison dissolved out before the plant is edible. The bitter and sweet cassava varieties are often confused. The bitter is more poisonous than the sweet, but both require careful preparation to be free of cyanogen.

Name: Elderberry. *Scientific Name: Sambucus canadensis. Other:*

American elderberry, black elder; red-berried elder (*S. racemosa*).
Toxicity: 4.
Location: It is found in the eastern and central United States and Canada. It grows six to twelve feet high in woods, waste places, and along streams. The red-berried elder is found in the northern United States and Canada.
Deadly Parts: Although cooked elderberries are safely eaten in jam and pies, the leaves, shoots, bark, roots, and raw berries are poisonous. The poison is cyanogenic glycoside.
Effects and Symptoms: Dizziness, headache, nausea, vomiting, stomach cramps, gastroenteritis, respiratory difficulty, convulsions, tachycardia, and possible death. The American Medical Association says it has found no documented cases of cyanide poisoning from the genus, but other sources disagree.
Reaction Time: Several hours.
Antidotes and Treatments: Gastric lavage and symptomatic treatment.
Notes: The ripe fruit, as used in elderberry wine, is harmless when cooked.
Name: Mandrake. *Scientific Name: Mandragora officinarum. Other:* Devil's apple, loveapple, mayapple.
Toxicity: 4.
Location: The yellow plumlike fruit is found in the Middle East. During wheat harvest time, it is ripe and smells sickeningly sweet.
Deadly Parts: The rootstock, stem, flower, leaves, and unripe fruit. When completely ripe (yellow and soft), the fruit can be eaten without harm but not in quantity. The plant contains several hallucinogenic alkaloids, including hyoscyamine (atropine) and mandragorin.
Effects and Symptoms: Primary symptoms are severe diarrhea with vomiting, insensitivity, heavy sedation, coma, and death. The atropine tends to reduce secretions, decrease gastric juices, and shut down the intestines. Mandrake also causes pupil dilation and some of the same symptoms as scopolamine, including slowed heart rate.
Reaction Time: A few minutes to a half-hour.
Antidotes and Treatments: Gastric lavage and symptomatic treatment.
Notes: Mandrake was well known in biblical times as a fertility drug.
In the Middle Ages, mandrake was famous as a love-potion and was used in incantations and considered a charm against evil spirits. Others believed elves would find its strange odor unbearable.

In 1630 in Hamburg, Germany, three women were executed for possession of mandrake root, supposed evidence that they were involved in witchcraft.

The mandrake has a large root, dark brown and rugged, resembling, to some, the male organ. According to superstition, it would kill a man to touch it fresh, and so a dog was used to pull it out of the ground. Supposedly, the mandrake would shriek and the dog would die.

Mandrake is now regarded as an anesthetic, cathartic, emetic, hypnotic, narcotic, and nervine.

Part of the mandrake family is mayapple (*Podophyllum pelatum*), which causes severe gastroenteritis, headache, giddiness, and collapse. [The poison is especially potent when combined with alcohol, and death can occur in fourteen hours. The taste is rather bitter. Workers handling the root often develop dermatitis. The oil is used externally for removing warts.]

Name: Moonseed. *Scientific Name: Menispermum canadense. Other:* Yellow parilla.

Toxicity: 5.

Location: A woody twining vine with smooth stem and alternate palmately veined and lobed leaves, it grows on the banks of streams, fence rows, and thickets in eastern North America. It is cultivated in other parts of the United States.

Deadly Parts: The bluish-black fruit resembles the wild grape but contains alkaloids with picrotoxinlike activity, which makes it poisonous. The leaves are also poisonous. The pits, with their sharp ridges, cause mechanical injury to the intestines.

Effects and Symptoms: Bloody diarrhea, convulsions, and shock, followed by death.

Reaction Time: Several hours.

Antidotes and Treatments: Gastric lavage and symptomatic treatment.

Notes: Several cases of poisoning have occurred from mistaking the plant for wild grapes. The rootstock is bitter.

A close relative, also called moonseed (*Cocculus ferrandianus*) is native to Hawaii and is used as a fish poison.

Name: Rhubarb. *Scientific Name: Rheum rhaponticum. Other:* Pie plant.

Toxicity: 4.

Location: The plant grows in sandy soil of northern climes. A common perennial, it was introduced from Asia and is now grown in many gardens. It is frequently seen in the northern United States and Canada and southward to Hawaii.

Deadly Parts: The leaves contain oxalic acid, potassium and calcium oxalates, as well as anthraquinone glycosides. The leaves in most varieties are the only poisonous part of the plant and must be removed before cooking or eating.

Effects and Symptoms: If a person unwittingly cooks the leaf blades in with the rhubarb, the digestive irritant may cause stomach pains, nausea, vomiting, hemorrhage, weakness, difficulty breathing, burning of mouth and throat, kidney irritation, and anuria, which then leads to a drop in the calcium content of the blood and cardiac or respiratory arrest.

Reaction Time: Several hours.

Antidotes and Treatments: Gastric lavage along with emesis. Calcium in any form (even milk or lime water) will help to precipitate the oxalate. Calcium salts and calcium gluconate are often given along with extra fluids and supportive care.

Notes: The stalks in some varieties contain oxalic acid, but the leaves contain much more. A woman in early pregnancy aborted before dying from rhubarb poisoning.

Medicinal Plants

Name: Bryony or white bryony. *Scientific Name: Bryonia dioica, B. alba, or B. cretica. Other:* Devil's turnip, British mandrake.

Toxicity: 4. Assuming there is a delay in treatment, the estimated lethal dose for an adult is forty berries.

Location: A common climbing plant in public gardens with decorative berries. The flowers, which bloom in June and July, are greenish-yellow. Found in England, Wales, and other northern climes.

Deadly Parts: The berries and roots are poisonous and contain glycosides, bryonin, and bryonidin.

Effects and Symptoms: Burning of the mouth after ingestion, nausea, and vomiting. The juice is an irritant and blisters the skin. Other symptoms include violent diarrhea, convulsive coma, and paralysis; death results from respiratory arrest.

Reaction Time: Several hours.

Antidotes and Treatments: Gastric lavage and keeping the victim warm and quiet. Demulcents such as milk and eggs are given. Fluid replacement and extra electrolytes are administered as needed. Pain medications are often used.

Notes: When the berries are distilled like an alcohol, the drink can cause abortions. The ripe fruit is a red berry with a dull surface containing flat black and yellow mottled seeds. The whole plant, but especially the root, has an acrid milky juice, the unpleasant odor of which persists after dying. The thick, fleshy, white roots can be mistaken for parsnips or turnips. Medically, it can be used as a diuretic.

Name: Cinchona bark. *Scientific Name: Cinchona ledgeriana.*
Toxicity: 4.
Location: It is native to the South American Andes, but is also found in Java, India, East Africa, as well as Australia and the Caucasus.
Deadly Parts: The bark. The poison is quinoline or quinine.
Effects and Symptoms: Nausea, vomiting, hemorrhage, tinnitus, giddiness, collapse, visual disturbances, coma, death from paralysis with respiratory arrest. Ingestion or injection of large doses causes sudden onset of cardiac depression — or heart failure.
Reaction Time: Several hours.
Antidotes and Treatments: Besides gastric lavage, the falling blood pressure is treated by injection of norepinephrine.
Case Histories: In 1971, a girl from a very strict family in Mexico, thinking she was pregnant, took numerous tablets. Six hours later, she suffered severe convulsions, causing respiratory distress and then death. The autopsy proved she was not pregnant.
Notes: This is also used as an abortifacient. Salt quinine tannate is absorbed slowly and is the least poisonous type. Quinine is used as bitter flavoring in many tonic drinks.

The curative properties were known after the sixteenth century. It was named after the Countess of Chinchon, wife of the Spanish viceroy of Peru. Legend has it that she was cured of malaria by this drug. Toward the end of the Thirty Years' War, the new drug came to Europe via Madrid.

Name: Colocynth. *Scientific Name: Citrullus colocynthis. Other:* Bitter apple, bitter cucumber.
Toxicity: 5.
Location: A pale yellowish-green, bitter-tasting fruit, it is native to the Mediterranean and now found in Central America.
Deadly Parts: The fruit is most deadly. Containing colocynthin, it

is used as an insecticide and sometimes as a purgative and as an abortifacient.

Effects and Symptoms: Blood-tinged diarrhea occurs on the first day, followed by cramps, headache, oliguria, kidney failure, and death.

Reaction Time: Several hours.

Antidotes and Treatments: Milk will relieve gastric irritation, and atropine will decrease the gastric secretions. Pain medications are given as necessary. Victims who live for forty-eight hours will probably recover.

Name: Croton oil. *Scientific Name: Croton tiglium. Other:* Mayapple, gamboge, purging croton.

Toxicity: 6.

Location: Native to Southeast Asia, it is now found in the southwest United States.

Deadly Parts: Seeds and extracted oil.

Effects and Symptoms: Externally, the oil causes blistering skin and irritation. (The blistering skin can last up to three weeks.) Internally, croton oil produces burning pain in the mouth and stomach, bloody diarrhea, violent purging, tachycardia, coma, and death. Autopsy shows blood in the stool and some blood in the urine.

Reaction Time: Immediately on skin contact, within ten to fifteen minutes for ingestion.

Antidotes and Treatments: Gastric lavage is said to be useless. Fluids are pushed and the victim is encouraged to drink as much as possible. Continuous intravenous infusion is used to correct the electrolyte imbalance along with symptomatic treatment of pain and kidney and liver damage.

Notes: It is said ten drops of croton, taken internally, will kill, but we found no cases to prove it.

Croton oil is easily identified if mixed with an equal amount of absolute alcohol and shaken. A reddish-brown color at the junction of the two liquids will slowly form. A diluted solution of oil will cause a blister to appear in four hours.

Croton oil in drinking alcohol is one form of a "Mickey Finn."

Name: Ergot. *Scientific Name: Claviceps purpurea. Other:* Ergot of rye, sansert, St. Anthony's fire.

Toxicity: 5.

Location: It originated in Europe but is now almost everywhere.

Deadly Parts: A fungus parasite, only a small amount is needed to be fatal. The fungus infests cereal grain, particularly rye. The alkaloids from the fungus disintegrate readily, and rye flour contaminated with the black fungus becomes less harmful toward spring. The poison stimulates the smooth muscles and exerts a paralyzing action on the sympathetic system.

Effects and Symptoms: Nausea, vomiting, severe headaches, numbness, anuria, pulmonary infiltration, coma, respiratory or cardiac arrest, and death. Coldness of the extremities and a tingling pain in the chest are caused by the contraction of the blood vessels. Ingestion of the drug tends to cause painful convulsions and contractions of the flexor muscles, which can cause permanent damage to the central nervous system. Psychosis (violent mood swings) can also occur. Gangrene of fingers and toes results when poisoning occurs over several days.

Reaction Time: Several days to weeks.

Antidotes and Treatments: Amyl nitrate is often used to relieve spasms. Gastric lavage should be followed by activated charcoal.

Notes: Ergot's odor and taste are fishy and unpleasant. It is usually parasitic on rye grass.

It is also used as an abortifacient since it causes the uterus to contract; however, the dose necessary to produce abortion is often fatal. Ergot is frequently found in obstetrical departments and is given to women after birth to help the uterus return to normal; seventeenth-century midwives used ergot for the same purposes. Migraine headaches and the pain of herpes zoster (which is related to genital herpes but causes an infection on the skin) can often be helped by ergotamine or methysergide, drugs created from ergot.

In the Middle Ages, the disease process caused by ergot often reached epidemic proportions. In A.D. 944, forty thousand people in France died from it. It was known as *mal des ardents, feu de Saint-Antoine* (also called St. Anthony's fire), and *gangrene des Solognots* and appeared in two forms: gangrenous (affecting the lower limbs especially) and convulsive (with hallucinations and sometimes paralysis). Supposedly only those who prayed to St. Anthony survived, but the true reason they lived was that they were taken to a monastery to be healed while they prayed and were fed bread without ergot.

This fungal disease is seldom seen today since measures have been taken to screen cereals for fungus, and preparations through medicine are relatively harmless. In hypersensitive persons, however, especially those with beginning vascular sclerosis, as little as

0.5 mg of Gynergen, an ergotamine tartrate extract, injected into the muscle can cause necrosis or gangrene. In cases of coronary symptoms, a cardiac infarction could be brought about by intramuscular injection of a small amount of the drug.

Poisoning through ergot can be cumulative.

Name: Foxglove. *Scientific Name: Digitalis purpurea, D. lanata. Other:* Fairy cap, fairy bells, fairy glove, fairy finger, fairy thimbles.
Toxicity: 5.
Location: Cultivated in gardens, foxglove is frequently found wild in north central and northeastern United States, along the Pacific Coast, and Hawaii. A biennial herb, the plant grows to five feet. It has downy stems with only a few leaves on the flowering side. Flowers are purple to white and bloom midsummer. The fruit is a dry capsule with numerous seeds.
Deadly Parts: All parts of the plant are toxic. *Digitalis purpurea* is a heteroside. The leaves contain digitalin, digitoxin, and digitonin. Severe poisoning comes from eating the leaves—either dried or fresh—which do not lose their toxicity by cooking.
Effects and Symptoms: Headache, nausea, vomiting, diarrhea, blurred vision, delirium, slow or irregular pulse, aberrant color vision, and death—usually from ventricular fibrillation. Increasing the force of the heart's contractions, in excess it irritates the heart and stimulates the central nervous system.
Reaction Time: Twenty to thirty minutes.
Antidotes and Treatments: Gastric lavage is followed by activated charcoal. Victims must be monitored constantly by electrocardiogram. Potassium chloride is given every hour unless urine output stops. Potassium level must also be monitored to avoid hyperkalemia and cardiac arrest.
Case Histories: Dr. Edmond de la Pommerais was the son of a French country doctor with pretensions to the title of Count. His medical practice gave him only modest support, and so in 1861 he married Mlle Dubisy for her considerable dowry. The money helped him maintain his mistress, Seraphine de Pawr. He worked out a plan to insure de Pawr's life for over a half-million francs. She was supposed to feign illness and scare the insurance company into paying an annuity as a price for canceling the policy.

De Pawr became ill according to plan but died, apparently of cholera, after being attended by her physician-lover. The insurance company began to investigate, and Madame de Pawr's body was exhumed. She had been given a massive dose of digitalis.

The doctor was arrested and tried for the double murder of his mother-in-law and his mistress. De la Pommerais was convicted of the second murder and guillotined in 1864.

Notes: Most poisonings are from therapeutic overdoses rather than by homicidal or suicidal intent.

Children have been poisoned by sucking on the flowers and swallowing the seeds.

Name: Indian tobacco. *Scientific Name: Lobelia inflata. Other:* Eyebright, bladderpod, asthma weed, lobelia.

Toxicity: 5.

Location: Found in waste areas, woodlands, and roadsides, it is native to eastern North America and less commonly found westward to Nebraska and Arkansas. It comes in blue, red, and white flowers.

Deadly Parts: The whole plant is toxic. The poisons are lobeline and related alkaloids. All parts of the plant contain a milky, toxic juice. All species cause human poisoning. Leaves, stems, and fruits are a frequent cause of skin rash.

Effects and Symptoms: Nausea, vomiting, exhaustion, prostration, dilation of pupils, stupor, coma, convulsion, and death. It is similar to nicotine poisoning. Convulsions lead to death by respiratory failure.

Reaction Time: One to several hours.

Antidotes and Treatments: Gastric lavage is done. Artificial respiration may be needed. Valium is given for convulsion. Atropine is administered as needed.

Notes: Indian tobacco is used medically in the treatment of laryngitis and spasmodic asthma. Overdoses act as narcotic poisons.

The plant is so-called because Indians dried and smoked the leaves. Eyebright is found in herb stores and is used to brew weak tea.

Name: Ipecac. *Scientific Name: Cephaelis ipecacuanha. Other:* Emetine.

Toxicity: 5.

Location: It is found throughout Europe and the Americas.

Deadly Parts: The berries and juice of the plant are most toxic.

Effects and Symptoms: The plant's juice causes nausea and vomiting and is used in medicine to rid victims of poison. However, an overdose will lead to fatigue, dyspnea, tachycardia, low blood pressure, collapse, loss of consciousness, and death from heart failure. Convulsions are also possible.

Emetine, the alkaloid extracted from the plant, weakens the heart, and the effect can be cumulative over a month or more; so the fictional killer can use chronic poisoning here.

The poison is also readily absorbed through injection, which can kill tissue. Oral absorption is uncertain since vomiting often interferes with this.

An autopsy shows congestion of stomach and intestine, and degenerative changes in the liver, kidneys, and heart. Kidney and liver damage can occur after massive doses.

Reaction Time: Immediate. Death may be delayed twenty-four hours to one week. Recovery may take as long as one year.

Antidotes and Treatments: Morphine and complete bed rest are advised after gastric lavage.

Notes: Used as an emetic in syrup form to rid the stomach of poisons, it is found in many houscholds.

The fluid extract from the plant is fourteen times more potent than the syrup sold over the counter and should never be used as a substitute for the syrup.

Name: Tansy. *Scientific Name: Tanacetum vulgare.*

Toxicity: 5.

Location: A perennial herb, a weed of the roadsides, waste places, and somctimes pastures, it is native to Europe but is now widely spread throughout the eastern United States and Pacific Northwest. It occurs chiefly on peat land and alluvial soils.

Deadly Parts: The leaves, flowers, and stem contain the toxic oil, tanacetin.

Effects and Symptoms: Convulsions, frothing at the mouth, violent spasms, dilated pupils, quick and feeble pulse, kidney problems, and death. Dermatitis is also caused by touching the plant.

Reaction Time: Several hours.

Antidotes and Treatments: Gastric lavage and symptomatic treatment.

Notes: "Oil of tansy" is used to kill intestinal worms, induce abortion, and encourage menstruation. Humans are often poisoned by taking overdoses of oil or tea made from the leaves. The herb has a very bitter taste and was commonly used in the Middle Ages for witchcraft.

Other Medicinal Poisons: Mistletoe *(Phoradendron flavescens/Vis-*

cum album) grows primarily in southern states but can be found elsewhere. While the whole plant is toxic (toxicity level 3), especially the pearl berries, and causes symptoms such as vomiting, slowed pulse, diarrhea, and some digitalislike symptoms, fatal poisonings are rare. Phoratoxin, the poison, inhibits synthesization of proteins in the intestinal wall.

White snakeroot or **white sanicle** *(Eupatorium rugosum,* toxicity level 3) causes a disease known as "milk sickness." The disease was traced to the ingestion of dairy products derived from livestock poisoned by the herb. The herb exists in eastern North America. The milk of cows that feed on snakeroot becomes poisonous. The toxic principle of white snakeroot is an unstable alcohol, tremetol, and is found in combination with an incomplete resin acid.

Drinking milk or eating other contaminated dairy products may result in weakness, nausea, vomiting, constipation, tremors, prostration, delirium, and even death in 10 percent to 25 percent of victims. Reaction time is several hours to several days.

"Milk sickness" was common in the early colonial days and became one of the most dreaded diseases from North Carolina and Virginia to the Midwest until the early nineteenth century. The massive loss of life of former times, however, cannot occur with current milk processing methods.

Flowering Plants

Name: Black hellebore. *Scientific Name: Helleborus niger. Other:* Christmas rose.

Toxicity: 5.

Location: It is found in the northern United States and Canada and is related to the American variety.

Deadly Parts: The entire plant is poisonous and contains helleborein, hellebrin, helleborin, saponins, and protoamemonie.

Effects and Symptoms: The poison has a blistering effect on the mucous membranes of the mouth, causes severe diarrhea, vomiting, and death from cardiac arrest.

Reaction Time: Symptoms begin within a half-hour, but death may take several hours.

Antidotes and Treatments: Cardiac and respiratory stimulants as amyl nitrate, strychnine, and atropine are often used.

Case Histories: In 1987, a Los Angeles emergency room saw a patient complaining of stomach pains and vomiting. No reason could be found for his distress, however, and he went away. He returned several hours later complaining he could not feel his arms. Before the nurse could check him out, he went into convulsions and died. Only later was it discovered that he had been poisoned by a friend, who was angry that the young man had given him AIDS.

Name: Black locust. *Scientific Name: Robinia pseudoacacia. Other:* Bastard acacia, black acacia, false acacia, pea flower locust.

Toxicity: 5.

Location: Native to eastern North America, it is found especially from Pennsylvania through Georgia and the Ozark Mountains.

Deadly Parts: Children and animals are especially susceptible when chewing on inner bark, seeds, and leaves. The poison is robin—a phototoxin, not the bird. The poison interferes with synthesis of protein in the intestine.

Effects and Symptoms: Purging, stupor, depressed heart action, weakened pulse, gastroenteritis, coldness of arms and legs, various features of shock, possible convulsions, and death.

Reaction Time: One hour.

Antidotes and Treatments: Gastric lavage and symptomatic treatment.

Name: Bloodroot. *Scientific Name: Sanguinaria canadensis.*

Toxicity: 4.

Location: A perennial herb with thick rootstocks and red juice. Shiny, white, poppylike flowers with eight petals and a yellow stamen appear early in spring. Found from southern Canada to Florida and as far west as Texas, it's frequently found in rich woodlands and among bushes along fence rows.

Deadly Parts: All parts are poisonous. Contact with the red sap may cause skin rashes. The poison is sanguinarine.

Effects and Symptoms: It reduces the heart's action and muscle strength and depresses the nerves. Death occurs from overdoses after violent vomiting, extreme thirst, great burning and soreness in that region, followed by heaviness of the chest with difficult breathing, dilation of pupils, faintness, coldness of skin, and cardiac paralysis.

Reaction Time: One to two hours.

Antidotes and Treatments: Gastric lavage and symptomatic treatment.

Notes: Bloodroot has a bitter and acrid taste. It causes a painful irritation when the prickles enter the skin.

Name: Dog mercury. *Scientific Name: Mercurialis perennis, M. annua. Other:* Herb mercury.

Toxicity: 5.

Location: Native to Europe, it is also found in waste places in the eastern United States.

Deadly Parts: All of the plant is toxic. The poison is mercurialine or oil of Euphorbia.

Effects and Symptoms: Mercury acts as an emetic and purgative. Irritant and narcotic symptoms also appear. The poison is cumulative in its effect, and death can result from cardiac depression.

Reaction Time: Several hours.

Antidotes and Treatments: Gastric lavage and symptomatic treatment.

Notes: The plants are poisonous when eaten fresh but not when dried or boiled. Apparently heat kills the poison.

Name: False hellebore. *Scientific Name: Veratrum alba, V. viride, V. californicum. Other:* Related to death camas; both are members of the lily family.

Toxicity: 5.

Location: It is found widely distributed in the northern temperate zone.

Deadly Parts: All parts are toxic.

Effects and Symptoms: The principal manifestations of poisoning are vomiting and rise and fall of blood pressure. Ingested, it causes nausea, severe vomiting, diarrhea, muscular weakness, visual disturbances, slow pulse (down to 30 or below), and low blood pressure.

Repeated use of small doses may produce tolerance to the blood pressure lowering effect but not to the raising effect.

Reaction Time: Within twenty minutes.

Antidotes and Treatments: Gastric lavage and symptomatic treatment.

Notes: The medical use of *Veratrum* alkaloids has caused myotonia, muscular spasms, and neuropathy.

Name: Cuckoopint. *Scientific Name: Arum maculatum. Other:* Adam and Eve, Lords-and-Ladies, wild arum, wake-robin.

Toxicity: 5.

Location: Native to southern Europe and northern Africa, it is also now found as far north as England. The North American variety,

Jack-in-the-Pulpit (*Arisaema atroubens*), is seen in the South, where it is a common houseplant.

The flower is about ten inches long, green, and often spotted with purple. The fruits are a brilliant red.

Deadly Parts: The whole plant is poisonous. The sweet-tasting berries, sour leaves, flowers, and roots are most deadly. The poisons are aroin, which is related to coniine (hemlock), and calcium oxylate.

Effects and Symptoms: Blistering, severe gastroenteritis, hemorrhages, convulsions, mydriasis, coma, and death.

Reaction Time: Several hours.

Antidotes and Treatments: No immediate treatment is known unless swelling of pharynx causes obstruction to breathing, which can be treated.

Name: Hydrangea. *Scientific Name: Hydrangea macrophylla. Other:* Hortensia, hills of snow.

Toxicity: 5.

Location: Native to Japan, the ornamental shrubs with their white, pink, or blue flowers are now found in Europe and the Western Hemisphere.

Deadly Parts: All parts, especially the flower buds, are toxic. The poison is a cyanogenetic glycoside (hydrangin).

Effects and Symptoms: Gastroenteritis, and other cyanide symptoms.

Reaction Time: Several hours before symptoms occur, as the glycosides must decompose by reacting with water in the gastrointestinal tract before releasing the poison.

Antidotes and Treatments: Gastric lavage and symptomatic treatment.

Notes: The public health departments list hydrangea as one of the most poisonous plants.

Name: Narcissus. *Scientific Name: Narcissus poeticus. Other:* Poets' narcissus, pheasant's eye.

Toxicity: 5.

Location: These flowers are native to Central Europe and North Africa.

Deadly Parts: All of the plant is toxic, especially the bulbs.

Effects and Symptoms: Nausea, severe vomiting for several hours, colic, tetanic convulsions, collapse, paralysis, and death.

Reaction Time: Several hours to a few days.

Antidotes and Treatments: Gastric lavage and symptomatic treatment.

Notes: Confusing the bulbs with onions or garlic cloves can cause poisoning. Soup is often made from them by mistake. Skin rashes occur in growers and others engaged in handling.

The jonquil *(N. jonquilla)* and daffodil *(N. pseudonarcissus)* are varieties of narcissus. All are grown as garden flowers.

Case Histories: A four-year-old girl died from sucking the juice from the flower's stem.

Name: Yellow jasmine. *Scientific Name: Gelsemium sempervirens. Other:* Yellow jessamine, Carolina jasmine, Carolina yellow jasmine, evening trumpet flower, Carolina wild woodbine.

Toxicity: 5.

Location: It is native to all continents except North America and Antarctica.

Deadly Parts: All parts are deadly. The poison is gelsemine, gelsemicine, and other related alkaloids.

Effects and Symptoms: Extreme weakness, frontal headache, intention tremor, giddiness, ataxia, dryness of skin or mouth, paralysis of tongue and aphasia, low body temperature, bradycardia, labored breathing, anxiety states, tetanic convulsions before death. In death, the face takes on a masklike expression. The pupils are completely dilated and fixed as if the victim were drugged.

Reaction Time: At high doses, death occurs in ten minutes; at low doses, after several hours.

Antidotes and Treatments: Gastric lavage and symptomatic treatment.

Notes: The drug is used mainly in liquid form against trigeminal neuralgia (jaw-nerve pain).

Miscellaneous Plant Poisons

The **Betel nut seed** *(Areca catechu)*, found in Central and Southwest Asia and South America, contains arecolin, a toxic alkaloid, arecain, and other poisons (toxicity level 5). Symptoms are vomiting, diarrhea, difficulty breathing, impaired vision, convulsions, and death within twenty minutes. Natives chew a less than toxic dose for its narcotic effect. Atropine is sometimes used as a treatment.

Celandine *(Chelidonium majus)* — also called felonwart, rock poppy, swallow wort, or wort weed — is deadly in all parts, but especially the leaves and stems. The poisons are celandine and isoquino-line (toxicity level 5). Symptoms take about fourteen hours and include nausea, vomiting, coma, and death.

Henbane (*Hyoscyamus niger*) — or insane root, fetid nightshade, poison tobacco, stinking nightshade, or black henbane — is known from Egypt to India and is now grown commercially in many parts of North America and California. It's most noted for hyoscyamine. The *H. reticulatus* variety of the plant grows only in India. All parts are poisonous, especially the roots and leaves. The seeds, with the highest scopolamine content, exert a central nervous system depressant. The poisons are hyoscyamine and atropine (toxicity level 5). Its symptoms are similar to those of atropine or deadly nightshade poisoning. It works in about fifteen minutes. A medicinal herb, the seeds and juice are deadly poison. This fact was known to the ancient Egyptians.

Horse chestnut (*Aesculus hippocastanum*) or buckeye is commonly found in northern England and northern United States. The poisons occur within the fruit. Symptoms include restlessness, severe vomiting, diarrhea, mydriasis, delirium, and death from respiratory arrest (toxicity level 5). It takes one to two days to work. Human poisoning has occurred when conkers are eaten in mistake for sweet chestnuts. Children have also been poisoned by making tea from the leaves or from eating the seeds. Honey made from California buckeye is also poisonous.

Larkspur (*Delphinium consolida, D. alpinum*) — also called delphinium or stagger weed — is similar to monkshood. A member of the buttercup family, it produces the same symptoms as monkshood poisoning, including the slowing of the heartbeat. Symptoms are a burning in the mouth, dermatitis, nausea, vomiting, respiratory distress, itching, cyanosis, and death. The entire plant is toxic; however, the young leaves eaten before the plant has flowered and the mature seeds, which contain concentrated doses of toxic alkaloids, are most deadly (toxicity level 4). The toxicity of the plant decreases with age. Symptoms begin immediately and death may occur in six hours. Larkspur is a great killer of livestock and is native to the United States.

Poinsettia (*Euphorbia pulcherrima*), a popular Christmas plant of the spurge family, the colorful leaves gathered at the top are often mistaken for flowers. They are bred in Hawaii and grow much larger in tropical climates. All parts of the plant contain a milky sap (toxicity level 4). Symptoms include abdominal pain with vomiting and diarrhea. Only two documented cases of death from poinsettia poisoning have been found in the literature.

It surprises some to know that the ordinary **potato** can be poisonous. Called *Solanum tuberoscum*, the poison (toxicity level 5) is contained in the green parts of the plant, the berries, and the sprouts of the unripe potato (which might make a good salad for some poor victim). Symptoms include burning and rawness in throat, headache, lassitude, vomiting, abdominal pain, diarrhea, cerebral edema, stupor, coma, convulsions, and death, much like its cousin deadly nightshade. Poison can be detected in the urine. Reaction time is fifteen to thirty minutes.

The **spindle tree** (*Euonymus europaeus*) is found in Europe and America. The leaves, seeds, and bark contain evomonoside, a cardiac glycoside (toxicity level 4). Symptoms are watery, blood-tinged diarrhea; colic; vomiting; fever; convulsions; and liver enlargement that can lead to death in eight to ten hours. The symptoms are similar to meningitis.

There are many poisons native to Africa and used as arrow poisons. *Buphane disticha* is also widely used in Africa by the medicine man. All parts of the plant are poisonous and contain buphanie, which reacts like scopolamine.

The **giant milkweed** (*Calotropis procera, C. gigantea*) is also used for arrow poisons in Africa. The latex contains the cardiac glycoside calotropin and is extremely potent. Minute amounts can cause death. It's a popular drug for suicides and murders in tropical America, as well.

Another African plant is *Albizia anthelmintica*. The bark of this plant is used as an anthelmintic and purgative, but a small overdose is said to cause death. Found in southwest Africa and Ethiopia, it's used for killing tapeworm by one tribe.

Passion flower (*Adenia volkensii*) is also considered a serious human poison in eastern Africa and may contain both a cyanogenic glycoside and a phytotoxin, like the southern African *A. digitata*. The Mau Mau used it in their oathing ceremonies. Other tribes used this plant to poison hyena bait. Symptoms include drowsiness and weakness increasing to paralysis and followed by death. The plant is a cortical depressant working on the higher centers of the brain. Minute quantities of *A. digitata* are sufficient to cause death.

In Guatemala and Panama, the leaves of the *Caesalpinia pulch-*

errima plant are used to poison fish and the seeds to poison criminals.

Africa also has the **African milk plant** (*Euphorbia lactea*). When the spine is broken, the poisonous juice comes out. It's reportedly used by women to rid themselves of evil husbands. There are several varieties of the Euphorbia family (*E. candelabrum, E. grantii, E. neglecta, E. giomgiecpstata, E. systyloides, E. tirucalli*) found all over Africa. Some are used medicinally, others are used for fish and arrow poisons. *E. candelabrum* is used in making arrow poisons, as is *E. neglecta*. *E. systyloides* is used as a remedy for hookworms, but too much will cause delirium, convulsions, and death within six hours.

F I V E

FRAGILE FUNGI

There are old *mushroom hunters and there are* bold *mushroom hunters but there are few* old, bold *mushroom hunters.*
— Anonymous

Like the other types of poisons, mushrooms have many myths surrounding them. One is that poisonous mushrooms — commonly called toadstools — can be detoxified by adding vinegar to the water and pouring off that water in which they've been boiled. Nor is it wise to have dogs or pigs root out the mushrooms, since a lethal dose for the animals differs greatly from a human dose, and many mushrooms have a delayed response time. Even if animals have eaten the mushrooms, what is edible for them might be fatal for a human. Often dried mushrooms are considered harmless and in some cases this might be true, but not for the Amanita family.

Folklore suggests checking for poison in mushrooms by slicing the fungus and rubbing a silver coin against the open surface. The coin will theoretically darken from the hydrogen cyanide or sulfide formation in the mushroom. The trouble with this test is that this reaction occurs with both edible and nonedible mushrooms, and some poisonous mushrooms will give no reaction at all.

There are reliable and fairly simple tests that can tell whether a given specimen is safe, reasonably safe, or very risky. Any good field guide will tell mushroom hunters what poisonous look-alikes an edible mushroom has, and what differences to look for (cap color, gill color, season, habitat).

The spore is the mushroom seed found in the mushroom's gill. Besides appearance, spore tests are the chief means of identification. The color of the spores gives the family type, and all mushroom hunters know that the Amanita family have white or colorless spores and so show up only on dark paper.

To see spores close up, you'll need a microscope. However, using dark and light papers as contrast, the spore color can be tested and the mushroom identified. Cut the mushroom, place it gill down on a half-dark, half-white piece of paper, then place a cover or a jar over the mushroom. Leave it for a short while and then lift the jar, checking to see the color left on the paper.

Each year a hundred or more people die from eating poisonous mushrooms. Most of these folks are amateur mushroom hunters who think they know what they're choosing, but some undoubtedly were fed mushrooms that seemed safe and were not.

Poisonous and nonpoisonous mushrooms often grow side by side. The mushroom brought in for identification may not be the only one eaten. It has been estimated that at least one hundred of the approximately five thousand species of mushrooms in the United States are poisonous. Since mushroom poisoning can be confused with other illnesses, the actual incidence of death by mushroom poisoning is not fully documented, but some sources estimate the amount as being up to a thousand cases a year or more.

Poisoning caused by mushrooms ranges from mild indigestion to death. The quicker help is reached, the better the chance of recovery. As with any poison, children and the ill and elderly are more likely to have fatal attacks with less of the fungus than a normal adult. Many of the "safe" mushrooms have a slight amount of poison in them. If they are not properly cooked before being eaten, they will cause stomach upset, and in children can be fatal. Some varieties will be fatal if allowed to stand for some time, and still others if prepared and rewarmed once or several times. There have been numerous cases of leftover casseroles being served day after day only to have the consumer hospitalized with severe gastrointestinal problems.

All the mushrooms are pleasant to taste and can be cooked in any way that edible mushrooms would be served. Until chemical analysis is done on the fungi or on the stomach contents, it's almost impossible to tell which mushroom has been eaten.

The poisons can sometimes be extracted and seem to be soluble in alcohol. Spilling infected alcohol on exposed body parts will often lead to absorption through the skin with almost the same effect as if the mushroom had been eaten.

The killer can never be sure of the effect the mushrooms will have, which makes them a difficult murder weapon.

Since the administration of the poison for all varieties of mushrooms usually comes from eating them, *location* will be substituted throughout the chapter for the *administration* subheading.

Amanita Family

The rule with Amanitas is **never** eat one. In fact, never eat any mushroom that might be one, unless you're an expert and are absolutely 100 percent sure of your identification. Particularly dangerous are the beautiful snow-white to pale-green or tan Amanitas.

The most certain means of quick identification — short of studies at the microscopic level — are spore print, gill type, and base type. In the earliest or eggsac stage, Amanitas might be confused with small (edible) puffballs. Simply cutting open the specimen will reveal whether the fungus in question is a gilled mushroom (and possibly an Amanita) or a solid, cheeselike puffball.

The spores may vary within the Amanita species, but they are still distinct from the edible mushroom. Field mushrooms (*Agaricus campestris*) have brown spores with pink gills turning tan and then chocolate with age. The gills are attached to the stem and can be seen when the mushroom is cut lengthwise.

Other Amanitas have white spores and white to very pale gills. The gills are not attached to the stem. When dug carefully from the ground, with dirt gently brushed off, Amanitas reveal a swollen bag or volva (small cup) at the base of the stem. In the early (button) stage, the entire mushroom is covered with a membrane (universal veil) from crown to base. Remnants of this veil may cling to the cap, appearing as a ring, a little skirt beneath the cap, or in patches along the stem.

Name: *Amanita phalloides* (death cap) is the most dangerous species. *Other*: Because of disagreements among mycologists in classification, and because of the close similarities between the related species, this general description also includes close relatives, *A. verna* (fool's mushroom), *A. virosa* (destroying angel or death angel), and *A. bisporiger* (smaller death angel).

Toxicity: 5.

Location: Abundantly available in America and Europe and known in ancient times (Pliny's writings ascribe numerous cases of poisoning to the fungi), Amanitas are usually found in the Mid-Atlantic States down to Florida, west to Texas. They flourish between October and December. *A. phalloides* prefers to grow singular in woods and likes damper, sandy soil at medium and lower elevations. Other versions of Amanita prefer dry pine woods. The smaller death angel likes mixed woods but can be found in wooded lawns, especially near oaks, and grows from May through October.

Form: The cap color varies from pale-green or yellow-olive in Europe and in some places along the two coasts of the United States, to colors ranging from white to light brown in the rest of the United States. Another amanitin, *A. mutabilis*, has an aniselike odor and reddish granules on its cap. Not as deadly as its sisters, the poison can still do serious damage if not caught in time.

Effects and Symptoms: The two main poisons involved are amanitin, which is slow acting, produces hypoglycemia, and is responsible for the major symptoms; and phalloidin, which acts much more quickly and produces degenerative changes in kidney, liver, and cardiac muscles.

Symptoms are slow to develop, usually six to fifteen hours after eating, sometimes as long as forty-eight hours later. The longer the delay, the more dangerous the results, since the toxin attacks the liver almost as soon as the toadstool is digested and, without symptoms, people seldom seek medical attention. Also, in the absence of any ill-effects, the subject will probably have additionally eaten the rest of the fungus, thus increasing the dose.

Amanitin can be detected in the blood almost immediately. The first physical symptoms are usually nausea, vomiting, and bloody diarrhea. After an early feeling of slight discomfort, there is a sudden onset of extreme stomach pains, violent vomiting, intense thirst, and cyanosis of extremities. If the liver is badly affected, jaundice occurs in the eyes and skin. The sufferer remains conscious almost to the end, with only brief periods of unconsciousness between long lucid intervals before lapsing into a final coma and dying.

Because of severe dehydration, it's only a matter of time before the potassium levels cause cardiac arrest.

Reaction Time: Six to fifteen hours after eating. Sometimes there may be no symptoms for forty-eight hours. Death may occur on the fourth or seventh day—or recovery may take up to two weeks.

Antidotes and Treatments: There are no known antidotes for Amanita poisoning; however, victims have survived after receiving liver transplants. The first recourse is to pump the stomach.

For amanitin-type poisoning, thioctic acid has been suggested and recently discarded as it is not approved in the United States. Still used in Europe, the drug has some unknown side effects not yet tested; therefore the medication has not been approved by the FDA.

Notes: Since poisoning by death cup is usually associated with complete disruption of the body metabolism, the symptoms often mimic hypoglycemia or Asiatic cholera.

Name: Panther mushroom. *Scientific Name: Amanita pantherina. Other:* Fly agaric (*A. muscaria*).

Toxicity: 3.

Location: Found in Europe, the Pacific Northwest, and other parts of the United States.

Form: The fly agaric mushroom is lovely to look at, resembling the "good luck" mushroom (red with white flecks) seen in many European paintings. Used in decoration around Europe, the mushroom was considered harmless. In the United States, the two related varieties come in an assortment of attractive colors—from chrome yellow to red to orange to grayish brown to cinnamon. The deep brown version is lovely and deadly in the Pacific Northwest. Those in other parts of the country have other color variants. All have distinctive white patches on the caps, though these may disappear with age. The fly agaric and the panther mushroom are related and the panther, because of the color variations, tends sometimes to be confused with the agaric.

All have the Amanita family's typical unattached, whitish gills with white spores. The bases, often underground, are usually bulbous with at least the remnants of the typical Amanita "cup" base.

Fly agaric, so-called because it's used to kill flies, is found in the summer along the roadside, on the border of fields, and in the groves of coniferous trees. Preferring a poor soil of sand or gravel in the northern and higher parts of the southern states, as well as much of Europe, these mushrooms often grow in arcs or fairy rings in hard woods or mixed woods during the late fall.

Effects and Symptoms: The chief poison is ibotenic acid affecting the central nervous system.

The symptoms associated with these mushrooms occur quickly, within a half-hour to three hours after ingestion. The main poisons involved are choline and muscarine, which cause a fall in blood pressure, slowed pulse, stomach upset, light-headedness, and profuse water loss from tears, saliva, sweat, and diarrhea. Ibotenic acid and muscimol cause dizziness, convulsions, delusions, violent headache, blurred vision, muscle cramps, staggering, and coma. Respiratory failure and death may occur but only after a large amount has been ingested and proper medical care has not been sought.

The fly agaric also causes copious mucus in the throat and closing of the throat. This may subside within twenty-four hours unless the victim has eaten a large quantity or was ill previously, in which case the mushroom could prove deadly.

Reaction Time: One-half hour to three hours.

Antidotes and Treatments: Pumping the stomach. Atropine is often used. Symptoms may subside in six to twenty-four hours. Death has been reported in several victims with concurrent diseases or who ate an abundance of the mushroom.

Notes: Thought safe until recently, the panther mushroom is more poisonous than the fly agaric. Its deadly powers were noticed in the 1946 Berlin outbreak, where fifteen hundred people were poisoned. Post-wartime Germany was hungry, and even though this was some time after the war had ended, food was still scarce. Mushroom hunters were out in full force that year, gathering what they could from nature to survive. Unfortunately, many did not survive.

Cortinarius Family

Name: Cort. *Scientific Name*: *Cortinarius orellanus*. *Other*: Cortinarious.

Toxicity: 5. One-and-a-half cups of this cooked mushroom is enough to make someone deathly ill.

Location: Found in Central Europe (largely Poland and surrounding areas).

Form: The family name comes from the cobwebby veil that often covers the gills of young mushrooms. Cap colors vary from shades of blue-violet (usually edible) to red and shades of brown or reddish-brown (some of the most deadly). With the spores ranging from gray-brown to orange-brown to orange, the family includes Inocybes, Hebelomas, Galerinas, Gymnopilus, and others of doubtful edibility.

Effects and Symptoms: The poison orellanin acts silently against the liver and kidneys.

Symptoms include nausea, vomiting, dizziness, rapid heartbeat, jaundice, urinary retention, blood-tinged urine, weakness, convulsions, coma, and eventual death.

Reaction Time: It often takes anywhere from three days to two weeks for the symptoms to show. By that time, the liver and kidneys are so damaged that very little can be done to save the victim.

Antidotes and Treatments: Pumping the stomach is good only if the victim is given emergency treatment immediately after ingesting the mushroom. By the time the symptoms show up, kidney and liver transplants are often the only lifesaving measures.

Notes: For a long time, it was thought that only the *Amanita* family of fungi were lethal, but *Cortinarius orellanus* has now been proven to be just as deadly.

Name: Galerinas. *Scientific Name*: *Cortinarius speciosissimus*, *C. gentilis*, and *C. orellanus*. *Other*: Deadly cort, deadly galerina, deadly lawn galerina.

Toxicity: 6.

Location: *C. orellanus* occurs mainly in Europe, while *C. gentilis* and *C. speciosissimus* occur commonly throughout the United States especially in lawns of the Northwest as does *Galerina venenata*. Deadly galerina (*G. autumnalis*) occurs throughout the United States and Canada.

Form: These deadly brown-capped fungi are all lethal. The cap colors range from brown to reddish-brown.

Effects and Symptoms: The poison involved, orellanin, causes acute or chronic kidney failure. Other as yet unidentified toxins may be involved, since those poisoned show severe damage to intestines, genital organs, liver, heart, nervous system, and kidneys.

Symptoms include acute gastroenteritis, headaches, pains in back and joints, and kidney failure. After several deceptive improvements, the last condition may lead to death several months later.

Reaction Time: It takes ten or more hours for the symptoms to show up, and sometimes there are no symptoms for as long as two weeks after ingestion.

Antidotes and Treatments: None known. The vomiting that normally occurs, if soon enough after, can sometimes expel the poison. Hospital treatment may save a victim.

Notes: A member of the Cortinarius family, it has some of the similar symptoms.

Name: Inocybe. *Scientific Name: Inocybe napipes, I. fastigiata. Other:* Caesar's fiber head, torn fiber head, scaly fiber head.

Toxicity: There are several varieties of this group, and the toxicity level can vary from 3 to 5.

Location: Abundant under conifers, especially white pines and in pine plantations, these mushrooms will occasionally be found under hardwoods in all parts of the United States.

Form: As do all corts, the Inocybes have brownish spores (from rush-brown to gray-brown, never purple-brown like the "good" mushrooms). The mushrooms tend to have small, brown fibrous caps.

Effects and Symptoms: The poison muscarine affects the autonomic nervous system and the liver. The other poison common with the cort family is orellanin.

The symptoms start with profuse sweating, salivation, stupor, and rapid loss of consciousness. The face takes on a bluish tinge, and the lips swell and become pinker as the blood vessels dilate. Muscles are flaccid, though from time to time twitching of the extremities will be noted. Reflexes are barely noticeable and pulse becomes difficult to find. Cardiac arrest occurs in the final stage only 4 percent of the time, since medical attention is usually reached soon enough.

Reaction Time: Sometimes as quickly as one hour after ingestion.

Antidotes and Treatments: Not as deadly as the Amanita group, it is possible to regurgitate the poison and recover shortly thereafter. Stomach pumping is the first recourse and then atropine can help, as it is an antidote for muscarine. A high protein diet will help the liver recover.

Notes: Of the Inocybe group, the most dangerous are *I. napipes* and *I. fastigiata.*

Gyromitra Family

Names: Turbantop. *Scientific Name*: *Gyromitra esculenta*. *Other*: False morel (*G. infula*). There is a variety called true morel, which is safe to eat but has pits.

Toxicity: Varies from 2 to 5, depending on the variety.

Location: Gyromitra is abundant in Central Europe, England, and Scandinavia, as well as North America. The ones in North America are almost all deadly. A few of the European varieties can be eaten safely.

Form: False morel is brown in color and looks like a brain folded over or a tumor gone wild. The stem is thick but hollow.

Effects and Symptoms: Hemolytic, it destroys the red blood cells. It also affects the kidney and central nervous system. Gyromitra mushrooms have the poison monomethylhydrazine (mmh), which causes vomiting, diarrhea, convulsions, destruction of red blood cells, and coma. Symptoms start eight to twelve hours after ingestion, and malfunction of the liver causes death in 20 to 40 percent of the cases.

Reaction Time: Anywhere from two to twenty-four hours.

Antidotes and Treatments: Pyridoxine seems to help gyromitrin-type poisoning. If the victim can keep fluids and food down, charcoal ingestion is successful, as well as vitamin K to control the bleeding from the damaged liver.

Notes: Very tasty to eat, some European varieties are safe but American varieties are poisonous.

Yet another type of fungus, this species breaks down the blood. *G. esculenta* (also called turbantop) and *G. infula* contain compounds similar to a common component of rocket fuel. Some toxins may be removed from Gyromitra mushrooms by drying, boiling, rinsing, and boiling again.

General Notes

In England, the chief fungi, apart from *Amanita phalloides*, are *Inocybe patouillardi*, *Amanita muscaria*, *A. pantheria*, and *A. rubescens*. In South Africa, *A. capensis* is the most common. In Central America, the hallucinogenic mushrooms are most prevalent. Similar effects arc had from Stropharia in East Africa. In the United States, *A. phalloides*, *A. verna*, and *A. virosa* are most common.

The smooth ink cap mushroom (*Coprinus atramentarius*) mimics Antabuse (a drug used to cure alcoholics by aversion therapy) so that, if alcohol is ingested at the same time (or within forty-eight hours) after eating the mushrooms, the result may be nausea, vomiting, heavy sweating, and respiratory difficulty, congestion of the face, and even tachycardia. Recovery can occur within a few hours, but if enough of the ink cap mushroom is taken in combination with alcohol, low blood pressure and sometimes cardiovascular collapse can occur. Symptoms appear almost immediately upon imbibing. This mushroom is found near the buried wood of hardwood.

In one case, when a family ingested a large quantity of unknown mushrooms and had slight symptoms nine hours later, the physician prescribed castor oil and charcoal to rid the stomach of its contents. Only one of the family took the medic's advice and recovered. The others, feeling better after vomiting, decided they were all right, only to rapidly deteriorate on the third day and die on the fourth.

Wilhelm Winter, a Marin County, California, amateur mycologist, "tasted death and found it delicious." He'd prepared gathered mushrooms for a friend and denied the symptoms could be from the plants. Sure his symptoms would go away shortly, he told his friend not to worry. She, however, sought medical attention. Even so, both lapsed into comas and liver transplants were necessary before they recovered.

The movie *The Beguiled* showed a young girl switching good mushrooms for poisonous ones so she could kill her chosen victim.

Agrippina, mother of ancient Rome's Nero, poisoned anyone who got in her or her son's way. When her husband, Claudius, tried to name someone else his heir, Agrippina fed Claudius poison mushrooms. He died within twelve hours and was subsequently deified. Nero decided that mushrooms must be the food of the gods, since that is what Claudius became.

Count de Vecchi, an Italian nobleman during the later Victorian era, died after eating fly agaric late in the season that he probably confused with royal agaric (*Agraicus caesarea*), a highly edible mushroom and one with features similar to fly agaric. His diary includes final notes on his agony and moments before death.

S I X

SNAKES, SPIDERS, AND OTHER LIVING THINGS

With thy sharp teeth this knot
intrinsicate
Of life at once untie; poor
venomous fool,
Be angry, and dispatch . . .
     —Shakespeare
     Antony and Cleopatra

When most people think of poison, they most likely think of how deadly it is, and many zoological toxins are among the deadliest. However, evaluating the killing power of zoological toxins is tricky because of the many variables involved. For the purposes of this chapter, only the most fatal will be discussed.

An interesting bit of trivia: When the whiskers of a tiger are ground up and fed to a victim, the reaction is the same as ingesting ground glass, causing internal bleeding. Of course, anyone with the nerve to get the whiskers off a tiger should be able to use a more direct means of dealing with problems.

Snakes

The majority of snakebites are not fatal because most attacks are by nonvenomous snakes. While snakes have often been used in murderous attempts, there is no guarantee of death since snakes don't always use all their venom on one strike. With the exception of the dangerously aggressive snakes, they seldom bite unless provoked and are secretive and timid, eager to avoid encounters with humans; they are quite as likely to bite the would-be murderer as the chosen victim.

In most cases, if medical care is administered quickly the victim will survive unless the bite connects with a vein, artery, or other vascular part of the body. If someone is allergic to any venom, however, the result is exaggerated and often deadly. Snake venom itself can cause allergies. Some cases of sudden death following snakebite are believed to have been caused by anaphylactic shock.

Reaction time can be anywhere from ten minutes to several days. The more vascular the area, the more severe the reaction. Other variables include the victim's body weight and amount of venom released. As they bite, snakes inject anywhere from 0 to 75 percent of the venom stored in their glands. The Crotalids, some Elapids, and tropical Viperidae are the most dangerous. Alcohol can sometimes mute the effects of the venom if the person is drunk prior to the bite.

A newly devised technique in Britain can show the exact type of snake venom present in the body. It is also possible to determine the type of snake by examining the bite and measuring the distance between the two punctures. Snake venom is yellowish, varying from amber to pale straw.

While poisoning by bite is the most common, a victim can also absorb the venom through injection, as well as through cuts and scratches. A few African snakes spit rather than bite. The jet of venom is toxic and can blind but seldom kills unless it comes into direct contact with the victim's bloodstream. Snakes can be milked for their venom, which can then be injected with equal effect. An injection into a vein or artery is most deadly. The victim can also accidentally drink the venom; however, symptoms and toxicity are usually lessened with oral administration.

Poisonous snakes were used in ancient Egypt to provide a prompt and reasonably painless death for select political prisoners. In early North America, snake venom or the pulped head of a snake was used as an arrow poison by several native tribes. The venom was often obtained by causing the snake to bite the liver of a deer or other animal. The poisoned organ was then allowed to putrify in a mix of toxic leaves and other purportedly lethal substances. Arrows and darts were dipped in this mixture. While the natives may have had the right idea, most unintentionally diluted the toxicity of their arrow poison by heating the mixture in an overzealous desire to deliver to their victim the greatest amount of damage possible.

The Bushmen of the Namaqualand region of southwestern Africa take the resin from a plant of the *Buphane* family and smear it on a stone. They then place the rock in the mouth of a snake — usually a spitting cobra — until the venom mixes with the resin. Carefully removing the stone, they dip their arrows and spears in the resultant lethal gum.

Other African poisoned-arrow techniques include the use of a toxic brew of puff adder heads, resin, beetles, and leaves of poisonous plants. This mixture is quite diluted, although the natives are unaware of the flaw in their brew. East Bengal natives prepare their arrows by securing bits of cobra-venom-soaked wadding to the tips. This is the only foolproof and quite deadly arrow poison.

Between 1830 and 1870, alcohol in the form of straight whiskey became the most popular snakebite remedy in the United States. During the last months of the Civil War, a Confederate quartermaster officer became incensed when the physician administered in a short period of time a full gallon of whiskey to a snakebitten soldier. The quartermaster argued that the barrel of whiskey, then priced at $450 in inflated Confederate currency, was worth more than the soldier himself.

In the Old West before the turn of the century, hard-liquor cures for snakebite were prevalent, and some people even believed whiskey or brandy made the imbiber immune to snakebite. One frontier physician reported in a prestigious medical journal how he had prescribed a pint of whiskey every five minutes until a quart had been consumed. In another case, he administered a gallon and a half of whiskey over a thirty-six-hour period. The physician complained in all seriousness that when the patient was fully recovered, he actually went out looking for another rattlesnake to bite him.

In ensuing years, science found alcohol of little use in combatting the effects of snakebite. In fact, medical experts discovered that drinking liquor is bad for the snakebite victim because alcohol in moderate to large quantities accelerates circulation and hastens the system's absorption of the venom. Only in the smallest amounts can alcohol be beneficial, since it then acts as a tranquilizer to reduce the fear and anxiety that can quicken the venom's spread.

Today, antivenin is the only specific antidote for snakebite.

While there are antiserums for most snake venoms, three factors play a crucial role in saving the victim: 1) correct identification of the snake, 2) the site of the bite, and 3) the amount of time lapsed between bite and antiserum administration. Most fatalities are attributed to the wrong type or too small a dose of antivenin being administered.

Antiserum can also cause heart or respiratory problems, and if someone who has not been snakebitten receives the antiserum, the result could be as dangerous as an actual bite.

Traditional snakebite kits at one time contained a sharp knife and a small hand-suction pump. Until recently, common practice was to make a shallow knife slit from fang-point to fang-point and then attempt to suck out the venom. An incision through the fang marks by an untrained person is both inadvisable and dangerous even as an extreme emergency measure. In most cases, more damage is inflicted, and at best only about 20 percent of the venom will be removed—and those removing the venom orally may cause themselves serious damage.

All snake venoms are complex proteins that affect the nerve center for senses, motor, heart, and lung. The venom results in cardiac weakening, harms the red blood cells, and affects the heart, kidney, and lung muscles, as well as preventing clotting. The venom attaches to the neural tissues even before symptoms occur.

The four basic snake families are the Crotalidae, Viperidae, Elapidae, and Hydrophidae, all of which have poisonous and non-poisonous members. The most common are listed below. The *form* category in the individual descriptions has been changed to *location/ description* in this chapter.

Name: Rattlesnake. *Family:* Crotalidae.
Toxicity: 4. (Death from rattlesnake bite in the United States is rare since medical help is usually given immediately.)
Location/Description: Found in the arid regions in the Americas from Canada to South America, they are called pit vipers because of the heat-sensing pit between each eye and nostril. These snakes have tail rattles that create a hissing or buzzing sound in most, but not all, rattlers.

North America—eastern diamondback (*Crotalus adamanteus*), the coastal plains from North Carolina to Mississippi; western diamondback rattlesnake (*C. atrox*), from Arkansas to Southern California, and northern and central Mexico; timber rattlesnake (*C. hor-*

ridus horridus), eastern United States from Minnesota to central Texas east; canebrake rattlesnake (*C. horridus atricaudatus*) southern United States version of timber rattler; Pacific rattlesnake (*C. viridis*), Southern California and Baja California; Mojave rattlesnake (*C. scutulatus*), west Texas to Southern California, northern and central Mexico.

Three rattlesnakes are from the family Viperidae: the sidewinder or horned rattler (*C. cerastes*), known for its sideways motion and found in the desert of the southwestern United States and northeastern Mexico; massasauga (*Sistrurus catenatus*) from the Great Lakes region southwest to southeastern Arizona and Mexico; pygmy rattlesnake (*S. miliarius*) with an ineffective rattle, southeastern United States west to Missouri and eastern Texas.

In Central and South America, the cascabel rattlesnake (*C. durissus*) is also known as the tropical or South American rattlesnake and found in tropical South America, and it is one of the two most dangerous rattlers; the Mexican West Coast rattlesnake (*C. basiliscus*) is the second most dangerous rattler, western Mexico; Brazilian (*C. durissis terrificus*) is found in southeastern Brazil, Argentina, Paraguay.

Effects and Symptoms: Rattlesnake venom causes excessive thirst, nausea, vomiting, shock, numbing and paralysis, swelling of lymph nodes, respiratory distress, anemia, drooping of the eyelids, and necrosis (dead tissue). Kidney shutdown is possible and with that, death occurs.

Rattlesnake bite, like that of most vipers, is painful and resembles a jab with a hot needle. Sometimes the area around the fang puncture is temporarily numb, which means a large injection of venom and a serious bite. Tingling around the mouth and a sensation of yellowish vision are other indications of severe poisoning. Vomiting and violent spasms will shake the entire body. The body will show small red spots (petechial hemorrhages) and extensive bleeding at the wound site. One or more puncture wounds or toothmarks will be found and the victim will have local pain, blurred vision, weakness, drowsiness, nausea, vomiting, salivation, faintness, and sweating. The skin will be discolored with local swelling.

Reaction Time: Fifteen minutes to an hour. Severe poisoning is indicated by swelling above the elbows or knees within two hours or by hemorrhages.

Antidotes and Treatments: Rattlesnake antivenin is available most places.

Case Histories: Representatives of the organization Synanon attempted to kill an opposing lawyer by putting a rattlesnake, minus its rattles, into the victim's mailbox. The lawyer was bitten on the hand and wrist, sought immediate medical attention, and survived the attack.

In a recent suicide, a despondent exotic dancer who used poisonous snakes and spiders in her act provoked a rattlesnake into biting her. She died four days later.

Notes: Of all the snakebites in the United States, 98 percent are from rattlesnakes and related species. While the reason for the rattles on the tail has never been proved, the theory is that rattles evolved to warn grazing herds away from trodding on them.

While acetylcholinesterase is the most active toxin in rattlesnake venom and that of many other snakes, crotamine—a toxin known to cause convulsions—is found in the venom of the deadly tropical rattlesnake in regions of southern Brazil. The tropical rattler also has the sinister reputation of being able to break a human's neck. Although the snake cannot literally snap a human's neck, the neurotoxin effect of its venom causes the neck muscles to relax to such a degree that the head will loll if not supported.

Name: Cottonmouth. *Family*: Crotalidae. *Other*: copperhead, cantil.

Toxicity: 5.

Location/Description: Found primarily in the Americas: North America—cottonmouth moccasin, or water moccasin (*Agkistrodon piscivorus*), an aquatic pit viper called cottonmouth because it threatens with its mouth wide open, showing its white interior, southeastern United States low marshlands; copperheads or highland moccasin (*A. contortrix*), a member of the Viperidae family, this reddish-colored pit viper with a copper-colored head and reddish-brown bands is found in swampy, rocky, and wooded regions of central and eastern United States; cantil or Mexican moccasin (*A. bilineatus*) is a brightly colored, extremely dangerous snake found from the low regions of the Rio Grande to Nicaragua.

Effects and Symptoms: Cottonmouth moccasin venom literally dissolves the tissue it contacts. The injection site is dark and oozes bloody fluid while swelling spreads outward from it. The region turns itchy and will cause the victim to scratch and rub and become irritable and hyperactive. After being bitten, a victim may experience a short period of near-normal activity followed by another quiet state that eventually terminates in collapse and death. An autopsy shows the injection site as gangrenous and often liquefied. There will be extensive hemorrhage under the swollen area and small hemorrhages in the heart, lungs, and other organs. The victim bleeds to death in his own tissues. The heart fails not because of direct injury but because it can no longer pump effectively through the riddled vascular bed.

Reaction Time: May begin within ten minutes.

Antidotes and Treatments: Antivenin is available in most hospitals.

Name: Fer-de-lance. *Family*: Viperidae (*Bothrops atrox*). *Other*: habu (*Trimeresurus flavoviridis*), jararaca (*Bothrops jararaca*), wutu (*B. alternus*), jumping viper or tommygoff (*B. nummifera*), Wagler's pit viper (*T. wagleri*).

Toxicity: 5.

Location/Description: From central Mexico south into South America, through tropical America, this extremely venomous pit viper makes its home in cultivated lands as well as tropical forests. The fer-de-lance — French for lancehead — is called "barba amarillo" (yellow chin) in Spanish, and it is gray or brown with black-edged diamonds on a lighter border. Other *Bothrops* and even some Asian *Trimeresurus* living in the tropical Americas are often called fer-de-lance. Most frequently confused with its cousin, the deadly jararaca is olive or gray-brown on darker blotches and prefers the grassy regions of Brazil. Another dangerous South American pit viper is the wutu, which can be recognized by its dark brown semicircles outlined in yellow over a brown body. Another aggressive cousin is the jumping viper of Central America, which is brown or gray with diamond-shaped crossmarkings.

The Okinawa hubu, a large, aggressive — but not quite as lethal — cousin, is found on the Amani and Okinawa groups of the Ryukyu Islands, sometimes boldly wandering into people's homes. Its body's dark green blotches form a wavy band lengthwise.

Effects and Symptoms: Local pain, bleeding from the bite, gums, nose, mouth, and rectum. Blood cannot coagulate and hemorrhages into muscles and nervous system. Shock and respiratory distress come before death.

Antidotes and Treatments: Antivenin is available.

Notes: The jumping viper lives up to its name, often attacking its victims so vigorously that it lifts itself clear off the ground. While people should give this snake wide berth, its venom is not as dangerous to humans as the venom of its cousins.

Name: Cobra. *Family*: Elapidae.

Toxicity: 6.

Location/Description: These are vipers that expand their neck ribs to form a hood. The king cobra or hamadryad (*Ophiophagus hannah* or *Naja hannah*) is the world's largest venomous snake and has been measured at up to eighteen feet long while averaging a little over twelve feet in length. Its bite is lethal about 10 percent of the time.

The Indian or Asian cobra or spectacle cobra (*Naja naja*) reportedly kills well over thirty thousand people a year, primarily because its venom is highly lethal and its feeding pattern is to seek out rats, which takes the cobra into populated areas — and sometimes homes — at twilight. Its markings, usually in the shape of spectacles on the extremely large hood in black and white, stand out on its yellow to dark brown body. It grows to be nearly six feet long.

The Egyptian and African cobra (*Naja haje*) in classical antiquity was known as the asp. A narrow, deep-hooded snake that, while described as small, grows to at least six feet.

The ringhals or spitting cobra (*Hemachatus hemachuatus*) has keeled scales and seldom strikes its victim, preferring to spit or spray venom into the eyes of its victim, often causing blindness.

The black-necked cobra (*Naja nigricollis*) is an extremely aggressive snake that can accurately spit a flow of venom into the eyes of a victim from seven feet away. While the venom is harmless to intact flesh, it is damaging to the eyes. If not washed away immediately, blindness ensues. This snake rarely bites, preferring to spit.

The tree cobra (*Pseudo haje*) is one of two arboreal elapids, along with the mambas.

Snakes in the cobra family that do not have a hood are:

The Indian or blue or common krait (*Bunguras caeruleus*) is a passive nocturnal feeder that rarely bites people. Growing to about five feet, its venom is powerful; nearly 50 percent of those bitten die if not treated with antivenin. It can be easily spotted, since it has shiny scales and strongly patterned yellow-and-black or white-and-black bands.

The banded krait or pama (*B. fasciatus*) is slightly larger than the Indian krait but is considered almost harmless since it appears docile. Few bites have been reported, although the venom is lethal.

The black mamba (*Dendroaspis polylepis*) is an extremely dangerous snake that sometimes hunts its prey in trees. Long and slender, the gray or greenish brown snake grows to about fourteen feet and has large scales and very long fangs. It is so aggressive that it rears up to strike and can land a bite on a human's head or torso. Its venom is 100 percent fatal without antivenin.

The green mamba (*Dendroaspis angusticeps*) is a smaller, less aggressive version and more arboreal than the black mamba. It grows to nine feet.

The taipan (*Oxyuranus scutellatus*) is another of the world's most dangerous snakes. The largest Australian snake of the cobra family, it grows to nearly eleven feet and is extremely aggressive. Yellow on the underside and brown on the top, its venom contains a clotting agent that proves fatal to humans within minutes. Attacking without warning, the snake inflicts several bites in succession with its unusually long fangs.

The death adder (*Acanthophis antarcticus*), while related to the cobras, has a thick body, a short tail, and a broad head. Its coloring is gray or brownish with dark crossbands. Its bite is fatal 50 percent of the time in untreated cases.

The tiger snake (*Notechis scutatus*), also called the Australian tiger snake, has yellow-and-brown bands and grows to no more than four feet in length, but it is quite dangerous and often fatal to humans. When readying to strike, it flattens its head and neck just as its cobra cousin does and appears to be jumping when it strikes. Preferring swampy regions of Australia, Tasmania, and islands in the immediate vicinity, the tiger snake is the most dangerous snake of southern Australia.

The Australian black snake (*Pseudeschis porphyriacus*) is a small-headed snake with blue-black body and a red underbelly. The most common of the Australian venomous snakes, it prefers marshy areas. It possesses a powerful anticoagulant. Others in this group include the spotted black snake (*P. guttatus*) and the mulga (*P. australis*), which is reddish brown on top and pink underneath.

The brown snake (*Demansia textilis*) is a slender, small-headed snake with a nasty temper. Growing up to seven feet in length, it will often rear up to strike, and its venom is highly lethal. Adapting to the color of its surroundings, it goes from light brown to dull green. A fast moving snake, it has caused more deaths in Australia than any other snake. Copperhead antivenin can be used for this bite.

The eastern coral snake or harlequin snake (*Micrurus fulvius*), a docile, nocturnal, burrowing snake is no more than three feet in length with wide bands of red and black separated by yellow bands. Quite a lot of venom, or a good bite in the right place, is needed for death to occur. Because there are nonvenomous coral snakes, a folk rhyme reminds people which one to stay clear of: "Red touching yellow, dangerous fellow." However, this rule is not always binding and caution should be taken with all these snakes.

The Arizona coral snake (*M. euryxanthus*) is a small and rare snake that is reluctant to strike at people.

The African coral snake (*Aspidelaps lubricus*) is quite small, with black-and-white bands over bright orange.

Other coral snakes include the black-banded coral snake (*M. nigrocinctus*), found in Central America. (Two fatalities were reported in Costa Rica within the past five years.) The Brazilian giant coral snake (*M. frontalis*), found in southern South America, is responsible for quite a number of deaths.

The cobra family is found from Africa through all Asia. The king cobra, southeast Asia from India to the Philippines to Indonesia; the Indian cobra, from Iran westward; the Egyptian cobra, North Africa; the ringhals, southern Africa; the tree cobra, equatorial Africa; the black-necked cobra, throughout Africa; the Indian krait, in open country from Pakistan and India to China; banded krait, Indochina; the black mamba, sub-Sahara Africa; the green mamba, East Africa; the taipan, Australia, around Queensland; death adder, Australia and nearby islands; tiger snake, southern regions of Australia's swampy lands; Australian black snake, Australia; brown snake, New Guinea and eastern Australia; eastern coral snake, from North Carolina to Missouri and down to northeastern Mexico; Arizona coral snake, limited to the southwestern United States deserts; African coral snake, South Africa; the black-banded coral snake, southern Mexico to northern Colombia; the Brazilian giant coral snake, Southern Brazil, Paraguay, Argentina, Bolivia, and Uruguay.

Effects and Symptoms: Symptoms start fifteen to thirty minutes after the bite. Symptoms are characterized by pain within ten minutes but with slow onset of swelling. Blood pressure falls and convulsions may occur. Death is caused by respiratory failure. The king cobra's bite may not affect the tissue around the bite site, while the vital functions of breathing and heartbeat are directly affected. An autopsy of a cobra-bite victim shows no reaction at the site of injection and no gross abnormalities of internal organs.

Lung paralysis can occur up to ten days after elapid (cobra family) bites. Symptoms are said to be similar to belladonna alkaloid poisoning.

Reaction Time: The venom paralyzes the nervous system and causes death within two hours if the antitoxin is not given. After a delay of four hours, the antiserum loses effectiveness; after twenty-four hours, it's useless.

Antidotes and Treatments: Only the specific antiserum will help. Before administering it, the victim should be tested for serum sensitivity since the antiserum itself can be life-threatening. Often the physician will wait for clear evidence of systemic venom toxicity before beginning treatment. If there is progressive swelling or numbness around the mouth, an initial dose of ten vials is needed via slow intravenous drip. This is combined with 5 percent dextrose in saline. Cardiopulmonary measures should be kept ready.

Case Histories: One bitten person said, "I was sinking into a state that could not be called unconsciousness, but one in which I was no longer aware of what was going on about me . . . I felt no anxiety; I felt no pain; it didn't even strike me as strange that the darkness was closing in on the light . . . I am certain I did not lose consciousness entirely at any time; I only felt a complete and utter lassitude in which nothing seemed to matter—not at all unpleasant if this is the way death comes from cobra poisoning."

Cleopatra remains history's most famous snakebite suicide. She probably employed the Egyptian cobra, as venom from the saw-scaled viper causes a prolonged and painful death.

A scientist who had been immunized against cobra venom some months before he was bitten suffered no neurotoxic or other generalized symptoms, but developed a gangrenous patch requiring skin grafting.

A generous sip of cobra venom could cause death, but an American bacteriologist chose a more scientific variant. He injected himself with a lethal dose of cobra venom.

In Florida, a young man was bitten by a coral snake and rested quite comfortably under hospital observation for about seven hours. Then he began having trouble breathing and moving his eyes. Soon almost all his muscles became paralyzed and he could respond to questions only by raising his eyebrows. Despite administration of antivenin and use of an iron lung, he died in a few hours.

Notes: Cobra venom is chemically different from other families. A neurotoxin, it brings on progressive paralysis, causing death when the poison spreads to respiratory muscles. Elapid venoms are more heat resistant than those of any other vipers and have the same toxicity as the yellow scorpion of the Middle East (*Leiurus quinquestriatus*). Elapid venom is also twice as toxic as strychnine, nearly five times as toxic as a black widow spider, but only half as deadly as the mushroom toxin amanitin.

Some coral snake venoms have powerful hemolytic effects—breaking down the red blood cells and liberating the hemoglobin, which appear in the urine. The autopsy will reveal gross hemorrhage, dead tissue (necrosis), cloudy swelling in the cells of the other organs, and destroyed kidney tubes.

The venom of the Wagler's pit viper is unique in that it remains almost fully toxic after heating in a sterilizer and causes exceptionally rapid collapse and death without local swelling or hemorrhage.

Name: Adder. *Family*: Viperidae. *Other*: Boomslang (*Dispholidus typhus*), bushmaster (*Lachesis muta*), gaboon viper (*Bitis gabonica*), horned viper (*Cerastes cerastas*), levantine viper (*Viper lebetina*), Palestina viper (*Vipera xanthina palaestinae*), sand viper (*C. vipera*), saw-scaled viper (*Echis carinatus*), Russell's viper (*Vipera russellii*).

Toxicity: 6.

Location/Description: The common adder or European adder (*Vipera berus*) grows to about three feet, and its body is gray with black zigzag bands on the back and black spots on the sides. This stout-bodied snake is rarely fatal to humans.

The puff adder (*Bitis arietans*) is thick-bodied and extremely venomous. Its name comes from the warning it gives when it inflates its body and hisses loudly. Gray to dark brown, it has thin yellow chevrons on the back. When approached, this highly lethal snake prefers to stand its ground rather than flee.

The boomslang, the only venomous member of the Colubridae family, is an arboreal predator. Lying in wait in a tree or bush with its forepart extended midair, it remains motionless for long periods of time. A master of camouflage, its body and eyes change color to suit the surroundings. When threatened, it inflates its neck, displaying the dark skin beneath its scales. Although it is rear-fanged, its venom is lethal even in the smallest quantities.

The bushmaster can be as long as twelve feet and is the longest pit viper in the New World. Pink or tan body spots contrast with the diamond-shaped blotches. This viper is extremely dangerous, and its bite can be lethal.

Found only in Africa (mainly Zululand, Rhodesia, East Africa, and French West Africa), the gaboon viper is the largest and heaviest of the venomous snakes. It is among the most dangerous of snakes. Colorfully marked in rectangles and triangles of brown, buff, and purple, it is thick-bodied and broad-headed. Two hornlike projections come from its snout. Often a bite goes unnoticed or is confused with an insect sting and only the ensuing pain draws the victim's attention to it when the administration of antivenin may be too late. The venom is less toxic than the puff-adder when bitten, but more toxic when injected intravenously. A nocturnal species, the snake becomes active toward sunset. The venom is a blood and nerve poison. It's sometimes called the king puff adder.

The levantine viper is extremely dangerous in northern Eurasia and north Africa.

The Russell's viper, tic polonga, or daboia is an extremely venomous terrestrial viper. Its bite is the major cause of snakebite death in regions it inhabits. Growing only about five feet in length, its bright markings stand out with its three rows of reddish brown spots being encircled by black and then white outline.

The saw-scaled viper, the most venomous of the Viperidae vipers, is a relatively small snake at no more than two feet, but its bite is usually fatal. It is renowned for its irritability and aggressiveness. Its rough scales, when rubbed together as a warning, produce a hissing sound. Gray or sand-colored with rows of white spots and pale zigzag lines as markings, it hides under rocks. It's found mainly in the Afro-Asian desert belt and the drier parts of Russian Asia, India, and Ceylon. The venom is unusually toxic for man, causing internal and external hemorrhages. Death may occur twelve to sixteen days after the bite. Fortunately, there are antivenins.

The Viperidae family is found throughout the world, with the majority in Africa. The common adder, throughout Europe and Asia, and even found north of the Arctic Circle in Norway; the night adder, south of the Sahara; the boomslang, in the scrublands and forests from the Amazon Basin as far north as Costa Rica; the gaboon viper, in sandy parts of central Africa; the Russell's viper, in open country from India to Taiwan and Java; the saw-scaled viper, northern and western Africa to the drier regions of India and Sri Lanka.

Effects and Symptoms: Victims of viper bites show symptoms of cobra bites in addition to bleeding from the gums and chills and fever. Severe poisoning is indicated by swelling or hemorrhages extending above the elbows or knees within two hours of the bite.

Following a bite on the hand, the whole arm will become swollen within a half hour and skin will become purple. The victim perspires heavily, vomits blood, and collapses within an hour. The nose and eyes bleed and loss of vision occurs, with subsequent loss of consciousness. Death is inevitable unless the antiserum is administered quickly.

Death usually comes from cardiorespiratory failure. The venom's powerful hemolytic effect breaks down the red blood cells and liberates hemoglobin, which may appear in the urine.

Reaction Time: Venom kills quickly, directly affecting the heart and lungs.

Antidotes and Treatments: Antiserum is given and the same measures are taken as for a cobra bite. Heart failure can rapidly occur, so cardiovascular resuscitation is kept available.

Case Histories: It is thought that Rudyard Kipling was probably referring to the saw-scaled viper when mentioning the "karait" in his renowned story "Rikki-Tikki-Tavi."

In *Death in the Air* by Agatha Christie, a boomslang snake was indirectly responsible for the death of a French moneylender. The tree snake's venom was put on a blow-gun dart, which was then shot at the victim in the middle of a plane ride.

Name: Beaked sea snake (*Enhydrina schistosa*). *Family*: Hydrophidae. *Other*: Yellow-lipped sea krait (*Laticauda colubrina*), olive-brown sea snake (*Aipysurus laevis*), yellow sea snake (*Hydrophis spiralis*), annulated sea snake (*H. cyanocinctus*), Hardwicke's sea snake (*Lapemis hardwickii*), Pelagic sea snake (*Pelamis platurus*).

Toxicity: 6.

Location/Description: The Indian Ocean, Pacific Ocean, Vietnam, the Philippines, and Malayan waters. They are often taken in fishing nets.

The distinctive feature is the form of the lower jaw. The shield of the chin tip, which is comparatively wide and large in most snakes, is reduced to a splinterlike shield buried between the first pair of lower lips. This gives greater flexibility to the lower jaw enabling the snake to seize and swallow large prey. A down-curved tip gives it its beaked look. A little under five feet, they are a dull olive green or pale greenish gray with dark crossbands. The belly and sides are cream to dirty white, while the tail is mottled with black. A shallow water snake, it is found both over mud and sand bottoms and found plentifully at the mouths of rivers, also in great deltas such as the Ganges and Indus. The snake has also been found in channels many miles from the open sea. It is awkward but not completely helpless on land.

Effects and Symptoms: The venom of sea snakes has a direct effect on the muscles, causing the release of the protein myoglobin. Its venom is extremely toxic.

Sea snake venom causes pain in the skeletal muscles, especially during motion, but only minor pain at the bite site. The victim's tongue and mouth will feel paralyzed, vision will be blurred, and there will be difficulty swallowing. The first evidence of trouble is weakness and soreness in the muscles. The eyelids droop, and the jaws become stiff, somewhat as in tetanus. Weakness increases until the patient can hardly lift a finger. Myoglobin and potassium from the damaged muscles stain the urine red, injure the kidneys, and cause irregularities of the heart.

Reaction Time: The bite itself is an innocuous-seeming pinprick and is symptom free for thirty minutes to eight hours. Death may come within hours of the bite but is usually delayed a few days.

Notes: Bites are rare but possible in warm water where fishermen catch the snakes with their hands. (Of course, a tank filled with sea snakes kept in the victim's house is handy for such murder plots.) The beaked sea snake is responsible for more serious and fatal bites than all other sea snakes combined.

The yellow sea snake yields litle venom, and while the toxicity is lower than most sea snakes' venoms, several deaths have been reported. The annulated sea snake has a higher toxicity than the yellow sea snake and causes more deaths than any other sea snake except the beaked sea snake.

Hardwicke's sea snake yields very little venom, but several fatal bites have been reported. It's found usually during the rainy season in the tropical countries mentioned above.

The pelagic sea snake is the most widespread of the species and can be found on the west coast of tropical America. Only one fatality (over a century ago) has been reported. Toxicity is about one-quarter that of the beaked sea snake.

Gila Monster

Name: Gila monster. *Scientific Name*: *Heloderma suspectum*. *Other*: Mexican beaded lizard (*H. horridum*).
Toxicity: 6.
Location/Description: The Gila monster is found in the desert areas of the southwestern United States and northern Mexico, while the Mexican version is found in dense forests of southern Mexico.

A thick-tailed lizard, it grows to twenty inches. The stout body has black and pink or orange blotches or bands and beadlike scales. The Mexican version is slightly larger and darker.

The deeply grooved and flanged teeth conduct the venom, a nerve poison, from the glands to the lower jaw.
Effects and Symptoms: Severe pain at the site of the bite. Systemic symptoms include blue-tinged skin; respiratory problems such as shallow, rapid breathing; erratic heartbeat; ringing in the ears; faintness; nausea; vertigo; and weakness. If a fatal dose is taken in, respiratory arrest causes death. Human fatalities are rare, but they do happen.
Reaction Time: Fifty minutes to a few hours after the bite. As with snakebites, the degree of severity varies with the amount of venom injected, the site of the bite, and the victim's general health.
Antidotes and Treatments: No specific antiserum is known.
Notes: In biting, the lizard is tenacious. Often the victim must be cut free from the animal.

Instead of fangs, the Gila monster has grooves in its front teeth to carry the venom. The lizard does not bite unless handled and provoked. The amount of venom to produce a fatal dose is not known, but toxicity is compared to snake venom since a small scratch from the teeth of the Gila monster can produce severe symptoms similar to rattlesnake poisoning.

No fatal cases have been reported in modern literature. Prior to 1900, however, the whiskey antidote that was popular for snakebites was used for Gila monster bites as well and was probably more responsible for the deaths than the actual bite.

The venom of the Gila monster is more heat resistant than that of any snake. The freshly extracted venom is a clear opalescent fluid.

Other Poisonous Amphibians

Numerous salamanders, newts, and toads secrete a venom toxic to humans, but because they have no means of injecting it, they rarely cause fatalities unless the venom comes in contact with a wound or sore, or passes into the body via a mucous membrane. A large dose of venom would be needed to cause death.

Indians of northern South America and southern Central America coat the tips of their arrows in an extremely potent poison secreted from the skin of a small, brightly colored tree frog aptly called arrow-poison frogs (*Dendrobates*, *Rana*, and *Phyllobates*).

The platypus, a playful creature found in Australia, also has the doubtful honor of being included in this list of venomous creatures. Their stings are nasty and painful but not deadly. A nocturnal animal, the platypus is shy and seldom comes into contact with man, though several fishermen have been gashed when they have hooked platypus instead of fish. "The result," said one fisherman, "is intense pain, with agonies shooting through you so you wish you'd never been born." If a swimmer were bitten, the pain might startle him so that he would lose control and perhaps drown.

Spiders

As with snakes, the toxicity and reaction time of spider bites depends on how vascular the area bitten (a bite in the genitals is far more serious than one on the lower leg), the weight of the person, and how much venom is injected. All the venoms are administered by bite but can also be singled out and given as intramuscular injections as well.

Name: Brown recluse. *Scientific Name: Loxosceles reclusa. Other:* Violin spider, fiddle-back spider, brown spider.

Toxicity: 4. Volume for volume, this venom is more deadly than that of many poisonous snakes.

Location/Description: The brown recluse is found in twenty-five states (primarily southern and midwestern) from Hawaii to New Jersey and Texas to Illinois and is by far the most dangerous of the spider family. Fawn to medium dark brown, the spider has a darker violin-shaped patch on its back and is found in dark, undisturbed places. The female is more dangerous than the male.

Effects and Symptoms: The initial bite is often painless, but by eight hours the victim may be in agony. Any place the spider bites the tissue dies and the area rots.

Pain develops in two to eight hours and is followed by blisters, redness, swelling, bleeding, or ulceration of the bite area. The untreated lesion increases in size for up to a week until blood appears in the urine. Symptoms also include fever, chills, joint pain, skin rash, nausea, vomiting, blue-tinged skin, and delirium. Blisters will form and drain. There will be large areas of necrosis near the bite, but the venom does not necessarily kill. Death, if it occurs, usually comes within the first forty-eight hours due to renal failure from coagulation of the blood, but medical help is usually sought before this.

Reaction Time: Two to eight hours.

Antidotes and Treatments: There is no specific antiserum known. Adrenocortical steroids, excision of the bite area, and exchange transfusion might be done. No other specific treatment is known.

Name: Black widow. *Scientific Name*: *Latrodectus mactans*. *Other*: Hourglass spider, button spider (South Africa), red back (Australia); Katipo (New Zealand) malmignatte (Mediterranean region), karakurt (Southern Russia). Brown widow (*L. geometrieus* found in all the tropics) has the same marks as the black widow but is brown. It is reluctant to bite humans. There are no widows in central or northern Eurasia.

Toxicity: 3.

Location/Description: Black widow spiders may be found throughout the United States and in parts of Canada, but are most numerous in warmer regions. Other members of the *Latrodectus* family are common through temperate and tropical zones. The spiders inhabit woodpiles, outhouses, brush piles, and dark corners of barns, garages, and houses. Only the female, shiny jet black with a globular abdomen marked with orange or red spots in the shape of an hourglass, is dangerous. The spider also hides under upholstery, cushions, and toilet lids, making bites in the genital organs the most common and deadly.

Effects and Symptoms: The bite is often not felt. Only later does the victim realize there is a problem. Flulike symptoms will predominate for several days. Abdominal or chest muscles become rigid, but unlike other stomach emergencies the patient is extremely restless. Chills, urinary retention, and sweating as well as nausea and vomiting are among the other symptoms. If this bite proves fatal, it will be from cardiac failure.

Reaction Time: Symptoms begin within an hour. Most bite victims recover without serious complications.

Antidotes and Treatments: Antiserum is available.

Notes: The danger of the famed female black widow "hourglass" spider causing instantaneous death is exaggerated. While both male and female can be deadly, the male's fangs are smaller and seldom penetrate human skin. In fact, of the six species, all of which are venomous, none are usually fatal.

Other Deadly Spiders: The brown spider (*Loxosceles laeta*) found in Chile; *Ctenus nigriventer* found in Brazil; and the funnel-web spider (*Atrax robustus*) found in Australia.

The tarantula or wolf spider (*Lycosa tarentula*), once thought to be fatal, belongs to a species of large, hairy spiders that are only mildly toxic. The largest tarantula may kill small vertebrates, but their food is usually other spiders. The bite can be painful but is seldom dangerous to humans, although in southeastern Europe it was assumed to be the cause of a nervous condition characterized by hysteria. A superstition dictated the best cure was dancing the tarantella to throw off the poison.

Scorpions

Name: Common striped scorpion. *Scientific Name*: *Centruroides vittatus*. *Other*: Brown scorpion (*C. gertschii*), sculptured scorpion (*C. sculpturatus*), devil scorpion (*Vejovis spinigerus*), giant hairy scorpion (*Hadrurus arizonensis*).

Toxicity: 4.

Location/Description: Poisonous scorpions of the United States — *Centruroides gertschii*, *C. vittatus*, and *C. sculpturatus* — live mainly in the arid Southwest (concentrating in Arizona) and other warm areas. In Mexico and Brazil, the poisonous ones are *Tityus bahiensis* and *T. serrulatus*. In dry areas of North Africa, India, and Pakistan, the most deadly are *Androctonus australis* and *Buthus occitanus*. While most prefer warm regions, there are species found in Mongolia and parts of Europe. Only New Zealand, Antarctica, and southern parts of Chile and Argentina are free of the creatures. Scorpions live near homes and like the dark warmth of shoes and other dark places.

The pale-yellow desert scorpion with slender claws is more

dangerous than the big black scorpion. The red ones are not lethal. Not aggressive toward humans, scorpions attack only when disturbed suddenly or annoyed. The scorpion's large front pinsers grab its victim, and the venomous tail is flung forward to sting once or repeatedly.

Effects and Symptoms: The neurotoxin destroys the nerve tissue and causes cardiac effects. The victim suffers intense pain, numbness, and increased bowel motility. Hemorrhage of intestine, stomach, and lung, along with periodic seizure activity is possible.

The sting of the nondeadly insect creates a burning sensation at the site of the wound and the area might become immediately swollen and discolored. A blister often forms where the skin is pricked, but the bite is seldom fatal. Effects last for eight to twelve hours.

The more dangerous insect gives little local evidence of the sting, except for mild tingling at the bite site. This tingling may progress up the extremity, but swelling and discoloration do not occur in a deadly species attack. In severe cases, throat spasms, thick tongue, restlessness, muscular spasms, stomach cramps, convulsions, high blood pressure, low blood pressure, poor cardiac rhythm, pulmonary edema, and respiratory failure occur. Symptoms starting as soon as two to four hours after sting indicate a poor outcome.

Reaction Time: The duration of symptoms is ordinarily twenty-four to forty-eight hours, but fatalities have occurred four days after the sting.

Antidotes and Treatments: Antiserum is available for immediate use. Treatment consists of applying a tourniquet proximal to the sting to limit absorption.

Notes: A popular belief holds that the sting of any scorpion means certain death. Not true. Very few species have poison strong enough to kill an adult human. Only one out of a thousand stings is fatal, so most scorpions are not as deadly as feared.

While scorpion venom is more toxic than that of many snakes, the amount released in a sting is usually minute; and if absorption is delayed, serious symptoms can be avoided. However, the venom can be collected separately and injected intramuscularly, making it quite deadly.

Bees, Wasps, Yellow Jackets

These insects are found throughout the world. Single stings can be dangerous if one is allergic or stung in a vein or artery. In a nonimmune person, multiple stings (thirty or forty insects) may cause chills, high fever, vomiting, pulmonary edema, severe fall of blood pressure, difficulty breathing, collapse, and blood in urine. A sensitivity reaction may cause bronchial constriction, swelling of face and lips, and itching. Death may occur in one hour. In children, respiratory and cardiac arrest often follows. Venom desensitization is possible. Diphenhydramine (Benadryl) 50 mg can stop or slow symptoms but must be given immediately. Hydrocortisone is given intravenously to prevent collapse.

The most lethal of these insects is the wasp, known for its long slender body and very long hind legs, and the vicious hornet or yellow jacket. The hornet, striped yellow and black, is quite aggressive and both stings and bites.

Deadly Aquatic Life

Name: Jellyfish. *Scientific Name*: *Chironex fleckeri* or *Chiropsalmus quadrigatus*. *Other*: Cube jellies, sea wasps, box jellyfish, cubomedusae.
Toxicity: 6.
Location/Description: Bluish, rosy, violet, or transparent open umbrellas with four, eight, or more tentacles dangling from the rim. There are numerous species of jellyfish. They float on or near the surface of the waves and often go unnoticed by humans until there is a rash of stings.

The *Chironex fleckeri*, named in 1956 for Dr. Flecker who determined that this species had caused the death of many swimmers, is considered one of the most deadly organisms anywhere. Its common name is sea wasp. Rather boxlike in shape, it is often quite small and has tentacles in clusters at the corners of its body. The stinging capsules within the sticky threads are nematocysts, each of which contains a minute amount of one of the most deadly venoms ever discovered.

They often invade beaches around the world in vast numbers. The Australian species are the most dangerous. They inhabit cool waters as well as tropical and are seen as far north as the central Atlantic seaboard in the United States.
Effects and Symptoms: In the dangerous varieties, the venom varies from mildly irritating to lethal. Symptoms are severe chest and abdominal pain, difficulty in swallowing, extreme pain, skin necrosis,

and respiratory and cardiac depression leading to death. The American variety will cause sickness, but probably not kill unless the victim already has a weak heart or other problems. Many an Australian-area swimmer has been found floating in the water — drowning was thought to be the cause of death until it was realized the victim had been stung by a sea wasp.

The initial pain and shock of the sting make the victim wrench away and this, in turn, stimulates the tentacles to release more poison, increasing the severity of the dose. On the beach, if the victim attempts to rip off the sticky threads where the poison comes from, more toxin is released. Victims look as if they've been beaten with a cat-o'-nine-tails made of barbed wire. On people who survive, the weals become disfiguring red blisters and may be permanent scars.

Reaction Time: The deadly variety is fatal in minutes.

Antidotes and Treatments: An antiserum exists but must be administered immediately and an occlusive tourniquet must be applied to all affected limbs. A copious amount of alcohol should be poured over the sticky tentacles to inactivate the nematocysts and shrivel the tentacles so they can be brushed off without releasing more venom. The theory is that the venom kills quickly through massive chemical shock. If the action is slowed, the body can cope.

Another type of jellyfish, bluebottle, or Portuguese man-of-war is of the *Physalia* species. It may cause hives, numbness, pain of extremity, and severe chest and abdominal pain, but deaths are rare.

Case Histories: On a warm Queensland (Australia) summer day in January 1955, a five-year-old and his family were at the beach. The boy was only in two feet of water when he screamed out in agony. His mother called him from the water and tried to drag the sticky threads off him. She was horrified to see the ugly weals scoring his thighs and legs. It was two minutes from the time he left the water until he collapsed and died.

Many a shallow-water swimmer near Queensland runs out of the water screaming as the sticky threads cling to him, and while bystanders watch helplessly, he turns blue and collapses.

The first jellyfish attack recorded was in 1884 in *Injuries to man from marine invertebrates in the Australian region* by Dr. Southcott. An eyewitness at Ross Island saw an eleven-year-old boy struck by a jellyfish and disappear while swimming. The body was recovered some hours later with "some living matter like transparent string clinging to him. I hastily rubbed some off the boy and in doing so got stung myself."

Notes: The Australian sea wasp (*Chironex fleckeri*) is possibly the most dangerous of all marine animals.

The live nematocysts are capable of discharging poisons for months after being beached if they are regularly moistened by sea water. Even air-dried nematocysts may contain considerable potency after a matter of weeks.

Name: Blue-ringed octopus. *Scientific Name*: *Hapalochlaena maculosa* or *Octopus maculosa*. *Other*: Australian spotted (*H. lunulata*), and North American West Coast octopus (*Octopus apollyon*).

Toxicity: 6.

Location/Description: Its brown-speckled coloration is distinguished by the blue bands around its tentacles, which give it its name. This small animal can be dangerous — when the bands around the tentacles glow blue, poison is about to be released. The octopus seldom bothers humans unless it is bothered first, but since it's so small, many humans think it harmless. No more than six inches across, it has a true octopus shape.

The Australian spotted octopus is found in Australia near Queensland, New South Wales, Sydney, and Victoria, and also in the Indian Ocean, Indo-Pacific, and Japan. It likes the bays and reefs.

Also found in North America from Alaska to Baja California is the *Octopus apollyon*, which is nearly as deadly.

Effects and Symptoms: Affecting the central nervous system, paralysis of the muscles goes from gradual weakness to paralysis of the whole body until breathing has stopped.

Reaction Time: Immediate.

Antidotes and Treatments: Maintaining respiration immediately with mouth-to-mouth resuscitation. Death comes in a high percentage of cases due to the neuromuscular poisons.

Case Histories: In 1967, a young soldier held an octopus on the back of his hand for a minute or two and had no sensation of a bite, but after putting the creature down, he noticed blood on his hand. A few minutes later he felt a prickling sensation around his mouth, which rapidly became generalized; within fifteen minutes he was almost completely paralyzed. He was hardly able to breathe. After an hour, he vomited and began convulsing. One hour after the bite, he was taken to the hospital, still breathing. He was fully conscious but completely paralyzed with no muscle tone and no reflexes. He couldn't even talk. In another hour, he had quit breathing and was put on a heart-lung machine and did, eventually, survive.

A lone fisherman, using the octopus for bait, was barely aware that he'd been bitten. Going into the water, he didn't realize his paralysis until it was too late and he drowned. When the body was later found, there was no sign of the fast-acting toxin in his body, and the bite — hard to find in good times — was nearly impossible to see in the water-affected body.

Notes: The octopus has killed at least two humans in recent years, both times because the person was playing with the creature.

Name: Geography cone. *Scientific Name*: *Conus geographus*. *Other*: There are over seventy different species including *C. magus*, *C. purpurascens*, tulip cone (*C. tulipa*), *C. catus*, and striated cone (*C. striatus*).

Toxicity: 5.

Location/Description: Cone shells are small venomous marine snails within spotted or brightly colored shells. The shell is one to four inches long, conical shaped with a large aperture. There are three types of cones — worm-eaters, mollusk-eaters, and fish-eaters. The fish-eaters are the ones that are deadly to humans. In some cases the harpoonlike teeth are a half-inch long and strong enough to pierce thin cloth.

The venom is white, gray, yellow, or black depending on the species.

They are found in the tropical waters of Australia (near Queensland), New Guinea, and notably on the Barrier Reef as well as tropical and subtropical waters of the Indo-Pacific. A few species are found in waters of the Mediterranean, Southern California, and New Zealand.

Effects and Symptoms: At the very least the cone shell poison causes temporary paralysis of the limbs and prolonged difficulty in breathing. A numb feeling starts with the lips and continues over the whole body. The victim complains of dizziness, tightness in the throat, and pain on breathing. The pulse is thready and rapid. Death occurs from respiratory arrest.

Reaction Time: Immediate first symptoms, and one to eight hours before death. If the victim survives the first ten hours, the prognosis is good.

Antidotes and Treatments: No antivenin is available. Supportive measures are taken as needed.

Case Histories: An Australian fatality occurred on Hayman Island in 1935. The victim, a young man in good health, held a cone shell in his hand as he scraped it with a knife. The snail inside extended its proboscis and stung him on the palm. Although just a small puncture wound, it caused almost immediate numbness. His lips became stiff, then his vision blurred. Within thirty minutes, his legs were paralyzed; within the hour, he had lost consciousness, drifting into a fatal coma.

Notes: All human victims were handling the shell before being stung. The snail usually comes out of the smaller end to sting, but it's best to handle the cone with forceps or not to pick up any shells at all. There have been several instances where the snail stung through cloth when being carried in a bag swinging against the victim's body.

Name: Sea anemone. *Scientific Name*: *Actinia equina*. *Other*: Hell's fire sea anemone (*Actinodendron plumosum*), rosy anemone (*Sagarita elegans*).

Toxicity: 2.

Location/Description: This polyp has a flowerlike appearance in the water and is usually found floating near the shore.

   Actinia equina inhabits the eastern Atlantic from the Arctic Ocean to the Gulf of Guinea, the Mediterranean Sea, the Black Sea, and the Sea of Azov. The hell's fire is found in the tropical Pacific, the Great Barrier Reef of Australia, and the Gilbert, Marshall, and Palau islands. The rosy anemone is found from Iceland to the Atlantic coast of France, the Mediterranean Sea, and the coast of Africa.

Effects and Symptoms: Anemones have stinging nematocysts or stinging tentacles that burst forth like a dart on contact with humans or other animals. Paralysis occurs progressing upward. Necrosis, skin ulceration, and secondary infection occur at the bite area— even when death does not occur. While death is rare, one may drown if stung while swimming.

Reaction Time: Immediate to a few hours.

Antidotes and Treatments: Symptomatically.

Notes: May also be poisonous when eaten. Because they are so pretty, children often pick them up and stick them in their mouths. Nudists often get genital injuries.

"Sponge diver's disease" is caused by the rosy sea anemone as it attaches itself to the sponge.

Name: Portuguese man-of-war. *Scientific Name*: *Physalia physalis*. *Other*: Australian bluebottle (*P. utriculus*).

Toxicity: 4.

Location/Description: This jellyfishlike creature inhabits the surface of the sea and is found in warm waters around the world. Tentacles of up to 165 feet in length hang downward. The float itself, which looks like an ancient Portuguese soldier's helmet, may be from three to twelve inches in diameter and is translucent but tinted pink, blue, or violet.

The *P. physalis* is most common in the gulf stream of the Atlantic and the subtropical and tropical regions of the Indo-Pacific.

Effects and Symptoms: The sting causes severe chest and abdominal pain, difficulty in swallowing, fever, and shock. Chest pains can cause problems while swimming, so drowning may be the actual cause of death.

Since they usually float in groups of a thousand or more, it's rare that the victim will receive only one sting. Therefore, enough venom can be administered to cause respiratory arrest.

Reaction Time: Immediate.

Antidotes and Treatments: Symptomatic.

Name: Stingray. *Scientific Name*: *Dasyatis pastinaca*. *Other*: Round stingray (*Urobatis halleri*), spotted eagle ray (*Aetobatus narinari*).

Toxicity: 4.

Location/Description: The stingray is found in the northeastern Atlantic, the Mediterranean Sea, and the Indian Ocean. The spotted eagle ray inhabits the tropical waters of the Atlantic, Red Sea, and Indo-Pacific. The round stingray is found from Point Conception in California to the Panama Bay.

Effects and Symptoms: The venom affects the heart muscle and causes erratic heart rhythm that sometimes brings on a fatal heart attack. The intense pain from the penetration of the skin with barbs in the tail starts a fall in blood pressure, nausea, vomiting, dizziness, profuse sweating, stomach pain, cramps, weakness, convulsions, and collapse. In some victims, there are multiple lesions from the sting which can become necrotic.

Reaction Time: Immediate. Recovery can occur in twenty-four to forty-eight hours.

Antidotes and Treatments: The wounds are surgically debrided and treatment is symptomatic.
Notes: In Colombia, over a five-year period, there were eight fatalities, twenty-three amputations of lower limbs, and one hundred and fourteen victims laid off from work for a long period of time.

Venomous Fish

Name: Scorpionfish or rockfish. *Scientific Name*: *Scorpaena guttata*. *Other*: zebrafish, butterfly cod, turkeyfish, firefish, or lionfish (*Pterois volitans*), stonefish (*Synanceja horrida*).
Toxicity: 5.
Location/Description: The scorpionfish can be found in Pacific waters from central California to the Gulf of California. Other varieties of this fish are found in most seas. The zebrafish is found in the Red Sea, Indian Ocean, and the western Pacific from Japan to Australia. The stonefish inhabits the Indo-Pacific and the waters around China, the Philippines, and Australia.

The stonefish looks like an irregular lump of flesh. It has a large upturned mouth to suck in prey. Closely related to the scorpionfish, it is sedentary, usually lying partially buried in the debris of a coral reef or in mud flats. Colors are subdued, matching their background to some extent. The spines and venom glands of these fish are well developed. The dorsal fins erect at the least disturbance, so if an unlucky swimmer or diver steps on the fish, there is an immediate sting.

The scorpionfish is about four to eight inches long with a large head, big mouth, and bright bands in reddish brown and white. Reef-dwellers, they are often found upside down in coral caves and other shelters. When annoyed, the fish tend to stand their ground and may actually approach the intruder, dorsal spines erect. All spines contain venom. The scratch is extremely painful and can cause a swimmer to be incapacitated. There are eighty different varieties of scorpionfish.

The zebrafish is beautiful with vivid colors and elegant fins like wings of a butterfly.
Effects and Symptoms: Marked swelling, convulsions, and intense pain may continue for hours, disabling the victim and even causing unconsciousness. Convulsions and unconsciousness, incredible pain, and paralysis of limbs can cause swimmers to drown. Cardiac arrest

is the final symptom. Secondary infection is common and gangrene sometimes occurs. A fluctuating fever with sharp highs and lows is another possibility that can lead to collapse and cardiac failure.

The zebrafish produces an intense pain with severe and lasting swelling. There is often respiratory distress and shock with a potentially fatal outcome.

Reaction Time: Instantaneous. Recovery is a slow and painful process of weeks and months. There may be a permanent scar.

Antidotes and Treatments: Stonefish antivenin is available, but in remote or tropical areas this may be unobtainable.

Notes: The most familiar aquarium species are among the most venomous.

Stonefish spines can penetrate flippers and thin tennis shoes as well as gloves. This fish often is found in aquariums.

Ingested Fish

Name: Pufferfish. *Scientific Name*: *Arothron meleagris*. *Other*: Toadfish, blowfish, swellfish, balloonfish, globefish, and toado.

Toxicity: 6. There is a mortality rate of 50 percent.

Location/Description: This fish is commonly found in warm or temperate regions around the world including the west coast of Central America, throughout the Indo-Pacific, around Japan, and from Australia to South Africa. There are over ninety species of pufferfish all belonging to the family Tetraodontidae. When disturbed, the fish inflates itself and becomes globular in form.

The poison tetraodontoxin is found in the fish's ovaries and is not destroyed by cooking. But the fish is usually harmless if the entrails are removed before cooking.

Effects and Symptoms: Difficulty speaking, talking, and other paralysis quickly move onto respiratory paralysis and death. The central nervous system is paralyzed. Death comes from convulsions or respiratory arrest within one to two hours.

People ingesting pufferfish often intentionally seek an exhilarated state characterized by mild numbness of the skin, tongue, and lips, flushing of the skin, a general warmth, and mood elevation.

Reaction Time: As rapid as ten minutes or delayed up to four hours. Survival past twenty-four hours is a sign of recovery.

Notes: In Japan, where it is called *fugu* and is considered the ultimate gastronomic experience, the fish must be cleaned and prepared by a specially trained and licensed chef. Even so, there are occasional fatal mishaps. There is a 57-percent mortality rate in those consuming the poisonous pufferfish. The poison is contained in the entrails and is not destroyed by cooking. From 1955 to 1975, of the three thousand people poisoned in Japan by eating *fugu*, over fifteen hundred died.

Also, this toxin was used in the movie *The Serpent and the Rainbow* to slow the respiration of the victim so that it appeared he was dead. After a quick burial, the victim was dug out and continued to be fed the drug at a lesser dose so that while his body functioned, his mind did not. He became a zombie or "living dead."

There is evidence that the toxin is used as part of the Haitian voodoo potion in the zombie ritual.

Name: Bivalve shellfish.

Toxicity: 6 during the toxic season (May to October).

Location/Description: Shellfish thrive in many marine locations such as California, Mexico, and Alaska. Mussels, clams, oysters, scallops, cockles, and other shellfish can become poisonous during the warm months of the year with potent nerve poisons when they feed on certain dinoflagellates, microscopic cellular beings, as *Gonyaulax catenella*, which carry the poison. These are rather rare.

Effects and Symptoms: A nitrogenous compound in the shellfish produces curarelike muscular paralysis.

After ingestion, numbness, tingling of lips, tongue, face, and extremities occur; nausea and vomiting follow. Convulsions may occur. Symptoms progress to respiratory paralysis and death.

Reaction Time: Symptoms start within a half hour. If victim survives for twelve hours, recovery is likely. Fatalities occur in 10 percent of the cases.

Notes: There are often warnings issued by the government agencies telling people not to eat particular shellfish at certain times of the year. The morbidity rate of those consuming toxic shellfish is high. Mussels produce the highest death rate of all the bivalve shellfish.

Other Fish: In tropical oceans, especially around Hawaii, there are poisonous fish such as porcupine, muki-muki, triggerfish, parrot fish, moray eel, surgeon fish, moon fish, filefish, goatfish, trunk fish, crown of thorn fish, and box fish all poisonous only part of the year, usually the warmer months.

There are two types of ingested fish poison: ciguatera and scombroid. These are usually the result of spoiled fish, and while they can make the victim quite ill, they are seldom fatal.

S E V E N

MEDICAL POISONS

If anyone ever gets a real dose of this, he's on his way to the next world.
— Ken Barlow, 1957
just before conviction for
the insulin murder of his
wife

In the eighteenth century, when medical science first stumbled forward, many doctors were reluctant to accept and use folk/plant lore for curing their patients. But the remedies they gave often killed the patients they intended to help. Nowadays, many medications are derived from plants.

Although no doctor will prescribe a deadly overdose, many fatalities result from bad combinations, as one doctor giving Valium and the other, not knowing what the patient is on, giving a barbiturate. Whether intentional or not, such mixtures and others like it can be problematic if not lethal. However, few reactions are guaranteed. Much depends on the size of the person, dose taken, and any other health problems he or she might have.

How the drug is taken can increase its lethal potential. For example, gelatin capsules or time-release capsules are meant to dissolve in the body slowly. But when alcohol accompanies them the capsules disintegrate rapidly, dumping the whole amount of drug into the body at once and causing a toxic and potentially fatal effect.

Deaths can also occur from an overdose when a drug is stopped too suddenly. Many times side effects will lessen as the body adjusts to the drug.

Amounts needed to kill depend on whether or not the victim has a tolerance or history with this drug or others in its same family. Many poisons, when constantly taken, tend to lose their effects because the patient becomes tolerant of the drug and therefore larger doses have to be given to produce the desired actions. This holds true, for example, if a victim takes Valium and the poisoner wants to use Librium. Because the person has developed a tolerance to Valium and the drugs act similarly, more Librium than the usual harmful dose will be needed to kill the victim. On the other hand, if a person does not have a history of using the drug, combining the two drugs would potentiate each other's effects.

All medications are possible poisons—some more so than others.

Medications here are grouped into categories. Symptoms here relate in general to the group and where they are located. Symptoms or notes specific to a particular drug within that category will be mentioned as will one drug if it stands out as being especially fatal.

Aspirin and Other Painkillers

Name: Aspirin. *Scientific Name: Acetylsalicylic acid. Other*: Bufferin, acetylsalicylics, Excedrin, Ecotrin, Bayer aspirin, Ascriptin, choline salicylate, methyl salicylate, and oil of wintergreen.
Toxicity: 3.
Form: Used orally or topically as an analgesic, it is a white powder with a slightly bitter taste. Aspirin is found in pill form and dermatologic ointments.
Effects and Symptoms: Aspirin stimulates the central nervous system and causes an accumulation of organic acids. It also interferes with Vitamin K utilization in the liver.

Among the symptoms are burning pain in the mouth, throat, or abdomen; lethargy; hearing loss; dizziness; fever; dehydration; restlessness; incoordination; cerebral edema; ecchymoses; pulmonary edema; convulsions; cyanosis; oliguria; uremia; coma; and respiratory failure. Chronic poisonings cause gastric bleeding or hemorrhages. Lab results show blood and protein in the urine as well as acidity in the blood.

Reaction Time: Four to six hours.

Antidotes and Treatments: Induce vomiting with syrup of ipecac unless respiration is depressed. Abnormal bleeding may have to be treated with fresh blood or platelet transfusion.

Notes: Aspirin may greatly increase the liver toxicity of acetaminophen (Tylenol). Aspirin also increases the activity of warfarin, the anticoagulation drug, so if someone is taking warfarin and receives a large dose of aspirin, there is a greater chance he might bleed to death if he falls down the steps, etc.

Vitamin C in large doses taken with aspirin can cause a poisonous, but not usually fatal, reaction.

Name: Cinchophen and Neocinchophen.

Toxicity: 5.

Form: An analgesic and antipyretic used in the treatment of gout, it is found in oral or injectable form.

Effects and Symptoms: Among the symptoms are gastrointestinal irritation, epigastric discomfort, anorexia, diarrhea, vomiting, hypernea, hyperthermia, delirium, convulsions, coma, and death. Since it damages the liver, autopsy findings include yellow atrophy of liver and fatty degeneration of heart and kidneys.

Reaction Time: Six to twelve hours.

Antidotes and Treatments: The treatment is the same as with salicylate poisoning. The damaged liver must be treated, and sometimes a liver transplant is necessary.

Notes: A high incidence of liver damage is associated with these drugs, which make their use in treatment of gout dangerous. Numerous fatalities have been reported.

Many painkillers like Fiorinal, which is used also as a muscle relaxant, increase sedation when taken with tranquilizers, antihistamines, antidepressants, sedatives, sleep inducers, alcohol, or narcotics. Fiorinal combined with codeine becomes more dangerous.

Name: Tylenol. *Scientific Name*: Acetaminophen. *Other*: Panadol, Anacin, Paracetamol.

Toxicity: 2.

Form: A white powder, it's usually taken in pill form, but there is a liquid version.

Effects and Symptoms: Tylenol's method of pain relief still has not been determined, but too much of it will injure the liver, kidney, heart, and central nervous system.

Nausea, vomiting, drowsiness, confusion, liver tenderness, low blood pressure, cardiac arrhythmias, jaundice, and hepatic and renal failure have resulted. Deaths have occurred from liver necrosis up to two weeks after ingestion.

Reaction Time: Thirty minutes up to four hours.

Antidotes and Treatments: Induce vomiting unless respiration is depressed. Activated charcoal is given to interfere with the drug's absorption. Efforts to remove the drug are useless after four hours. Fresh transfusions of plasma or clotting factors may be necessary. N-acetyl cysteine is an antidote if given within fifteen to twenty hours after ingestion.

Case Histories: Most analgesics and other over-the-counter drugs were, at one time, sold in capsule form, along with pills and caplets. In Chicago in the late seventies, someone inserted cyanide into several Tylenol capsules, thus sending the country into a panic. Shortly thereafter, all drug companies discontinued capsules and made their drugs as tamperproof as possible.

Notes: After three days evidence of liver damage is seen. Often the nausea experienced with the initial dose sends the victim to medical care.

It takes a large amount to kill with Tylenol alone, but in combination with other drugs or a central nervous system depressant, it could be fatal.

Vicodin, a pain reliever in this category, combines hydrocodone bitartrate (a variation of codeine) and acetaminophen, causing sedation, lethargy, anxiety, fear, mood changes, unhappy feelings, urinary spasms, and breathing problems. Drug dependence can result from this drug, and when used with MAO inhibitors or tricyclic antidepressants, the effects of this drug can be increased.

Norgesic, a muscle relaxant and pain reliever made up of orphenadrine, aspirin, and caffeine, has side effects such as excitation, hallucinations, increased bleeding, lightheadedness, and blacking out. Confusion, anxiety, and tremors can result from the combination of this drug and propoxyphene (Darvon). Many over-the-counter drugs for colds, coughs, and allergies also interact unfavorably with Norgesic. This drug often increases sedation when taken with tranquilizers, antihistamines, antidepressants, sedatives, sleep inducers, alcohol, or narcotics. Norgesic also increases the action of anticlotting drugs.

Anti-inflammatory Pain Relievers

Anti-inflammatory drugs — diflunisal (Dolobid); ibuprofen (Motrin, Rufen, Advil, Haltrain, Medipren, Nuprin, Trendar); fenoprofen (Nalfon); meclofenamate (Meclomen); naproxen (Anaprox, Naprosyn) — should not be taken in combination with aspirin or other nonsteroid analgesic drugs, or with warfarin or other oral anticlotting drugs, because bleeding time may be prolonged while on anti-inflammatory pain relievers and a simple fall could prove fatal. Antacids, however, may sometimes reduce the effects of an anti-inflammatory drug, nullifying the combination. So if the victim is surprisingly still alive, an antacid could be the culprit.

On their own, anti-inflammatory drugs are of low toxicity. Victims with gastrointestinal tract disease, peptic ulcers, poor heart function, or those taking anticlotting drugs should avoid them.

If the victim is allergic to aspirin or other nonsteroid analgesic drugs, especially if they have sniffling, nasal polyps, or asthma, these anti-inflammatory drugs can cause a fatal reaction.

Anti-inflammatory drugs easily become toxic when given to those with renal problems because the kidneys cannot cleanse the blood and the poisons build up. Overdoses cause renal failure and severe liver reactions including fatal jaundice.

Ibuprofen also negates the diuretics taken to get rid of excess body fluid. A moderately large dose of ibuprofen combined with a diuretic often increases the chance of congestive heart failure because neither the diuretic nor the ibuprofen is working.

Taken with lithium (to control manic-depressive symptoms), ibuprofen produces an elevation of lithium blood level. Lithium itself is quite toxic and needs to be constantly monitored. In the proper percentage, this could be a fatal combination.

It's not wise to take Anaprox (naproxen sodium) with Naprosyn (naproxen), as they both circulate the same anion in the blood and the mixture could be fatal. Naproxen also tends to increase the effects of antidiabetic drugs, so a person taking this could easily go into hypoglycemia and die.

Local Anesthetics

Local anesthetics first stimulate and then depress the central nervous system. No two anesthetics act the same, and the effects also

depend greatly on the physical makeup of the person taking them.
Name: Procaine and lidocaine. *Similar*: Marcaine, monocaine, nes-
acaine, nupercaine, duranest, xylocaine, carocaine, oracaine, un-
acaine, citanest, and novocaine. All of these are related to cocaine
and are synthetic versions of the coca bush alkaloids.
Toxicity: 5.
Form: Colorless liquids or thick gels, these drugs are given by injection or used topically for cardiac irregularity.
Effects and Symptoms: These drugs are rapidly distributed in the
body and numbness occurs locally.

At first giddiness develops, then feelings of oppression. These
are followed by severe collapse, coma, convulsions, and respiratory
arrest. After injection or large surface application, circulatory collapse comes about by direct depression of blood vessel tone or by
effect on the central nervous system. Dizziness, cyanosis, fall of
blood pressure, muscular tremors, convulsions, coma, irregular and
weak breathing, bronchial spasm, and cardiac standstill are other
symptoms. Rapid intravenous injection causes cardiac arrest. Hypersensitivity occurs with repeated topical applications. These reactions include itching, redness, edema, and blistering.
Reaction Time: Immediate. Efforts to remove the drug after thirty
minutes are useless. After survival of one hour, the victim usually
recovers.
Antidotes and Treatments: The ingested drug must first be removed and absorption from the injection site must be limited by
tourniquet and ice pack. Maintain the airway and give artificial respiration with oxygen until convulsions and central nervous system
depression are controlled. Procaine is considered the most dangerous of all the derivatives and has caused numerous fatalities.
Case Histories: A recent hospital scandal occurred when patients
at a VA hospital were given overdoses of procaine as a form of
euthanasia.
Notes: As with cocaine, states of shock with a possible fatal outcome can occur with very small doses of procaine. Procaine enhances the effects of muscle relaxants.

Volatile and Gaseous Anesthetics

Most of the gases act the same way and so have been lumped together.

Name: Ether, chloroform, Vinethene, Fluothane, Penthrane, Fluoromar, ethylene, cyclopropane. *Scientific Name*: diethyl ether, ethyl ether, divinyl ether, ethyl chloride, halothane, methoxyflurane, fluroxene. *Other*: Found as gases are ethylene, cyclopropane, and nitrous oxide.

Toxicity: 5.

Form: They are used to produce general anesthesia. At cold temperatures, these drugs are volatile liquids before they become gases and as such can be ingested or inhaled.

Effects and Symptoms: All functions of the central nervous system are depressed; excessive use stops respiration, causes liver necrosis, and causes trouble with the autoimmune system. The principal manifestations are unconsciousness and respiratory failure. Cyanosis and cardiac irregularities are seen.

Reaction Time: Patients die after several days.

Antidotes and Treatments: Force ventilation, remove gas, maintain respiration, and keep the body warm. If fever occurs, body temperature is lowered by the application of wet towels. For malignant hyperthermia, dantrolene sodium 1 mg/kg every fifteen minutes to a total of 10 mg/kg and procainamide 15 mg/kg intravenous over ten minutes.

Notes: Liver damage caused by chloroform may progress to cirrhosis and death. Often uncontrolled hyperthermia shows up. This is a genetic response that occurs in about 10 percent of the population, driving their temperatures up over 110 degrees, and occurs during or after anesthesia. Cyclopropane and halothan increase the effect of blood pressure medications and taken together can cause the blood pressure to fall dangerously low.

Name: Nitrous oxide.

Toxicity: 5.

Form: A nonflammable, nearly odorless gas, nitrous oxide will not produce complete anesthesia at safe concentration and so is used primarily as an analgesic or as an adjunct to more potent anesthetic agents. Often inhaled for its euphoric effects, this gas is easily obtained.

Effects and Symptoms: The gas is a central nervous system depressant. Nitrous oxide without adequate oxygen can cause heart palpitation, irregular heart rhythms, brain damage, and death. Headaches, cerebral edema, and permanent mental deficiency can also result.

Reaction Time: A few seconds to several minutes.

Antidotes and Treatments: Oxygen is given and other symptoms are treated as they occur.

Case Histories: A dentist purposely suffocated several of his clients with nitrous oxide.

Notes: Discovered in 1776, nitrous oxide was not used as an anesthetic until 1799 and did not come into general use until 1860.

Narcotic Analgesics

Most narcotic analgesics come in oral, injectable, and topical forms; some can be inhaled. The oral version is usually a white powder. These drugs are all used to control severe pain and work by depressing the central nervous system. Death from respiratory failure may occur immediately after intravenous overdose or within two to four hours after oral or subcutaneous administration. The reaction time and amount needed depends on the victim's size, prior health, and drug tolerance.

General symptoms from ingestion or injection are unconsciousness; pinpoint pupils; slow, shallow respiration; cyanosis; weak pulse; low blood pressure; spasm of gastrointestinal tract; pulmonary edema; spasticity; and twitching of the muscles. Convulsions may accompany codeine, meperidine, apomorphine, propoxyphene, or oxymorphone. The toxicity is usually 5. Antidotes and treatments include use of the drug Naloxone, which binds up the narcotics and helps eliminate them from the body. Treatments must be started within two hours of administration. Sometimes the drug absorption in cases of injection can be delayed by use of a tourniquet.

Name: Codeine. *Scientific Name*: Methylmorphine.

Toxicity: 6.

Form: Codeine is a nearly transparent, odorless substance with a fairly bitter taste. It is found as a powder or a liquid.

Effects and Symptoms: An addictive sedative and analgesic, it's symptoms include sleepiness, floating sensation, giddiness, unbalanced gait, slowing heartbeat, respiratory difficulty, coma, and death. Since it suppresses reflexes, it is often used as an anticough medication.

Reaction Time: Immediate for injections; within twenty minutes for ingestion.

Antidotes and Treatments: Naloxone is used and other symptoms are treated as they occur.

Notes: Codeine is a dangerous fire hazard when exposed to heat or flame.

Codeine comes in combination with many other drugs such as acetaminophen (Tylenol), aspirin, caffeine, other painkillers, or cough suppressants. Canada has a drug 222 (and various versions of it) sold over the counter that contains one-fourth grain codeine.

Name: Morphine. *Other*: Laudanum, opium, narcotine, protopine, meconidine, laudanoisine, and lanthopine.

Toxicity: 6.

Form: A white crystalline alkaloid, morphine is found as a liquid or a tablet and can be ingested or injected.

Effects and Symptoms: An addictive sedative and analgesic, it's symptoms include sleepiness, sense of physical ease, quickening of the pulse, floating sensation, giddiness, unbalanced gait, dizziness, heaviness of the head, nausea, slowing heartbeat, contracted pupils, loss of muscle power, respiratory difficulty, unconsciousness, coma, and death.

Reaction Time: Twenty to forty minutes when ingested; five to ten minutes for injection. If the victim survives forty-eight hours the prognosis is favorable.

Antidotes and Treatments: If Naloxone is used, recovery can be as quick as one to four hours.

Case Histories: In May 1947, Dr. Robert Clements called another physician to his Southsea, Hampshire house to attend his fourth wife, who had fallen into a deep coma. Dr. Clements told his colleague that Mrs. Clements had suffered from myeloid leukemia. The disease was listed on the death certificate when Mrs. Clements died the following morning. Two other physicians, however, were unhappy about the situation, for they noticed that Mrs. Clements's eyes had retracted into the typical pinpoint state associated with narcotic poisoning. A third medical man performed the autopsy and pronounced the cause of death as leukemia. Still, the coroners were not happy. They reported their suspicions to their superiors.

The police began inquiries and noted the couple had not been getting along. In addition, Mrs. Clements had been subject to bouts of unconsciousness, though her husband always seemed to predict when they would occur. He had also recently had their telephone removed from the home — a rather odd action for a busy physician with a chronically ill wife. Her health had deteriorated over a period of time, she had vomited regularly, and her complexion had a yellowish tinge. She was also lethargic — a sure sign of morphine overdosing.

It was then discovered Dr. Clements had prescribed a high dose of morphine for a nonexistent patient, and a second autopsy was ordered. Before the results could be released, Dr. Clements, himself, died of morphine poisoning. His suicide note read, "I can no longer tolerate the diabolical insults to which I have recently been exposed." Clements was found guilty of killing his fourth wife, an heiress, and inquiries showed his other three wives had also been rich. All three had died of illnesses diagnosed by Clements himself — and he had signed all their death certificates.

Notes: Morphine is the poisonous part of opium. Used as a painkiller since 1886, morphine was commonly found in the Chinese opium dens and popular especially in Victorian times for women with "anxieties."

Liquid morphine, a bluish syrup given to cancer patients for pain, can be mixed with blue liqueur like creme de menthe to strengthen the effects of the drug.

Morphine increases the effects of sedatives, analgesics, sleep-inducing drugs, tranquilizers, antidepressants, and other narcotic drugs. If mixed with alcohol or other solvents, it works faster. Death occurs between six to twelve hours and is almost always due to respiratory failure.

Name: Percodan. *Scientific Name*: Oxycodone.

Toxicity: 5.

Form: A narcotic analgesic, it is often available in combination with aspirin, phenacetin, and caffeine. Oral or injectable, it is often prescribed to control coughing.

Effects and Symptoms: A central nervous system depressant, Percodan can cause drowsiness, constipation, unsteady walking, light-headedness, dizziness, sedation, nausea, and vomiting. As many others, this drug is capable of producing stupor, coma, muscle flaccidity, severe respiratory depression, hypotension, and cardiac arrest.

Reaction Time: One-half hour or less.

Antidotes and Treatments: Naloxone is a specific antidote.

Case Histories: A man took Percodan for a toothache and then went scuba diving. He died while in the water as a result of the drowsy effects of the drug.

Notes: Sedation may increase when taken with tranquilizers, antihistamines, antidepressants, sedatives, sleep inducers, alcohol, or narcotics. Combining this drug with phenytoin (Dilantin) may decrease brain functions and might cause brain death.

Other Depressant Drugs and Their Lethal Levels

There are many addictive drugs, and several work in the same way as the narcotics. Depending on the hospital, these may or may not be locked up. If they are, they will be found in the narcotic box since even though they are technically not narcotics, they are drugs of abuse. Nurses carry the narcotic keys and usually only one nurse per shift will be the medication nurse. Doctors do not often have access to the keys or to the narcotic box unless they specifically ask for a certain drug, and then the process of accounting for each drug at the end of each shift makes stealing such drugs difficult for the average poisoner. Despite what many may think, the majority of doctors' offices do not carry narcotics, and from the physician's office the best a villain can do is to steal a prescription blank. All of these drugs are or can be addictive.

Some of these drugs and their effects are:

Fentanyl or **Sublimaze** has a toxicity of 6 and causes muscle rigidity before death much the same as strychnine.

DFP or **diisopropylphosphate** is an eye drop with a toxicity of 5.

Numorphan (oxymorphone) causes restlessness before death.

Dilaudid (hydromorphone) is for pain.

Hycodan or **Dicodid** is hydrocodeine and is often used to control coughs. A derivative of codeine, it causes tremors when overdosing. Death can occur.

Lorfan (levallorphan) causes restlessness before death.

Levo-Dromoran (levorphanol) is injectable.

Darvon (propoxyphene) is a painkiller that is sometimes mixed with acetaminophen, aspirin, or caffeine for further effect as in Darvon Compound, Darvon 100, or Darvon 65, which have mixtures of aspirin, caffeine, and propoxyphene. An odorless, crystalline powder with a bitter taste, it is freely soluble in water. Among the overdose symptoms before the lethal dose are nausea, vomiting, skin rash, drooping of the eyelids, and convulsions. Darvon is classed as a mild narcotic analgesic. It can cause coma and respiratory depression and is quite addictive as well. A warning in the *Prescription Drug Encyclopedia* indicates it should not be given to suicidal people as it will increase their depression. Of course, this could aid the killer if he wants the death to look like suicide. This is always given orally as a pill. Sedation may increase when taken with tranquilizers, antihistamines, antidepressants, sedatives, sleep inducers, alcohol, or narcotics.

Talwin (pentazocine) is an addictive painkiller that can be given in oral form, but is usually injected or given intravenously, and causes extreme nausea. Talwin causes withdrawal symptoms. Sedation increases when taken with tranquilizers, antihistamines, antidepressants, sedatives, sleep inducers, alcohol, or narcotics. It's often found on the black market and sold as a street drug.

Flexeril (cyclobenzaprine) is used as a muscle relaxant and for pain caused by muscle spasms. It causes drowsiness, dizziness, increased heart rate, weakness, fatigue, nausea, and should not be used by those recovering from recent heart attacks, congestive heart failure, or those who've taken MAO inhibitors (a type of antidepressant) in the past fourteen days. Convulsions may result with this last situation.

Demerol (meperidine) and **Dolantin (pethidine)** have a toxicity of 4 and will cause generalized edema (swelling), coma, and hypertension in addition to other symptoms above. Sedation increases when taken with tranquilizers, antihistamines, antidepressants, sedatives, sleep inducers, alcohol, or narcotics. Serious reactions can occur if MAO inhibitors are taken within fourteen days of Demerol.

Ritalin is another drug that can be quite addictive and is usually kept locked up. While it is a stimulant, it seems to have the opposite effect on hyperactive children and is commonly given to them to calm them down. Tolerance or drug dependence may develop with long-term use. A central nervous system stimulant for most adults, it can cause nausea, vomiting, tremors, coma, and convulsions. Toxicity level is 4. Blood pressure can be greatly increased if this drug is taken with MAO inhibitors. If taken with anticonvulsants, changes in seizure patterns may occur. The effects of anticlotting and antidepressants are also increased when taking Ritalin.

Drugs with a level-three toxicity (out of a rating of six) in this list that would need quite a bit to kill—but could be very dangerous in combination with another depressant or barbiturate—are **Nisen-**

til; **Leritine**; **Apodol** (anileridine); **Stadol** (butorphanol), **Romilar** (**dextromethorphan**), which causes dizziness; and **Norvad** (**levopropoxyphene**).

Sometimes given to cancer patients, the Bromptom Cocktail or Bromptom Mixture includes a variety of drugs like morphine, cocaine, alcohol, chloroform, a tranquilizer, and/or an antiemetic mixed into a syrup.

Sleeping Pills

Those who use sleeping pills often build up a tolerance. As with any drug where a tolerance has developed, more is usually needed to obtain the desired effect. But each day the drug companies develop more varieties and each seems to be more potent than the next.

Almost all texts agree that combining ethyl alcohol with these drugs multiplies the effects, but there is no agreement on how much alcohol is needed to exacerbate the lethality of any drug.

Name: Chloral hydrate. *Other Names*: Triclos, triclofos.

Toxicity: 5.

Form: Given orally, chloral hydrate is a clear liquid; the gelatin capsules are often tinted red.

Effects and Symptoms: The central nervous system is depressed. Symptoms include sleepiness, mental confusion, unsteadiness, followed rapidly with coma; slow, shallow respiration; flaccid muscles; hypotension; cyanosis; hypothermia or hyperthermia; and absent reflexes. Duration of coma is dependent on the amount of medication taken. In prolonged coma, moist rales are heard in the lower lung fields and can be an indication of pulmonary edema. Carbon dioxide retention under these conditions causes acidosis. Death occurs from pneumonia, pulmonary edema, hypotension that will not go away, or respiratory failure.

Chronic poisoning from ingestion causes skin rash, mental confusion, ataxia, dizziness, drowsiness, hangover, depression, irritability, poor judgment, neglect of personal appearance, and other behavior disturbances.

Reaction Time: Within a half hour the victim will begin to react. Death may occur in a few hours.

Antidotes and Treatments: Pump the stomach, maintain the airway, and increase oxygen intake.

Case Histories: Agatha Christie's *Secret Adversary* and *The Clocks* both used chloral hydrate (or Mickey Finns) to poison the victims.

Her famous *Ten Little Indians* also used chloral hydrate in Emily Brent's coffee to render her unconscious. (Though it was the injection of cyanide that finally did her in.)

Notes: With the introduction of chloroform as an anesthetic by James Young Simpson in 1847, interest in painkillers increased. Chloral hydrate, brought out as a derivative of chloroform by Oscar Liebreich in 1862, is now the oldest prescription hypnotic currently available. Like barbiturates, chloral hydrate has anticonvulsant effects, but the doses necessary are likely to completely sedate the victim and it has few analgesic properties.

Chloral hydrate, a popular drug of abuse in the late nineteenth century, was common in the thirties' hard-boiled detective stories as "knockout drops" or "Mickey Finns." The drug also enters breast milk to induce lethargy in children.

Mixed with alcohol, chloral hydrate can be lethal. Fesules are the English version of the drug.

Name: Dalmane. *Scientific Name*: Flurazepam. *Other*: Nitrazepam and other benzodiazepins. In Britain it's Dalinanc.

Toxicity: 5.

Form: Sleeping pills.

Effects and Symptoms: A muscle relaxant used to relieve anxiety and anticonvulsant, Dalmane is less potent than diazepam (Valium), more like chlordiazepoxide (Librium). Because the victim's central nervous system is affected, there is decreased respiratory drive and breathing is impaired. The victim doesn't take in enough oxygen and becomes groggy.

Drowsiness, sleep, and unconsciousness are the primary symptoms. If taken with alcohol or other central nervous system drugs, it will potentiate the effect of the drug.

Reaction Time: Ten to twenty minutes.

Antidotes and Treatments: Pump stomach, give Ipecac syrup, maintain airway, increase oxygen, maintain blood pressure.

Notes: Suicides often use this in conjunction with other methods as gassing, hypothermia, or drowning. Withdrawal psychosis (craziness) is possible.

Substantial amounts of the drug are detected in the blood with decreasing amounts up to twenty-five hours after swallowing. The drug can be detected in the urine for up to 120 hours after taking it.

Name: Dilantin. *Scientific Name*: Diphenylhydantoin. *Other*: Phenytoin.

Toxicity: 4.

Form: Found as tablets or a colorless liquid, Dilantin is given orally or injected.

Effects and Symptoms: Used as an anticonvulsant and sleep aid, some of the symptoms include swelling of gums, fever, liver and kidney damage, anemia, pulmonary changes, lymph gland enlargement, epidermal necrosis, cardiac irregularities, peripheral nerve damage, tremor, drug psychosis, and muscle rigidity. Other symptoms include slurred speech, confusion, dizziness, mild nervousness, excessive facial hair growth, and low blood sugar that can cause insulin shock and death.

Reaction Time: Fifteen minutes to an hour, depending on administration.

Antidotes and Treatments: Gastric lavage.

Notes: This drug should be discontinued gradually. Barbiturates may increase this drug's action. Blood thinners, antidepressants, or alcohol will reduce its effectiveness.

Other Common Sleeping Pills

The majority of sleeping pills were not developed until the late forties or early fifties, so if you're doing a period piece you'll want to check the dates on the following drugs before using them. All the symptoms are the same as chloral hydrate, except where noted, since they're all central nervous system depressants. Reaction time is usually from ten minutes to a half hour, depending on the dose and the weight of the person. Almost all are given only in pill or capsule form. Toxicity for the following are level 4 unless otherwise mentioned, as with Mogadon, which is a 5.

Mogadon (nitrazepam) is commonly used in European countries.

In addition to the regular symptoms caused by chloral hydrate, **Soma (carisoprodol)** causes paralysis, visual disturbances, excitement, skin rash, asthma, fever, and high blood pressure. **Placidyl (ethychlorvynol)** causes fatigue, headache, confusion, nausea, vomiting, pulmonary edema, destruction of red blood cells, liver damage, and an acid imbalance in the body (acidosis). **Valmid (ethinamate)** works in similar ways and also lessens the number of red blood cells, causing cyanosis and liver impairment.

Doriden (glutethimide) and **Restoril (temazepam)** are often prescribed in hospitals and for postsurgical patients returning home. Doriden was first introduced clinically in 1954 and causes nausea, an increased white blood cell count, numbness in the limbs, toxic psychosis, dry mouth, widening of the pupils, swelling of the brain tissue, and convulsions. Restoril, which is commonly used to relieve insomnia, most frequently causes dizziness, confusion, lethargy, loss of balance, an awareness of the heartbeat, hallucinations, and excessive anxiety. Restoril, as with many of these others, can be addictive.

Halcion (triazolam) is commonly found in the psychiatric ward and its side effects include lightedheadness, nervousness, incoordination, nausea, vomiting, increased heart rate, an excessive feeling of happiness, memory loss, cramps, visual disturbances, altered taste, dry mouth, tingling sensation, ringing in the ears, poor urinary control, changes in sex drive, liver failure, and hallucinations. When this is withdrawn suddenly, there can be bizarre personality changes (psychosis) and even paranoia. This can be physically and psychologically habit-forming.

Two other popular drugs are **Noludar (methyprylon)** and **Tegretol (carbamazepine)**. The latter is classed as an anticonvulsant and pain reliever, but is also used for sleeplessness and treating epilepsy when other drugs have failed. Sometimes it's also used to treat nerve pain in the facial region. The symptoms for Tegretol overdose include urinary retention, skin rash, iron deficiency, stomach upset, jaundice, low blood pressure, and heart failure. If that doesn't get the victim, the fatal hepatitis will. People taking MAO inhibitor antidepressants should not be taking Tegretol since it zooms the blood pressure way up. Victims with high blood pressure, active liver disease, or serious mental or emotional disorders will be adversely affected by Tegretol.

The sleeping drug **Ethotoin (peganone)** and **Mesantoin (mephenytoin)** cause infections in the lymph glands; **Milontin (phensuximide)** causes blood to appear in the urine and kidney infections as well as muscle weakness.

Celotin (methsuximide) and **Zarotin (ethosuximide)** cause swelling of the limbs, liver failure, and fatal bone marrow aplasia. There is a delay of one to several days in the onset of the coma mainly because it takes several hours for the above symptoms to kick in.

Phenurone (phenacemide) causes liver damage, a decrease of white blood cells, behavioral effects, kidney impairment, skin rash, and psychotic breaks as well as suicidal tendencies. Someone might even commit or try to commit suicide while under the influence of this drug.

Mysoline (primidone) causes painful gums and excessive fatigue.

There is no specific antidote for sedative and hypnotic drugs. Analeptic drugs like caffeine, Emivan, Metrazol, and amphetamine can cause further problems such as irritability and hypertension and even death if they are overdone. Sometimes special problems like hypothermia or hyperthermia develop, in which case, avoid rapid warming or cooling of the victim.

Barbiturates

Barbiturates are derived from barbituric acid, discovered by Adolph von Baeyer in 1864, and are a key factor in twenty-five hundred derivatives, fifty of which are used medically. Overdose of barbiturates is a common cause of death.

Name: Many of the barbiturates like Veronal aka Carbutol (barbital); Luminal aka purple hearts, goof balls, or downs (phenobarbital); Amytal aka blue heaves (amobarbital); Butisol (butabarbital); Nembutal aka yellow jackets (pentobarbital); Seconal aka reds, red devils, red birds (secobarbital); Pentothal (thiopental); Dialog (allobarbital); Alurate (aprobarbital); Medomin (hexobarbital); Mebaral (mephobarbital); Brevital (methohexital); Gemonil (metharbital); and Surital (thiamylal) are used for sedation.

Toxicity: 4 to 5. It depends on if the barbiturate is long-, medium-, short-, or ultra-short-acting. The ill effects from overdose such as severe shock or respiratory failure tend to be more frequent and serious with medium- and short-acting. Some combination drugs as Tuinal contain a short-acting barbiturate (quinalbarbitone) combined with a medium-acting one (amylobarbitone).

Form: Depending on the drug, barbiturates can be administered orally, by injection, intravenously, or rectally.

Effects and Symptoms: All cause unconsciousness—either in sleep or surgical anesthesia. The affects of these drugs also depend on the liver's ability to metabolize and use them. Because the drugs are not properly excreted, patients with acute hepatitis (liver damage) develop sedation sooner, especially during intravenous administration. So someone with liver disease should be careful using sedatives, hypnotics, or barbiturates. The major symptom is sedation, but dizziness, headache, irritability, confusion, irregular heartbeat, shallow breathing, and low blood pressure can also be a problem. Sedation may increase when taken with tranquilizers, antihistamines, antidepressants, sedatives, sleep inducers, alcohol, or narcotics.

Reaction Time: A few minutes to half hour.

Antidotes and Treatments: All barbiturates tend to be well absorbed and so in cases of ingestion, gastric lavage is needed immediately. Other treatment is symptomatic.

Notes: Phenobarbital is often given to control seizures. Phenobarbital and Doriden will potentiate each other.

The ever-popular Seconal (secobarbital) is another common drug. Most who die by Seconal are in a coma for several days, unless drug was combined with another which would increase its toxicity from 3 to 4 or 5, depending on what it had been combined with.

Coadministration with other drugs may alter the victim's metabolism of barbiturates. Ingested alcohol may decrease the rate of metabolism and increase the toxicity of the drug. Abuse is also a problem.

Many of the drugs when taken in small repeated doses may accumulate in the system and act as if a larger dose has been given. Intravenous injection of any barbiturate may cause severe respiratory depression, severe fall of blood pressure, and combination with alcohol will make barbiturates more dangerous. When blood pressure falls too low, life can end because no oxygen is circulated.

In small doses, barbiturates may actually increase sensation of pain.

Sudden withdrawal from barbiturates may increase emotional disturbances and can prove fatal.

Ultrashort-acting thiobarbital, used also as an intravenous anesthetic, has quickest response on the brain. According to *Prediction of Suicide*, by Drs. Beck, Resnick, and Lettierri, this last drug is the most widely used of all drugs for suicide among doctors.

Those who overdose on barbiturates usually go into a coma which lasts one to five days. The toxicity level is 5 for most of these, but combined with other drugs or with alcohol, they may be fatal.

Alcohol with any drug will increase potential. Taking barbiturates may decrease the effects of anticlotting drugs or adrenal hormones. In this case more than just a single dose would be needed for the mystery writers to kill their victims.

Intravenous barbiturates may cause decreased cardiac output, increased heart rate, or other changes. Barbiturates may decrease gastric secretions and affect the intestinal muscles, kidney function, and blood flow, as well as blood pressure.

Name: Veronol. *Scientific Name*: Barbital.

Toxicity: 5.

Form: Veronal is a colorless liquid that can be injected, taken orally, or used as a gas in surgical anesthesia.

Veronol inhibits seizure activity. It is also a respiratory depressant, affecting the nerve impulses and the victim's responses to lack of oxygen, carbon dioxide tension, and blood acidity.

Effects and Symptoms: Unconsciousness.

Reaction Time: Immediate.

Case Histories: Veronol is thought to be the first true barbiturate and used commonly until 1912, when Luminal (phenobarbital) was discovered by Alfred Hauptmann.

Other Hypnotics

Oral hypnotic doses have little effect on the cardiovascular system to reduce heart rate and blood pressure. A victim could be convinced to use these hypnotics to suppress his cough and then die, since the amount needed to affect the cough reflex would also have a major effect on the respiratory system.

Name: Paral. *Scientific Name*: Paraldehyde.

Toxicity: 5.

Form: Oral and injectable, Paral is used as a sedative or hypnotic and is administered in small doses.

First used in 1882 in obstetrics, it is an aromatic liquid at room temperature, but it slowly decomposes to an acetic acid upon exposure to air.

Effects and Symptoms: Believed to work in the liver and to oxidize into acetic acid, Paral has produced hypotension, tachycardia, cyanosis, rapid and shallow breathing, coughing, coma, and death — even with therapeutic amounts. Chronic use can result in addiction, which resembles that of alcohol. It is seldom used in the United States now.

Reaction Time: Immediate.

Antidotes and Treatments: Giving oxygen and maintaining respiration are the most important, and then symptomatic treatment.

Antihistamines

There are no antihistamines that are fatal on their own, but in combination with other drugs, some may cause fatal reactions. **Dimetapp** and **Entex**, for example, are combinations of antihistamines and decongestants. Both adversely affect blood pressure and a large dose can lead to a severe rise in blood pressure, which may then produce a stroke. Sedation increases when these drugs are taken with tranquilizers, other antihistamines, antidepressants, sedatives, sleep inducers, alcohol, or narcotics.

Often antihistamines are combined with phlegm looseners, which, if victims have high blood pressure already, can adversely affect them. The risk is greatest to victims who have thyroid or heart disease. However, toxicity is about 4, so quite a bit would be needed.

If MAO inhibitor antidepressants are taken concurrently or within fourteen days of taking some of these antihistamines, the blood pressure may rise dramatically, again causing a stroke.

Some antihistamines are **Benadryl (diphenhydramine)**, **Optimine** or **Azatadine (trinalin)**, **Dimetane (brompheniramine)**, **Chlor-Trimeton (chlorpheniramine)**, and **Tavist (clemastine)**. Benadryl and others in this group are often used to combat anaphylactic shock caused by severe allergy attacks.

Another drug in this category is **Naldecon** (a combination of phenylpropanolamine, phenylephrine, phenyltoloxamine, and chlorpheniramine) that when combined with MAO inhibitors causes a rise in blood pressure. Beta blockers, another type of drug, increase the effect even more.

Phenergan expectorant may also lower the convulsion threshold of anticonvulsants and increase the severity of convulsions. Effects of atropine and related drugs may be increased when using Phenergan. Most of the other over-the-counter drugs for allergies and colds negatively interact with this drug in the same way.

Phenylpropanolamine is used as a decongestant, antihistamine, and as an appetite suppressant. Contained in many over-the-counter drugs for colds, allergies, coughs, and diet aids, it reacts negatively to many other similar drugs. And if the recommended dose is exceeded there may be a large rise in blood pressure. If a person takes a diet aid such as Acutrim and then something for his cold, chances are he'll have an adverse reaction.

People sensitive to epinephrine, ephedrine, terbutaline, and amphetamines may also be sensitive to phenylpropanolamine. Taking this drug can increase the effects of epinephrine and decrease the effects of blood-pressure reducers so that even though the victim is taking a blood pressure reducer, he might still have a fatal stroke. If taken with digitalis preparations, the blood pressure might rise dramatically. Tricyclic antidepressants may react to cause excessive stimulation of the heart and blood pressure. MAO inhibitors can do the same if taken within fourteen days of having taken the drug.

Tussi-Organidin, an anticough phlegm loosener and antihistamine, and **Tussionex**, an anticough medication, can both cause major problems with overdose. Convulsions, low breathing rates, sedation, and loss of consciousness can occur with the former. The latter may increase the thyroid hormone, lowering the effects of antithyroid hormones as well as the drug lithium (used for manic-depressive syndrome).

Major Bronchial Tube Relaxers

Name: Ventolin or Proventil (albuterol) are used as bronchial tube relaxers to provide relief during asthma, bronchitis, and emphysema. *Other*: Alupent (metaproterenol) is used to relieve spasms in asthma, bronchitis, and emphysema, as well as tightness in the chest. Aminophylline, Theolair (theophylline), Choledyl (oxtriphylline) and Slo-Phyllin are all used to treat bronchial asthma and other lung disorders.

Toxicity: 4.

Form: Found in a liquid or gaseous state, these drugs are often administered into the air by nebulizers in closed rooms or by hand-held inhalers.

Effects and Symptoms: With large doses, bronchial fluid builds up and causes inflammation, pounding heartbeat, dizziness, nervousness, bad or unusual taste in the mouth, dry mouth, headache, insomnia, anxiety, tension, and blood pressure changes. Loosening the congestion of the bronchial tubes, these drugs also cause flushing of the skin, sweating, or angina-type chest or arm pain.

With overdose, convulsions, hallucinations, serious breathing problems, fever, chills, vomiting, and cold perspiration occur. A sharp rise in blood pressure may cause stroke or external bleeding. Serious side effects happen if the drug is taken with or soon after taking another bronchial-tube relaxer or decongestant in pill or liquid form.

Reaction Time: Immediate.

Antidotes and Treatments: Oxygen is given and other treatment is symptomatic.

Notes: Fatalities have been associated with excessive use of inhalers.

For people with heart disease, congestive heart failure, high blood pressure, or diabetes, these drugs could be dangerous since they often interfere with the rhythm of the heart, especially when rauwolfia drugs (used to reduce high blood pressure) are also taken. (Some of these are Enduronyl, Rauzide, Diupres, Hydropres, Regroton, Ser-Ap-Es, Salutensin, rauwolfia serpentina, deserpidine, and reserpine.)

The elimination of lithium can be increased by these drugs, causing a manic or depressive attack in which a patient may have a suicidal depression or grandiose ideas they can fly and jump from a window, killing themselves.

If taken with beta blockers, the effects of both drugs are diminished.

Epinephrine or other bronchial tube relaxers will cause increased effects.

If taken with antidepressants, there may be severe blood pressure changes, especially with MAO inhibitors.

Name: Dyphylline. *Scientific Name*: 7-dihydroxypropyltheophylline. *Other*: Lufyllin, Neothylline, glyphylline.

Toxicity: 5.

Form: Supplied in time-released tablets or syrup for oral use, Dyphylline is water soluble.

Effects and Symptoms: A bronchial dilator, symptoms include headache, nervousness, insomnia, nausea, vomiting, tachycardia, hypotension, convulsions, and circulatory failure. An autopsy reveals the drug through an analysis of the biological fluids.

Reaction Time: Peak concentration is reached within one hour.

Antidotes and Treatments: After pumping the stomach, symptomatic care is given.

Notes: Introduced in 1946 as a bronchodilator.

Antianxiety, Antidepressants, Stimulants, and Psychomimetic Agents

Chlorpromazine and related drugs are synthetic chemicals derived from phenothiazine and used as antiemetics, tranquilizers, and potentiators of analgesic and hypnotic drugs.

The symptoms and effects of these drugs—for the purposes of this book—are essentially the same, and only a few of the more common ones are mentioned.

Most of the drugs in this category are used to treat schizophrenia, and manic-depressive illness, and psychotic manifestations. They're also used before surgery to relieve apprehension, for the treatments of tetanus, and behavior disorders in children.

A nurse discovered to her chagrin that one of the patients receiving a high dose of Thorazine liquid, mixed in cranberry juice to hide the bitter taste, wasn't responding the way he should. When she switched to orange juice, it worked like a charm. Apparently many of the "zine" drugs in this category are negated by cranberry juice or other juices of that acidity. While this has never been properly studied, several nurses report that unsweetened orange juice in the can is the only juice these drugs can be safely combined with. There is a bitter aftertaste if they're given in liquid form.

Name: Thorazine. *Scientific Name*: Chlorpromazine.

Toxicity: 5.

Form: Found as tablets, syrup, injectables, or suppositories, Thorazine is usually given either orally, intramuscularly, or intravenously.

Effects and Symptoms: A central nervous system depressant, Thorazine is used mainly to control manic-depressives, but is also found in the treatment of hiccups, tetanus, and severe behavior problems—both in children and adults. Since Thorazine reduces the cough reflex, aspiration of vomit can occur if the victim is already sedated. Overdose causes drowsiness, fainting, hypotension, tachycardia, tremor, dizziness, EKG changes, coma, and convulsions. A syndrome known as "phenothiazine sudden death" has been noted among psychiatric patients who receive large doses of thorazine or other phenothiazines. The mechanism is believed to involve asphyxiation during a convulsive seizure, ventricular fibrillation, and cardio-vascular failure during a hypotensive crisis.

Reaction Time: Ten minutes to one hour.

Antidotes and Treatments: Stomach pumping and symptomatic treatment. Severe hypotension is treated by giving fluids but the use of norepinephrine is contraindicated.

Notes: The patient builds up tolerance to the drug. Acutely disturbed patients can receive large amounts, but using it with a comatose victim or combining with barbiturates or alcohol can be dangerous.

First used in 1952, Thorazine was found effective in psychotic disorders and still is one of the most common psychiatric drugs available.

Patients who are receiving an overdose often have extrapyramidal symptoms such as unsteady gait, slobbering, stuttering, rigid back muscles, restlessness, contraction of the face and neck muscles, and hand tremors. Artane, Benadryl, and Cogentin are some of the drugs given to combat this.

Name: Stelazine. *Scientific Name*: Trifluroperazine.

Toxicity: 5.

Form: Found as tablets, liquid, and injectables, Stelazine is used in the treatment of psychotic anxiety and agitated depressions.

Effects and Symptoms: A central nervous system depressant, Stelazine overdoses produce somnolence, agitation, convulsions, fever, coma, hypotension, and cardiac arrest.

Reaction Time: Immediate, if injected. Twenty minutes or longer if taken orally.

Antidotes and Treatments: Cogentin is used to remove the extrapyramidal symptoms and the stomach is pumped. The rest of the treatment is symptomatic.

Name: Haldol. *Scientific Name*: Haloperidol.

Toxicity: 5.

Form: Haldol is found as tablets, syrup, injectables, and suppositories.

Effects and Symptoms: A central nervous system depressant, Haldol is used for psychotic states and is a major tranquilizer. Adverse reactions include drowsiness; blurred vision; extrapyramidal symptoms such as unsteady walk, drooling, and slurred speech; tachycardia; hypotension; muscle rigidity; coma; and collapse. Other symptoms can be depression, low blood pressure, headache, confusion, grand mal seizures, rapid heartbeat, exacerbation of psychosis, hypotension, skin rash, pain in the upper respiratory tract, excessively deep breathing, and sudden death. It can also cause psychotic reactions in those previously not crazy.

Reaction Time: If a large enough overdose is given death can come immediately, but chronic poisoning takes several days. However, this is a cumulative action and it builds up quickly.

Antidotes and Treatments: Artane or Cogentin is used to combat the extrapyramidal (Parkinsonlike) symptoms (like unsteady gait, slobbering, slurring words, shuffling feet), but the only other way to treat this is to stop the drug. Sudden withdrawal after a high dose, however, can cause psychosis and/or death.

Notes: In recent years numerous patients have died while using Haldol. No explanation could be found.

An antipsychotic drug first used in the United States in 1967, it's also used to treat Tourette's syndrome and severe behavioral problems in children.

Name: Lithium. *Scientific Name*: Lithium carbonate (pill) or lithium citrate (liquid).

Toxicity: 5.

Form: Used to treat manic-depressive cases, lithium is given orally.

Effects and Symptoms: If a toxic level is reached—and it can quickly—fatal acidosis or alkalosis may be seen. First noted symptoms are tremors, muscular twitchings, apathy, difficulty speaking, confusion, and finally coma and death. Also seen are exaggerated reflexes and jerking upon noise or light stimulation.

Reaction Time: Fifteen minutes to an hour.

Antidotes and Treatments: Stop the drug. Ample sodium chloride should be given as an intravenous drip. If potassium level is low, that should be given as well.

Notes: Absorption of lithium ions may cause disturbance in the sodium and potassium levels. This is especially the case if the victim is on a low-salt or salt-free diet.

The blood level must be monitored constantly. Patients on this drug will have their blood drawn every few days to determine that they do not overdose since this drug accumulates rapidly in the body.

Lithium should not be used with Moduretic (a blood pressure reducer) since it causes a severe decrease in blood pressure.

Lithium increases the toxicity of Haldol; sodium restriction and diruetics that induce sodium loss increase the toxicity of lithium.

Other Psychometric Drugs

Name: Permitial (fluphenazine); Serentil (mesoridazine); Levo-prome (methotrimeprazine), which causes prolonged dizziness and fall of blood pressure when one stands; Trilafon (perphenazine); Sparine (promazine); Dartal (thiopropazate); Mellaril (thioidazine); Navane (thiothixene); Stelazine (trifluoperazine); and Versprin (triflupromazine).

Toxicity: 5.

Form: Mainly found as pills, a few are injectable.

Effects and Symptoms: Marked sedation occurs with all these drugs. The symptoms include drowsiness, severe postural hypotension, hypothermia, tachycardia, dryness of mouth, nausea, ataxia, anorexia, nasal congestion, fever, blurring of vision, stiff muscles, urinary retention, coma. Hypotension and ventricular arrhythmias are the most common cause of death. Extrapyramidal symptoms from an overdose on a psychiatric drug include spasmodic contractions of face and neck muscles with swallowing difficulties, intolerable motor restlessness, salivation, convulsions, and endocrine disturbances as abnormal lactation in someone not lactating—even a male—interference with menstruation, and increase in thyroid activity. Prolonged effects at high doses show a purple pigmentation on face, hands, and neck. Lab tests show poor liver function. Phenothiazine compounds can be detected by the addition of a few drops of tincture of ferric chloride to urine acidified with nitric acid. A violet color results if phenothiazine compounds are present.

Reaction Time: Several hours.

Antidotes and Treatments: Benadryl is often used to reverse the extrapyramidal signs. Phenytoin is given for ventricular arrhythmias. Lidocaine is contraindicated.

Name: Norpramine, Pertofrane. *Scientific Name*: Desipramine. *Other*: Tofranil (imipramine), Vivactil (protriptyline), Aventyl (nortriptyline), Flexeril (cyclobenzaprine).

Toxicity: 5.

Form: A central nervous system depressant, Norpramine was first used in 1963 and is supposed to be faster acting and better tolerated than others in this class. Used as antidepressants, these drugs are found as tablets, and in some cases, syrup counterparts.

Effects and Symptoms: Used as antidepressants and sedatives, the side effects include seizure, coma, hypotension, and EKG abnormalities. Overdose shows coma, hypothermia, clonic movements or convulsions, fall of blood pressure, respiratory depression, dilation of pupils, disturbances of cardiac rhythm, and conduction. Death may occur after apparent recovery, giving the killer an alibi. A heart attack immediately precedes death.

Reaction Time: Symptoms usually appear within an hour but death may take several hours.

Antidotes and Treatments: Stomach lavage.

Notes: These drugs should not be given within two weeks of having taken MAO inhibitors. High fever, severe convulsions, and death have occurred when combining the two. Abrupt withdrawal can precipitate psychosis.

Name: Elavil. *Scientific Name*: Amitriptyline.

Toxicity: 5.

Form: Found in oral and injectable forms, Elavil is used to treat illnesses such as depressive neurosis, manic-depression, and anxiety associated with depression. Sometimes Elavil is given to alcoholics to relieve their withdrawal depressions.

Effects and Symptoms: Tingling sensations, tremors, seizures, ringing in the ears, dryness of mouth, blurred vision, urinary retention, changed sex drive, weight gain, jaundice, drowsiness, dizziness, fatigue, headache, and loss of balance begin the symptoms. They continue with hallucinations, delusions, anxiety, agitation, insomnia, manic behavior, and end with changes in blood pressure, skipped or pounding heartbeat, heart attacks, congestive heart failure, stroke, and death.

Reaction Time: Fifteen to forty minutes.

Antidotes and Treatments: Pump stomach, put in airway, and maintain blood pressure.

Case Histories: A patient mistakenly given an Elavil dose meant for another patient (who had developed a tolerance and was getting a much higher dose) developed psychotic symptoms and killed himself.

Notes: People who have a history of seizures can have their seizures increase while taking this. Convulsions will also result when taking MAO inhibitors at the same time. If taken with blood pressure reducers, Elavil could nullify the effect of the blood pressure medication, inadvertently causing a stroke. Blood levels of and possible toxicity from tricyclic antidepressants are increased by the use of aspirin, chloramphenicol, haloperidol, chlorpromazine, perhenazine, and diazepam.

Amitriptyline increases the absorption of coumarin anticoagulants.

Tricyclics alter catecholamine levels in the brain, interact dangerously with MAO inhibitors, and may cause agitation, tremor, coma, and death. Tricyclics also inhibit the work of antihypertensive drugs so that if a victim is on both and takes his high blood pressure drug, he will still have the high blood pressure.

Name: Sinequan. *Scientific Name*: Doxepin hydrochloride. *Other*: Adapin.

Toxicity: 5.

Form: Oral concentrate and tablets are the way this medication is found.

Effects and Symptoms: Overdose causes agitation, hallucinations, drowsiness, tachycardia, hypertension, dizziness, and coma.

Reaction Time: Within an hour.

Antidotes and Treatments: Stomach lavage and supportive therapy is needed.

Notes: In the past few years at least seventeen fatalities have been reported.

First used as an antidepressant in 1963, it is a derivative of amitriptyline.

Antianxiety Drugs and Selective Antidepressants

The **benzodiazepine** class of drugs is used to relieve short-term anxiety caused by trauma or stress. They're also used to relieve agitation and delirium in alcohol withdrawal, as muscle relaxants, and to help sleep.

Among them are Xanax (alprazolam), Librium (chlordiazepoxide), Tranxene (chlorazepate), Valium (diazepam), Dalmane (flurazepam), Ativan (lorazapam), Seraz (oxazepam), Centrax (prazepam), and Halcion (triazolam). Dalmane and Halcion have been discussed already in the sleep section.

Most of these drugs can be addicting and all of them potentiate the others. All are available in oral or injectable varieties; some are available as suppositories. *The Physician's Desk Reference* can give exact details on ones not mentioned here.

The general symptoms include drowsiness, weakness, nystagmus (crossed eyes), diplopia (double vision), incoordination, and lassitude progressing to convulsions with coma, cyanosis, and respiratory depression. Chronic symptoms include a skin rash, gastric upset, headaches, and blurred vision. Reaction time on all of these is a few minutes to several hours. Toxicity level is 5.

Taking **Tagamet** (ulcer medication) with these drugs can cause an increased effect.

Some of those not specifically listed are **Xanax** (alprazolam), a fast-action drug that is about half as potent as Valium or Librium. **Trancopal** (chlormezanone), which in addition to the other symptoms common to this class causes vertigo, flushing, and depression. **Clonopin** (clonazepam), which causes hair loss and contradictory excess hair growth (hirsutism), gastrointestinal disturbances, sore gums, and painful urination. **Ativan** (lorazepam), causes nausea, change of appetite, headache, sleep disturbances, and is very addicting. **Dantrium** (dantrolene), can cause liver damage, gastrointestinal upset, and bleeding.

Others are **Equanil** (meprobamate), used to tranquilize and induce sleep, causes drowsiness, incoordinated movements, loss of balance, headache, low blood pressure, skipped heartbeat, fluid retention, fever, restricted breathing, and shock. **Inapsine** (droperidol) causes symptoms such as hallucinations, hypotension, and respiratory depression, especially when used with narcotics. Drug dependence can easily result with either of these. Sudden withdrawal from Equanil can trigger severe anxiety, tremors, hallucinations, convulsions, and possible stroke. If taken with anticonvulsants, Equanil will alter the seizure patterns.

Name: Depakene. *Scientific Name*: Valproic acid. *Other*: Depakote (sodium valproate or divalproex).

Toxicity: 4.

Form: Used as an anticonvulsant drug since 1967, it is a colorless liquid at room temperature with a characteristic sweet odor. The drug comes as capsules, syrup, or free salts and is given orally.

Effects and Symptoms: A central nervous system depressant, Depakene causes symptoms such as gastrointestinal disturbances, hair loss, psychosis, slower clotting time, and hepatic failure leading to death.

Reaction Time: Within a half hour.

Antidotes and Treatments: The stomach must be pumped and symptoms treated as they occur.

Name: Librax. *Scientific Name*: Chlordiazepoxide hydrochloride and clidinium bromide. *Other*: Librium (chlordiazepoxide hydrochloride).

Toxicity: 3.

Effects and Symptoms: A tranquilizer, Librax is given also to control nervous effects of a spastic colon. Symptoms include drowsiness, incoordinated movements, skin rashes, confusion, menstrual irregularities, unsteady standing, fainting, and blurred vision.

Reaction Time: Normally a half hour or more.

Antidotes and Treatments: Pumping the stomach and symptomatic treatments.

Notes: While Librax and Librium can be habit-forming, in and of themselves they are seldom fatal. Mixed with other drugs, they can be deadly. Withdrawal symptoms include nervousness, tremor, and convulsions. Suicidal tendencies can come to the surface in depressed patients. If taken with MAO inhibitors, extreme sedation and convulsions can occur.

Name: Quaalude. *Scientific Name*: Methaqualone. *Other*: Mandrax.

Toxicity: 5.

Form: Quaalude is commonly found in pill form, but it can be injected as well.

Effects and Symptoms: Quaalude is used to relieve anxiety and tension as well as inducing sleep. Symptoms include nausea, gastric irritation, vomiting, paresthesia, pulmonary edema, convulsions, and death.

Reaction Time: Five to thirty minutes, depending on how given.

Antidotes and Treatments: Stomach pumping and symptomatic treatment.

Notes: Quaaludes have been taken off the American market.

Name: Valium. *Scientific Name:* Diazepam.

Toxicity: 5.

Form: Often found in tablets, it is also given intravenously and as intramuscular injections. It is only slightly soluble in water.

Effects and Symptoms: Used as an antianxiety agent, Valium is a muscle relaxant and anticonvulsant. Symptoms include drowsiness, ataxia, muscle weakness, tinnitus, excitability, rage reaction, hallucinations, coma, and cardiac arrest. It potentiates other antidepressants. Traces are found in the urine.

Reaction Time: Five minutes to one hour.
Notes: Can quickly be abused, as tolerance develops. Most reported cases of fatalities have been with Valium combined with other drugs, most notably alcohol and barbiturates.

Monoamine Oxidase Inhibitors (MAO Inhibitors)

A different class of psychiatric drugs, **MAO inhibitor drugs** work on the central nervous system and liver. Primarily a central nervous system stimulant, these drugs like the other antidepressants are supposed to change the chemical composition of the blood reportedly responsible for the depression. They usually come oral or injectable and are used for hypertension as well as depression. General symptoms include nausea, vomiting, lethargy, dry mouth, ataxia, stupor, rise or fall in blood pressure, fever, tachycardia, acidosis, convulsions, liver damage, and jaundice. Death is usually from cardiac or respiratory failure.

Some common names are Parnate (tranylcypromine), Nardil (phenelzine), and Eutonyl, (pargyline).

The toxicity is 4, but the reaction time is immediate. And since they do not mix well with other drugs, any combination can cause problems. For example, if these drugs are combined with Tofranil (imipramine) or an opium derivative, they arc more likely to cause extreme reactions like fatal hyperpyrexia (a high body temperature above 106 degrees). In addition, eating cheese or drinking alcohol while taking MAO inhibitors can cause severe hypertension, leading to a stroke and possible death. Mentioned in the individual notes of other drugs are cautionaries against combining them with MAO inhibitors.

Unfortunately, many patients who take this medication outside the hospital are not fully informed of the dietary restrictions, or if they are, don't understand just what going to a wine and cheese party would mean to them.

Several other MAO inhibitor drugs such as iproniazid, isocarboxazid, pheniprazine, and nialamide are no longer marketed in the United States because of toxicity, since they are particularly potent in dangerous combinations with other drugs. However, all drugs in this category need to be watched carefully.

MAO inhibitors potentiate the action of barbiturates, antihis-

tamines, other antidepressants, merperidine, morphine, and amino-
pyrine among others.

Neuromuscular Blocking Agents

Neuromuscular blocking agents are given as intramuscular or intravenous injection. They are used to promote muscle relaxation during
surgical anesthesia and occasionally to control convulsions. An effective dose of any of these is potentially fatal if respiration is not
properly maintained by artificial means.

Other names include **Tracium** (atracurium); **Flaxedil** (galla-
mine triethiodide), not to be confused with Flexeril, also a muscle
relaxant but much milder; **Pavulon** (pancuronium); **Norcuron** (vec-
uronium bromide); **Tubarine** (tubocurarine chloride); **Anectine**
(succinylcholine chloride).

The general effect is to block the neuromuscular transmissions
and depress respiration as in respiratory failure and circulatory collapse. Symptoms include heaviness of eyelids; diplopia; difficulty in
swallowing and talking; and rapid paralysis of the extremities, neck,
intercostal (rib) muscles, and diaphragm. Reaction time is usually
immediate. Symptoms will continue for one to ten minutes after the
injection is discontinued. Toxicity for all of these is 6.

Antidotes can include either edrophonium (Tensilon) or neostigmine (Prostigmin).

The chance of death is greatly increased if several neuromuscular blocking agents are used at the same time. Cardiac arrest has
occurred during succinylcholine administration after a head injury.

All central nervous system depressants—including alcohol—
enhance the central nervous system action of another. Tolerance to
one indicates tolerance to another. Hypnotics, antihistamines, and
narcotic analgesics slow intestinal absorption.

Name: Tubarine. *Scientific Name*: Tubocurarine chloride.

Toxicity: 6.

Form: Injectable. The drug is supplied as a chloride salt in ampules
that must be mixed with sterile water before injection. It is a curare
alkaloid derived from the South American plant.

Effects and Symptoms: Accidental overdose causes hypotension
and respiratory failure. Concentration of the drug remains in the
liver for a short time after death.

Reaction Time: Immediate.

Antidotes and Treatments: Endrophonium or neostigmine are antidotes.

Case Histories: The use of Tubarine as a homicidal poison was suspected in a series of eastern United States hospital deaths. The victims supposedly all had heart attacks, but when an empty vial of drug was found in the intern's locker, the bodies were checked. The drug was detected in decomposed tissue. This is a popular poison for use by medical personnel and those who have access to hospital drugs.

Notes: Quinidine and procainamide increase the victim's susceptibility to curare poisoning. Quinidine, procainamide, lidocaine, propranolol, and phenytoin reduce cardiac contraction and thus increase the possibility of heart failure during anesthesia.

Name: Pavulon. *Scientific Name*: Pancuronium.

Toxicity: 6.

Form: Injectable, it is usually administered intravenously.

Effects and Symptoms: Eighty percent paralysis has been noted with only a small amount of the drug. Pavulon works most quickly in patients with kidney or liver problems.

The dose is eliminated in the urine as unchanged drug and can be detected in autopsy only if the pathologist acts quickly.

Reaction Time: Immediate.

Antidotes and Treatments: Endrophonium or neostigmine are antidotes.

Notes: Developed in 1964 as a neuromuscular blocking agent, it is used as an alternative to tubocurarine. It is often used in the operating room.

Name: Anectine. *Scientific Name*: Succinylcholine.

Toxicity: 6.

Form: An ultrashort-acting drug that affects the skeletal muscles, succinylcholine chloride is a white, odorless, slightly bitter powder and very soluble in water. The drug is unstable in alkaline solutions but relatively stable in acid. Solutions should be stored in the refrigerator to protect potency. The drug is administered intramuscularly or intravenously.

Effects and Symptoms: Respiratory paralysis.

Reaction Time: Immediate.

Antidotes and Treatments: None.

Notes: Often used in the operating room and for homicidal poisonings. When patients on digitalis are given succinylcholine, because of the extra potassium often prescribed for them or given at the same time, they often have irregular heartbeats that can lead to heart attacks.

Name: Atropine. *Scientific Name*: Dl-hyoscyamine. *Other*: Hyoscine, hyoscyamine, belladonna, scopolamine.

Toxicity: 6.

Form: Available in tablets as the sulfate salt, as capsules, injectable solutions, inhalants, and eye solutions, these potent anticholinergic agents are sold by prescription. However, there arc a number of over-the-counter treatments for colds, hay fever, gastrointestinal diseases, and asthma that use small amounts of atropine. As a group, these drugs have been used for centuries as drugs and poisons. As a preanesthetic medication, they reduce salivary and bronchial secretions, relax the gastrointestinal tract in certain spastic conditions, and are used as an antidote to cholinesterase inhibitors. *See plants*.

Effects and Symptoms: The effect is to paralyze the parasympthetic nervous system by blocking the action of acetylcholine released at nerve endings. Kidney function must be normal to eliminate the drug.

The signs and symptoms of atropine poisoning develop quickly and are described by one victim as being "hot as a hare, blind as a bat, dry as a bone, red as a beet, and mad as a wet hen." The first manifestation is an immediate sensation of dryness and burning of the mouth and intense thirst. Talking and swallowing become difficult or impossible. Blurred vision and a marked aversion to light reflect in the dilated pupils. There is an inability for the eyes to accommodate to changing light. Mania, delirium, psychotic behavior, hallucinations, aggressive behavior, and disorientation may occur in a few hours or days. Also found are rapid pulse and respiration, urinary retention, muscle stiffness, fever, convulsions, and coma. A rash sometimes appears, followed by the shedding of skin, especially in the region of the face, neck, and upper trunk. The circulatory and respiratory systems collapse, causing death.

Reaction Time: Quickly. If a patient survives twenty-four hours, he will probably recover.

Antidotes and Treatments: Physostigmine salicylate is sometimes given intravenously. Oxygen is often given to improve respiration. Valium helps the convulsions.

Case Histories: Thc well-known mystery author Charlotte MacLeod used atropine eye drops to poison the victim in one of her books. Hyoscine poisonings have been responsible for many deaths.

A notable Victorian case is that of Dr. Crippen. He had apparently sacrificed a great deal to his wife's ambition, while she openly flaunted affairs. He purchased the vegetable drug hyoscine hydrobromide, now used in treatments of motion sickness. He knew from working with psychiatric patients in the United States that it dampened the sexual ardors of those who took it, and it's supposed he bought it to stop his wife's philanderings. However, he accidentally killed her instead. The hyoscine traces were found at postmortem examination. He appears to be the first recorded murderer in history to use the drug.

In Henry Wade's *No Friendly Drop*, the sudden death of a Lord is caused by hyoscine.

Hyoscine is also used in Agatha Christie's play *Black Coffee*.

Notes: Patients taking atropine are especially susceptible to heat exhaustion.

Linneaus named the deadly nightshade shrub *Atropo belladonna* after Atropos, eldest of the three fates, the one whose duty it was to cut the thread of life.

It is a 2:1 ratio for oral versus injected atropine.

Hallucinations occur in 50 percent of users.

Name: Epinephrine. *Other*: Norepinephrine, naphazoline, amphetamine, ephedrine, oxymetazoline, tetrahydrozoline, and xylometazoline. Gangrene of the extremities has occurred after Intropin (dopamine) injection.

Toxicity: 5.

Form: Epinephrine can be administered by ingestion, inhalation, and intramuscular or subcutaneous injection. It can also be applied to mucous membranes.

Effects and Symptoms: A sympathomimetic agent, it affects the autonomic nervous system. Symptoms are nausea, vomiting, nervousness, irritability, tachycardia, cardiac arrhythmias, dilated pupils, blurred vision, chills, pallor or cyanosis, fever, suicidal behavior, spasms, convulsions, pulmonary edema, gasping respiration, coma, and respiratory failure.

Reaction Time: Immediately.

Antidotes and Treatments: Treatment is directed at relieving the cardiac problems and other systemic reactions.

Notes: Inhalation of gaseous decomposed epinephrine will cause a psychosislike state with hallucinations and morbid fears. Subcutaneous injection causes necrosis and shedding of skin.

Epinephrine is found widely in over-the-counter drugs like cough syrups and nasal decongestants. Levodopa, or Sinemet, is also in this group. It can cause nausea, loss of appetite, tachycardia, depression, agitation, hypotension or hypertension, hallucinations, toxic psychosis, and flaying movements. A combination of carbidopa with levodopa can cause psychosis, depression, convulsions, cardiac irregularity, gastrointestinal ulceration, and hypertension. Continued use of the drug often leads to acidosis and death.

Should the victim survive, he will have continued life-threatening hypertension.

Parasympathomimetic Agents

Name: Physostigmine, pilocarpine, neostigmine, methacholine.
Toxicity: 5.
Form: Used for treatments of myasthenia gravis, for atonic conditions of bladder where there is a lack of muscle tone, and certain heart irregularities, these drugs work on the parasympathetic nervous system and are administered by ingestion, injection, or application to mucous membranes.

Acetylcholine, urecholine, Tensilon, stigmonerne, and mecholyl are given by injection; Mytelase, muscarine, and Prostigmin are given orally; Humorsol, phospholine, and pilocarpine are administered topically; Miostat is given by injection or topically; Antilirium is given by injection or orally.

Effects and Symptoms: The basic manifestation is respiratory difficulty. Symptoms include tremor, marked peristalsis with involuntary defecation and urination, pinpoint pupils, vomiting, cold extremities, hypotension, bronchial constriction, wheezing, twitching of muscles, fainting, slow pulse, convulsions, death from asphyxia, or cardiac slowing. Autopsy findings include congestion of brain, lungs, and gastrointestinal tract. Pulmonary edema may occur. Repeated small doses may reproduce the symptoms of acute poisoning.
Reaction Time: Immediate.
Antidotes and Treatments: If atropine can be given, recovery is immediate.

Nitrites and Nitrates

Nitroglycerin (glyceryl trinite), amyl nitrite, ethyl nitrite, mannitol hexanitrate, sodium nitrite, isosorbide dinitrate, and trolnitrate are used medically to dilate the coronary vessels and reduce blood pressure.

In some instances, nitrites such as bismuth subnitrate or nitrate from well water may be converted to nitrite by the action of intestinal bacteria. Nitrites are also used to preserve the color of meat in pickling or salting. The allowable residue in food is 0.01 percent. Nitrates and nitrites can interact with amines (produced by items as fried bacon and other cooked preservatives) either alone or in the body to cause nitrosamines, which are carcinogenic. These nitrosamines are used in fertilizer, industrial cutting fluid, plastics, toiletries, and pesticides. They also occur in surface water near industrial parks. The toxicity level for most of these mentioned is 4. The reaction, except in the case of cancer, is immediate.

Name: Nitroglycerin. *Scientific Name*: Glyceryl trinitrate. *Other*: Nitrobid, Nitrostat, Nitropaste, amyl nitrate, ethyl nitrate, sodium nitrate, mannitol hexanitrate, pentaerythritol tetranitrite, isosorbide dinitrate, and trolnitrite phosphate.

Toxicity: 4.

Form: Used medically to dilate coronary vessels and reduce blood pressure. Nitroglycerin is found as tablets (Nitrostat or Nitrobid) and aerosol spray (nitrolingual). Administration is by ingestion, injection, inhalation, or absorption from skin or mucous membranes.

Effects and Symptoms: The drug dilates blood vessels throughout the body by direct relaxant effect on smooth muscles. It also causes headache, flushing of skin, vomiting, dizziness, collapse, a marked fall in blood pressure, cyanosis, coma, and respiratory paralysis.

Reaction Time: Immediate.

Antidotes and Treatments: Remove overdose by ipecac emesis and activated charcoal.

Notes: Ethylene glycol nitrate and nitroglycerin are used to make dynamite!

Lab results will show chocolate-colored blood due to conversion of hemoglobin to methemoglobin and congestion of all organs. Exam must be quick since methemoglobin disappears in standing blood.

When taken with alcohol or blood pressure reducers, nitroglycerin can cause a severe drop in blood pressure. Yet, since blood pressure problems many times occur simultaneously with heart problems, doctors often give drugs together without realizing the problems or in spite of the danger, knowing that high blood pressure is more life threatening.

Anticoagulants

These drugs are used to keep the blood from clotting too quickly.
Name: Warfarin. *Other*: Dicumarol, ethyl biscoumacetate, heparin, phenindione, diphenadione, acenocoumarol, Valone, Talon, and Racumin.
Toxicity: 4.
Form: A coumarin derivative, Warfarin is used medically to inhibit the clotting mechanism. These drugs are oral or injectable.
Effects and Symptoms: Warfarin inhibits the formation in the liver of a number of the clotting factors whose formation is dependent on Vitamin K.

Symptoms include hemoptysis (a sudden attack where blood suddenly arises from hemorrhaging of the larynx, trachea, or lungs; there is a salty taste and bright, red, frothy blood), hematuria, bloody stools, hemorrhages in organs, widespread bruising, and bleeding into joint spaces. Repeated use leads to acute poisoning. Clotting time is prolonged, so with an overdose the victim can bleed to death from a severe cut. Jaundice and liver enlargement may be seen. Skin rash, vomiting, bloody diarrhea, orange-staining urine, kidney damage, and fever are also found. The kidney and liver injuries are often fatal.
Reaction Time: Fatalities have been reported after repeated daily doses of anticoagulants. Death may occur up to two weeks after discontinuing the drug. However, adequate therapy with Vitamin K will bring the prothrombin (a plasma protein that affects blood coagulation) level back to normal in twenty-four to forty-eight hours.
Antidotes and Treatments: Mephyton is given along with absolute bed rest to prevent further hemorrhages and internal bleeding.
Notes: Coumarin anticoagulants enhance the effects of the thyroid hormone. Many other drugs listed in the medical chapter interact with Warfarin, causing the effect to be stronger and more dangerous. Being an anticoagulant, it's quite easy for someone to bleed to death.

Bromadiolone, Talon, Racumin, coumachlor, and Warfarin are used as rodenticides.

Potassium, Calcium, and Sodium

These are several of the body elements, which given alone can throw off the body function to such a degree that respiratory acidosis can occur leading to cardiac arrest and death. Some of the drugs that contain **potassium** are potassium alum, potassium bichromate, potassium bromate, potassium carbonate, potassium chlorate, potassium chloriese, potassium cyanate, potassium cyanide, potassium iodide, potassium permanganate, and potassium thiocyanate.

K-Lyte or potassium bicarbonate is an orange-flavored pill dissolved quickly in water and given to patients who are on diuretics such as Lasix. Other forms of potassium come as Kay-ciel, K-Lor, Klotrix, K-Tab, Micro-K, and Slow-K (potassium chloride).

Some of the **calcium** drugs are calcium arsenate (similar to arsenic), calcium carbimide (similar to cyanamide), calcium disodium edetate, calcium hydroxide, calcium oxide, and calcium phosphate.

The most famous **sodiums** are sodium chloride, or salt, and sodium bicarbonate. While salt has a definite taste, sugar can sometimes be used to mask the flavor, and enough salt in a susceptible person can raise his blood pressure high enough to cause a stroke.

Varieties of these drugs can be injected, taken orally, or given as suppositories.

The first symptoms are slight paralysis of the limbs, nausea, abdominal discomfort, vomiting, diarrhea, mental confusion, unusual weakness, shortness of breath, and then respiratory failure since the action is quick. Consciousness is fully preserved until the end. The toxicity rating for Potassium (K), Calcium (Ca), or Sodium (Na) is 4. In a kidney patient, quite a bit less would be needed. People taking salt substitutes already are getting a large dose of potassium.

Spironolactone or triamterene (Dyrenium, a blood pressure reducer) when taken with potassium supplements may cause an excessive rise in blood potassium levels that can be fatal.

Antiseptics

These drugs, when not used to poison, remove microorganisms that cause disease, fermentation, or putrefaction.
Name: Chloramine-T.

Toxicity: 6.

Form: Ingested, inhaled, or applied to the skin, Chloramine-T is a water-soluble compound containing about 12 percent chlorine. The chlorine is slowly released on contact with water. In solid form, it is used as a water purifier and in solution as a mouthwash.

Effects and Symptoms: The effect is not known, but it is postulated that poisoning may occur through the conversion of Chloramine-T to a cyanide derivative under certain circumstances. Cyanosis and respiratory failure, collapse, and frothing at the mouth occur. Death is within a few minutes.

Reaction Time: Immediate.

Antidotes and Treatments: Sodium nitrate and sodium thiosulfate, the same as for cyanide poisoning.

Notes: If the patient lives twenty-four hours, he will likely recover.

Name: Silver nitrate.

Toxicity: 5.

Form: A water-soluble salt that is fatal as a salt or a liquid.

Effects and Symptoms: It damages the kidney and liver. From ingestion, the victim will have pain and burning in the mouth; blackening of the skin, mucous membranes, throat, and abdomen; increased salivation; vomiting of black material; diarrhea; anuria; collapse; shock; and death from convulsions or coma. Repeated application or ingestion causes argyria, a permanent bluish-black discoloration of the skin, membranes of the eyes, and other mucous membranes.

Reaction Time: Immediate.

Antidotes and Treatments: Dilute with water containing table salt, remove the drug from intestines via an enema, and give milk and pain medication to relieve gastric distress.

Notes: Recovery has been reported at higher than the usual fatal dose. It varies greatly with individuals.

Name: Boric acid. *Other*: Sodium borate, borax, Pentaborane, decaborane, and diborane are used as repellents.

Toxicity: 5.

Form: A white compound, boric acid dissolves slightly in cold water and decomposes in hot water. It can be ingested, or absorbed through skin or mucous membranes.

Effects and Symptoms: Boric acid is toxic to all cells. The effect on an organ is dependent on the concentration reached in that organ. Highest toxicity usually occurs in kidneys.

Boron oxide dust is irritating to mucous membranes and can cause excitability, narcosis (an unconscious state due to narcotics, which in this case, may be delayed up to forty-eight hours), vomiting, diarrhea of mucus and blood, lethargy, twitching of facial muscles and extremities, followed by convulsions, cyanosis, fall of blood pressure, collapse, coma, and death.

In chronic poisoning, the victim will suffer anorexia, weight loss, vomiting, alopecia (hair loss), convulsions, anemia, and skin rash, as well as the other symptoms.

Autopsy findings in fatal cases are gastroenteritis, fatty degeneration of the liver and kidneys, cerebral edema, and congestion of all organs.

Reaction Time: Immediate. Deaths occur frequently following the swallowing or excessive skin exposure of boric acid powder or solution.

Antidotes and Treatments: Remove boric acid from skin or mucous membranes by washing. Remove poison by ipecac emesis and by activated charcoal.

Notes: Boron oxide is also used in industry. It was formerly used as an antiseptic and to make talcum powder flow freely. Sodium borate (borax) is used as a cleaning agent. Sodium perborate is used as a mouthwash and dentrifice.

Name: Iodine. *Other*: Iodoform, iodochlorhydroxyquin, chiniofon, iodides.

Toxicity: 5.

Form: A bluish-black powder, it is soluble in alcohol and slightly soluble in water. Iodoform, a slightly yellowish powder or crystalline material with a penetrating odor, is insoluble in water but soluble in alcohol. Sodium and potassium iodides are white crystals soluble in water.

Effects and Symptoms: Iodine acts directly on the cells by precipitating proteins. The affected cells are often killed. The effects are similar to acid corrosives. Iodine depresses the central nervous system.

Ingestion causes severe vomiting, frequent liquid stools, abdominal pain, thirst, a metallic taste, shock, fever, anuria, delirium, stupor, and death occurs from uremia or poisoning of the body from toxic wastes the kidneys cannot expel. A patient who recovers might have esophageal stricture. Nausea, respiratory distress, and circulatory collapse have also been reported. Application to the skin may cause weeping, crusting, blistering, and fever.

Injection of iodine compounds may cause sudden fatal collapse (anaphylaxis) as a result of hypersensitivity. Symptoms are dyspnea, cyanosis, fall of blood pressure, unconsciousness, and convulsions leading to death.

In autopsy, the kidneys show necrosis.

Reaction Time: Immediate. Survival is likely if the victim lives one hour.

Antidotes and Treatments: Sodium thiosulfate will immediately reduce iodine to iodide.

Name: Potassium permanganate.

Toxicity: 5.

Form: A water-soluble, violet, crystalline compound, potassium permanganate is used as a disinfectant and oxidizing agent. It has an undeserved reputation of causing abortions when used in the vagina. Possible errors in concentration of the crystals and water make any use of potassium permanganate hazardous. It is used topically or can be ingested.

Effects and Symptoms: Potassium permanganate acts by destroying cells of the mucous membranes by alkaline caustic action.

Ingestion of solid or concentrated potassium permanganate causes brown discoloration, necrosis, and edema of mucous membranes of the mouth, larynx, and pharynx. Other symptoms are cough, stridor, slow pulse, and shock with fall of blood pressure. If death is not immediate, jaundice and oliguria or anuria may appear and later cause collapse.

Solid or concentrated potassium permanganate solution applied to the mucous membranes of the vagina or urethra causes severe burning, hemorrhages, and vascular collapse. Perforation of the vaginal wall may occur, resulting in peritonitis with fever and abdominal pain. Examination reveals a chemical burn that is stained brown.

Autopsy findings are necrosis, hemorrhage, and corrosion of the mucous membranes that potassium permanganate has touched. The liver and kidneys show degenerative changes.

Reaction Time: Immediate.

Antidotes and Treatments: Remove poison from mucous membranes by washing repeatedly with tap water. Perforations are treated surgically.

Cardiovascular Drugs

There are some twenty-five commonly used drugs for treating heart failure, angina, and blood pressure abnormalities. All of them are available by prescription only.

The three types of cardiovascular drugs are cardiac glycosides (used to treat heart failure), vasodilators (used for angina), and catecholamines (used for abnormal blood pressure).

Physicians order cardiac glycosides for patients who have congestive heart failure. Among them are digoxin, digitoxin, digitalis, deslanoside, and ouabain. These are used to strengthen the contractions of the heart. As a result, the heart pumps stronger, more blood flows to the kidneys, leading to elimination of more salty fluids, and in turn venous congestion decreases, easing the workload of the heart. Patients taking digoxin and digitoxin may have exaggerated problems with hypokalemia (not enough potassium). These cardiac glycosides are also used to treat irregular electrical impulses from the heart and help to stabilize the heart rhythms.

Those that are used mainly to prevent and treat angina are nitrates such as nitroglycerin and isosorbide dinitrate. These expand the veins and venules so that more blood collects in the vessels before returning to the heart. Because the amount of blood going into the heart is reduced, the heart needs less oxygen to empty its chambers and is less likely to develop a myocardial oxygen deficit that causes angina or myocardial ischemia.

These drugs are given sublingually, or under the tongue. Nitroglycerin is used this way just before or as soon as angina-producing activities begin. Some of these activities might be exercising (especially in cold weather), eating a heavy meal, or dealing with a stressful situation. When an attack starts, the patient usually takes a tablet every three to five minutes. If relief does not come within ten minutes, it's probable the person is experiencing a heart attack. If there is an overdose of nitroglycerin, death comes in two to six hours. Toxicity level is 6.

Name: Digitoxin. *Other*: Lantoxin, Crystodigin (oral), Purodigin (IV).

Toxicity: 5.

Form: Tablet or liquid, digitoxin can be given orally, intramuscularly or intravenously.

Effects and Symptoms: Used for congestive heart failure to regulate the heart rhythm, all the cardiac drugs work on the heart muscle to increase contractions and reduce fluid retention.

An overdose causes nausea, vomiting, diarrhea, blurred vision, and cardiac disturbances as tachycardia, premature contractions, aterial fibrillation, and atrioventricular block.

Reaction Time: Immediate.

Antidotes and Treatments: The stomach is washed with tannic acid or strong tea and the victim is kept lying down. Stimulants such as caffeine, ammonia, or atropine are given. If the pulse falls below fifty per minute, morphine is given.

Case Histories: Agatha Christie's *Appointment with Death* and *Postern of Fate* used digitoxia, a drug of the digitalis series, as the cause of death. The overdose slowed the pulse, retarded the heart contractions, and increased the amount of blood flowing to the heart, giving the person a heart attack.

Marissa Piesman in her *Unorthodox Practices* had her victims killed with digitalis powder in the food.

Strophanthin, another cardiac drug, similar in effect but found mainly in Europe, was used in Christie's *Verdict* to dispose of the burdensome wife.

Notes: Intake of food affects the oral absorption time. The risk of toxicity from digitalis is increased by administration of reserpine, succinylcholine, laxative abuse, or calcium and potassium loss induced by diuretics.

Some doctors have used digoxin to treat obesity, but it is dangerous and can have adverse effects, leading to death.

Dilantin (used for seizures) may alter the body's requirements for digitalis medicines and increase the body's need later.

In England, during the early 70s, when several patients of one doctor mysteriously died, digitoxin was identified by bioassay (a chemical checking process) and found in the skeletal muscle of nine out of fourteen victims all dead for seventeen to forty months. These victims were suspected of having accidentally received digitoxin in place of estradiol.

Digoxin (Lanoxin) has the same symptoms as digitoxin and is also used in treatment of congestive heart failure. Alone, the toxicity level is 5 and reaction time is six hours. Digoxin is potentiated by mixing with Quinidine or Quinine.

Other cardiac drugs are ouabain, Isordil, amyl nitrate, nitrostat, nitrospan, nitro-bid ointment, and tridil.

Name: Persantine.

Toxicity: 4.

Form: Given in tablet form, Persantine is an odorless, yellow crystalline powder with a bitter taste and is soluble in dilute acids, methanol, and chloroform, but insoluble in water.

A blood vessel enlarger, Persantine is used to dilate or enlarge the coronary arteries and increase the blood flow to the heart. Given orally, it is used to prevent the pain of angina pectoris, but does not stop an acute angina attack.

Effects and Symptoms: Headache, dizziness, nausea, flushing or reddening of the skin, weakness, blackouts, and aggravation of angina.

Reaction Time: Immediate.

Antidotes and Treatments: Caffeine and ergot are used to constrict the blood vessels, the stomach is pumped, and all other symptoms are treated as they occur.

Notes: In cases of low blood pressure, this will make the pressure fall even lower.

Name: Sodium azide. *Other*: Hydrazoic acid, sodium hydroxide, and other azides.

Toxicity: 4.

Form: The drug version can poison through ingestion, skin contact, subclavian administration (an IV going directly into the heart), intravenous administration, or under the skin (subcutaneous) administration, as well as interperitoneal administration (into the stomach via a tube). The acid version is mildly corrosive and used for cleaning metals and other products.

Sodium azide comes in salts and liquids. A cardiovascular drug, it is often used to reduce high blood pressure, but too much of it will cause hypotension. It is usually found in solutions as Natural Buffered Saline, the type which killed the girl described in the case history. Since it is mildly corrosive, the amounts given normally would not kill.

Effects and Symptoms: 0.1 mg/kg is known to cause hypotension. The tissues are destroyed by direct chemical action and the blood (hemoglobin) is broken down. A central nervous system affector, the drug also inhibits enzyme actions and acts similarly to nitrates and cyanide.

Reaction Time: Immediate, but effects from the ingestion of a corrosive acid have been known to occur up to a month after exposure.

Antidotes and Treatments: None.

Case Histories: Dawn had been a bright and eager student, willing to please her instructor who'd been teaching the class about sodium's effects on the body. In the lab, several students, Dawn among them, volunteered to assist by drinking a saline solution. Unfortunately, the lab assistant, not wanting to take the time to prepare the saline solution, had taken a premixed "Normal Saline Buffer" from the shelf, thinking that would do the trick.

The prepared solution had sodium azide in it. Since the bottle had no poison markings on it, the lab technician was unaware of the fatal effects of this drug. While Dawn's friend took a few sips and put her glass down because of the salty taste, Dawn drank more than a quart.

Within moments, the girl was on the floor writhing in pain. She knew something had happened to her, but even when they brought her into the emergency room and realized what she had consumed, the doctors felt things would be all right. After all, the chemical company claimed there wasn't enough sodium azide in the solution to kill anyone.

Yet four days later, Dawn was dead and the doctors had been unable to save her.

Notes: Insoluble in ether, it is soluble in liquid ammonia. The salts are highly explosive and cause toxic fumes when heated. All salts and acids in this category are unstable.

Beta Adrenergic Blocking Agents

These drugs used to reduce blood pressure include Sectral, Tenormin, Lopressor, Visken, Inderal, and Timolide. They all have similar symptoms and toxicity ratings.

If beta blockers are suddenly withdrawn heart failure may result, especially in people with aorta problems.

Name: Inderal. *Scientific Name*: Propranolol.

Toxicity: 5.

Form: The pills are ingested.

Effects and Symptoms: Inderal reduces or blocks cardiac and bronchial response to excessive stimulation. It affects the central nervous system and causes hypotension.

Symptoms include slow pulse; nausea, vomiting; numbness in the hands, arms, or feet; hypotension (faintness on rising); dryness of mouth; diarrhea; fall of blood pressure; hallucinations; headache; sleeping problems; difficulty in breathing and disorientation; hypoglycemia; respiratory depression; convulsions; bronchospasm; coma; catatonia; delirium; and death.

Reaction Time: Within a half hour.

Antidotes and Treatments: Give isoproterenol.

Notes: Myocardiac infarction—heart attack—can occur after abrupt withdrawal. If treatment is being given for overactive thyroid, low blood sugar, diabetes, kidney, or liver disease, this drug should be carefully monitored since serious complications, including many of the side effects, could be exacerbated. Asthma or hay fever patients may experience more problems with breathing and a dangerously low heart rate. If alcohol is consumed, the blood pressure may drop to a hazardous level. The properties of antidiabetic drugs (like insulin) are increased when taking this medication and so the patient could go into insulin shock.

Propranolol and other beta-blockers enhance the effects of quinidine, procainamide, antihypertensives, insulin, tricyclic antidepressants, and muscle relaxants. Levodopa can cause hypertension, especially in the presence of the MAO inhibitors. Atropine-like compounds delay absorption of the drugs.

Diuretics are also given in congestive heart failure. One of the major diuretics is Lasix.

Name: Lasix. *Scientific Name*: Furosemide, chlorothiazide, or hydrochlorothiazide. *Other*: Diuril, water pills, HydroDIURIL, Hygroton, Esidrix, Enduron, Zaroxolyn.

Toxicity: 4.

Form: Taken orally as tablets or liquid or injected, Lasix is used as a diuretic and antihypertensive. It is usually given in cases of congestive heart failure, pulmonary edema, liver or kidney problems, or other swelling to help the tissues release fluid. In general, it eliminates excess fluid from the body.

Effects and Symptoms: It works on the kidney tubules and decreases the fluid in the cells. Symptoms include nausea, vomiting, frequent urination, dizziness, headache, hypotension, blurred vision, tingling sensations, weakness, bleeding under the skin, sensitivity to light, fever, difficult breathing, congestion in the lungs, shock, high blood sugar, uremic poisoning, muscle spasms, and death.

All patients receiving these drugs are usually monitored for fluid and electrolyte depletion. (An I & O record, or intake and output flow chart, is done if the patient is in then hospital. This measures how much liquid is taken in compared to how much urine is excreted.) Too much of the drug can cause acidosis or alkalosis and subsequent heart failure. Patients with kidney disease must be watched especially closely as they are most affected by any slight electrolyte change.

Reaction Time: One to eight hours, if ingested. Ten minutes or more if injected.

Antidotes and Treatments: Potassium is given to combat symptoms.

Notes: It's quite possible to faint and become quite ill with just a little too much Lasix. Most people who take a diuretic on a regular basis also have a supply of potassium pills or tablets in the house. Those who have poor kidney function or liver disease need to be careful as the Lasix will build up quickly. People taking diuretics are more prone to sunburn.

Since these are blood-pressure reducers, they can combine with other blood-pressure reducers to create havoc in some patients. While it's important to keep up enough potassium in the body, patients on diuretics often have drugs like spironolactone, triamterene, or amuloride in the house, which help them retain potassium in their bodies. Taking them makes potassium supplements harmful since too much potassium can be deadly. A "well-meaning friend" who offers a potassium supplement should be watched carefully. Pain relievers and barbiturates may increase the effects. Lithium taken in combination with these drugs can quickly reach a poisonous level.

Diabetics taking water pills will also have problems since the properties of both the insulin and the diuretic are increased.

Antihypertensive Drugs

Antihypertensives, used medically to lower blood pressure, also called catecholamines, enhance the effects of central nervous system depressants, anesthetics, diuretics, MAO inhibitors, and tranquilizers.

Name: Aldomet. *Scientific Name*: Methyldopa.

Toxicity: 3.

Form: Found as a liquid or a tablet, it's usually a white or off-white preparation.

Effects and Symptoms: Used to lower blood pressure, Aldomet's symptoms include drowsiness, headache, dizziness, weakness, tiredness, lightheadedness, skin rash, joint and muscle pains, impotence, bone-marrow depression, fever, nightmares.

Reaction Time: Twenty minutes to one hour.

Antidotes and Treatments: Stimulants like caffeine or atropine are used.

Notes: If taken with alcohol, the sedation effect is increased and the blood pressure is lowered excessively. The effects of other blood pressure pills are increased if taken with Aldomet, as are anticlotting drugs, tolbutamide, or lithium, which quickly reaches a dangerous level in the body. If taken with Haldol, behavior disturbances could result. Taken with MAO inhibitors or tricyclic antidepressants, the blood pressure will zoom up. The effects of the medication are also increased with diuretics, even though this is a common dual prescription.

Name: Catapres. *Scientific Name*: Clonidine. *Other*: Hyperstat, Apresoline, Loniten, Regitine, phentolamine, minoxidil, hydralazine, captopril, Capoten, prazosin, dopamine, Intropin, and dopastat.

Toxicity: 6.

Form: Used for hypertension, Catapres is a white, crystalline powder, slightly soluble in water, and is given either by tablet or injection.

Effects and Symptoms: Symptoms include bradycardia, drowsiness, gastrointestinal upset, possible hepatitis, heart failure, rash, increased sensitivity to alcohol, coma, hypotension, and depressed respiration.

Reaction Time: Within a few minutes if by injection; a half hour if taken orally.

Antidotes and Treatments: Atropine can be helpful. The cardiac and respiratory system must be watched carefully. The victim must be kept in a supine position. Kidney function also must be monitored.

Notes: A hypertensive crisis can occur with an abrupt withdrawal of the medication. This can also trigger hyperexcitability, psychosis, cardiac arrhythmias, rapid rise of blood pressure, and death.

Name: Minipress. *Scientific Name*: Prazosin hydrochloride.

Toxicity: 5.

Form: Found as a capsule, Minipress is a white, crystalline substance, slightly soluble in water.

Effects and Symptoms: A blood pressure reducer, Minipress can cause headache, drowsiness, lack of energy, weakness, pounding of the heart, nausea, vomiting, diarrhea, abdominal discomfort or pain, shortness of breath, blackout, nervousness, rapid heartbeat, incoordinated movements, depression, tingling sensations, rash, itching, loss of hair, blurred vision, loss of consciousness, and death.

Reaction Time: Thirty to ninety minutes.

Antidotes and Treatments: Same as Catapres.

Notes: Blood pressure may drop suddenly causing loss of consciousness and subsequent falls and/or death. If taken with other blood pressure reducers, the effect would be increased.

Dopamine, Intropin, or dopastat are one and the same. They support blood pressure when shock is due to myocardial infarction, during open heart surgery, and in congestive heart failure.

Nitroprusside or Nipride is given intravenously not only for hypertensive crisis but to control blood pressure and bleeding during an operation. It takes effect in two minutes and lasts about ten minutes. Other drugs should not be mixed with it at the same time. If a patient needs it for more than forty-eight hours, one nursing journal states, blood must be drawn to check for lab levels of metabolite thiocyanide, as the drug is potent and toxic.

Name: Procainamide. *Scientific Name*: Procainamide hydrochloride.

Toxicity: 5.

Form: Found as a clear liquid and given intravenously, procainamide is given for irregularities of ventricular contraction including tachycardia or fibrillation.

Effects and Symptoms: The pulse becomes irregular and suddenly disappears, and with it the blood pressure collapses and falls. Almost immediately there is an onset of convulsions and death.

Reaction Time: Immediate. Death caused by hypersensitivity or rapid injection.

Antidotes and Treatments: Treat for cardiac arrest.

Name: Quinidine. *Scientific Name*: Cinchonan-9-ol, 6'-methoxy-, (9S)-, mono-*D*-gluconate. *Other*: Conquinine, Pitayine.

Toxicity: 6.

Form: A white, water-soluble alkaloid obtained from the cinchona bark, it is used in the treatment of cardiac irregularities. Usually given orally, it can also be administered intravenously or intramuscularly. The latter two can be quite painful.

Effects and Symptoms: Quinidine depresses the metabolic activity of all the cells, but its effect is mostly on the heart. Principal effects are fall of blood pressure and nausea. Poisoning from ingestion includes ringing or noise in the ears; headache; nausea; diarrhea; fall of blood pressure with disappearance of pulse; involuntary, rhythmic movement of the eyeball; bradycardia; and respiratory failure. Sudden death may result from ventricular fibrillation.

Reaction Time: Immediate.

Antidotes and Treatments: Gastric lavage and support for the cardiac system.

Notes: Quinidine enhances the effects of muscle relaxants.

Name: Sodium thiocyanate/potassium thiocyanate.

Toxicity: 5.

Form: Given orally, this drug was formerly used for treatment of hypertension, but now has been replaced with "safer" drugs. Sodium thiocynate can still be found and is still sometimes prescribed, especially by older doctors. Also, it can still be found in many hospitals.

Effects and Symptoms: Sodium thiocyanate depresses the metabolic activities of all cells, but acts most noticeably on brain and heart just like regular sodium or potassium would. Symptoms include disorientation, weakness, low blood pressure, confusion, psychotic behavior, muscular spasms, convulsions, and death.

Reaction Time: Immediate.

Antidotes and Treatments: Remove by peritoneal dialysis.

Notes: Psychotic behavior is commonly seen and someone could be committed on the basis of that, or have a "suicidal" accident.

More than twenty fatalities have been reported from sodium and potassium thiocyanate.

If kidney disease is present, the drug is urinated out slower than with a healthier patient, and therefore toxic symptoms are seen quicker.

The patient can show recovery when the medication has stopped, but even after several days of improvement, a relapse can occur and death has been known to happen as long as two weeks after taking the drug.

Appetite Suppressant Drugs

Some of these drugs—Didrex (benzphetamine), Tenuate (diethylpropion), Fastin or Ionamin (phentermine), and Preludin (phenmetrazine)—will not only reduce the appetite but elevate the blood pressure, disturb the heart rhythm, cause overactivity, restlessness, insomnia, euphoria, tremor, headache, dryness of mouth, unpleasant tastes, diarrhea, upset stomach, changes in sex drive, and impotence, as well as depression and psychosis. Overdoses cause hallucinations, aggressiveness, and panic, which might result in an "accidental" death.

These drugs should not be taken by people suffering heart disease, having high blood pressure, or other blood vessel problems. These drugs may decrease the action of blood pressure reducers, and so combined, the victim may think he's taking his pills but still suffer a fatal stroke. If MAO inhibitors are taken with this, the blood pressure can increase dramatically. Some alcoholic drinks, chocolate, and meat may cause the blood pressure to rise when taken with these drugs.

Name: Preludin. *Scientific Name*: Phenmetrazine hydrochloride.
Toxicity: 5.
Form: Found as tablets or injectables, Preludin is a white, water-soluble crystalline powder used for diet control in obese people.
Effects and Symptoms: Similar to amphetamines, actions here include central nervous system stimulation and rise in blood pressure. Tachycardia and addiction are common. The drug causes circulatory collapse and coma.

Tolerance develops within a few weeks of using this drug. Among the symptoms are appetite suppression, impaired judgment, incoordination, palpitation, elevation of blood pressure, restlessness, dizziness, dryness of mouth, euphoria, insomnia, tremors, confusion, assaultiveness, headache, hallucinations, panic states, fatigue, and depression. Psychotic episodes can occur even at therapeutic doses. An unpleasant taste in the mouth is noticed as well as diarrhea or constipation and other gastrointestinal disturbances, like nausea and vomiting. Impotence and changes in libido occur as well. Circulatory collapse, coma, hyper- or hypotension, and death can result from an overdose. Abrupt cessation causes extreme fatigue, mental depression, irritability, hyperactivity, and personality changes. The psychosis shown here is often confused with schizophrenia.

Reaction Time: Within an hour.

Antidotes and Treatments: Sedate with a barbiturate.

Case Histories: One patient trying to lose weight was committed to a mental institution by her family until they realized it was the drug that was causing her problem.

Miscellaneous Drugs

Name: Atophan. *Scientific Name*: Phenylquinoline carbonic acid. *Other*: Cinchophen, Atochinol. Composite preparations in which atophan is hidden and which are particularly dangerous are Uro-Zero, Arkanol, and Gorum.

Toxicity: 6.

Form: Administered orally, it is widely used in rheumatic disease and podagra or true gout.

Effects and Symptoms: It promotes uric acid excretion in the body and does general liver damage. The victim's urine has a *very* yellow color. Vomiting, jaundice, and poor clotting time occur, as well as hemorrhages throughout the body. Deaths are usually from acute yellow liver atrophy.

Reaction Time: Several days.

Antidotes and Treatments: Medication must be discontinued immediately. No other treatment is known.

Name: Barium.

Toxicity: 5.

Form: Barium is administered by ingestion or inhalation. An absorbable salt, barium carbonate, hydroxide, or chloride are largely used in the paint industry and to kill pests. Barium sulfate is sometimes used for depilatories and soluble barium sulfate salt is used as radiopaque contrast medium, especially for lower gastrointestinal x-rays, to help "illuminate" the insides of the intestines and stomach for the pictures. It's also used to color fireworks.

Effects and Symptoms: The barium ion induces a change in permeability or polarization of the cell membrane that results in stimulation of all the muscle cells indiscriminately.

The symptoms include tightness of muscles in face or neck, nausea, vomiting, diarrhea, abdominal pain, anxiety, weakness, difficulty in breathing, cardiac irregularities, convulsions, and death from cardiac and respiratory failure.

Reaction Time: One hour.

Antidotes and Treatments: Magnesium or sodium sulfate.

Case Histories: One death came when an unobservant assistant mixed the bariums up and gave the patient the wrong one.

Notes: Poisoning often comes from using the soluble salts in place of the insoluble sulfate.

Name: Caffeine. *Other*: Aminophylline, dyphylline, pentoxifylline, theophylline, Trental, No-Doz, Cafergot, and in compound with numerous other drugs.

Toxicity: 3. Fifty percent of patients with theophylline convulsions die. Caffeine convulsions are less fatal, but combined with theophylline or other convulsion-encouraging drugs they could be fatal.

Form: Besides the fact we drink caffeine, it is used for the treatments of shock, asthma, and heart disease. It is also a good diuretic. It's also administered through injection intravenously, orally, or rectally as suppositories or an enema solution.

Effects and Symptoms: The general public isn't aware just how dangerous caffeine can be. Caffeine works on the central nervous system to increase the stimulation to a point of hyperexcitability, possibly convulsions, and death.

Caffeine taken orally causes gastric irritation, projectile vomiting, muscle twitching, alternating states of consciousness, sweating, insomnia, inability to walk, rapid heartbeat, palpitations, photophobia, and convulsions. There are also cases of caffeine-induced manic-depression, and caffeine-induced psychosis.

Oral theophylline causes vomiting, coma, hyperflexia, and ventricular arrhythmias including fibrillation, hypotension, convulsions, and respiratory arrest.

Reaction Time: One to two minutes. Administration of intravenous aminophylline is sometimes followed by sudden collapse and death. Toxic symptoms begin after one gram, though much more is needed for a lethal dose.

Antidotes and Treatments: The main effort is to control the convulsions and keep an airway open.

Notes: Injection of aminophylline in hypersensitive subjects causes immediate vasomotor collapse and death. There are more people sensitive to caffeine than many of us know. As people get older they tend to be less tolerant of the drug, but there's always the odd case of the woman who at eighty would continue to consume fifteen to twenty cups of coffee a day, despite what her doctor warned. Rapid intravenous injection causes cardiac inhibition. In large doses aminophylline depresses the central nervous system whereas caffeine stimulates it.

Historically sources of caffeine included the coffee bean and coffee in Arabia, kola nut of West Africa, tea of China, cocoa bean in Mexico, the ilex plant in Brazil, cassina (the Christmas berry tree), and yaupon (the North American tea plant), which was used during the Confederacy blockade as a coffee substitute.

While an average cup of coffee contains only sixty to one hundred fifty milligrams of caffeine, caffeine is hidden in a variety of products and medications.

Name: Camphor. *Other*: Vicks Vaporub.

Toxicity: 5.

Form: Used in moth-damage preventives, camphor oil is a respiratory aid and a stimulant. It's also in mothballs. As a medication, it can be administered topically, orally, or intramuscularly by injection.

Effects and Symptoms: Early symptoms include headache, sensation of warmth, excitement, nausea, and vomiting. There is a camphor odor on the breath, the skin becomes clammy, and the face alternates between being flushed and pale. Symptoms include burning in mouth and throat, epigastric pain, thirst, feelings of tension, dizziness, irrational behavior, unconsciousness, rigidity, rapid pulse, slow respiration, twitching of facial muscles, muscle spasms, generalized convulsions, and circulatory collapse. Convulsions occur by stimulating the cerebral cortex cells. Autopsy findings include congestion, edematous changes in the intestinal tract, and destruction of the kidneys and the brain.

Reaction Time: Fifteen minutes to one hour. Absorption through the mucous membranes occurs rapidly. Toxic levels may be achieved after prolonged vapor inhalation and within a few minutes after ingestion.

Antidotes and Treatments: Gastric lavage and administration of activated charcoal. Vomiting is not induced since it might cause seizures. Valium is given for agitation or convulsions and hemodialysis is sometimes done to help with the elimination of the drug.

Notes: There is a pleasant smell.

Name: Cantharidin. *Scientific Name*: Cantharis vericatoria. *Other*: Spanish fly.

Toxicity: 6.

Form: A white powder with very little taste, cantharidin is used as a skin irritant or vesicant (blister inducer). The drug can be administered topically or orally.

Effects and Symptoms: A potent irritant to all cells and tissues, Spanish fly has an undeserved reputation for being an aphrodisiac.

The principal manifestations are vomiting and collapse. Other symptoms are severe skin irritation, blister formation on the mucous membranes, abdominal pain, nausea, diarrhea, vomiting of blood, severe fall in blood pressure, hematuria, coma, and death due to respiratory failure. Autopsy findings are necrosis of esophageal and gastric mucous membranes, intense congestion of blood in the genital and urinary organs, damaged cells in the renal tubules, and hemorrhagic changes in the ovaries.

Reaction Time: Immediate.

Antidotes and Treatments: None.

Case Histories: One of the most sensational cases involving cantharidin was in London's Old Bailey in 1954 when a chemist, Arthur Ford, was tried on the charge of manslaughter of the two women who worked for him. Apparently happily married, he had heard while in the army of the aphrodisiac qualities of Spanish fly. One day discovering that cantharidin was the technical term for Spanish fly and that supplies were available at his shop, he asked the senior pharmacist for some, saying one of his neighbors bred rabbits and thought that the drug might be useful in the mating process. He was told the drug was a number one poison and that if administered to a human in anything but a minute dose, it could be fatal. Ford bought a bag of pink and white coconut ice candy and back at the office pushed quantities of Spanish fly into the candy with a pair of scissors. He gave a piece to each of the women and then took one himself. Within an hour, all three were violently sick. The two women died shortly, though he survived somehow. The autopsies showed the internal organs had literally been "burned away" by the drug.

Name: Flagyl. *Scientific Name*: Metronidazole.

Toxicity: 2.

Form: Found as vaginal suppositories, Flagyl is an antibacterial and antiprotozoa and is used to treat vaginal infections.

Effects and Symptoms: The most frequent symptoms are nausea, headache, and loss of appetite. Vomiting, diarrhea, abdominal cramping, constipation, metallic taste in mouth, sore throat, dizziness, vertigo, changes in heartbeat, seizures, incoordination, irritability, depression, confusion, fever, dark-colored urine, and decreased sex drive may also be experienced, as well as other symptoms.

Reaction Time: Thirty minutes to several hours.

Antidotes and Treatments: Symptoms are treated as they occur.

Case Histories: One young woman who was taking Flagyl attended a friend's wedding party. Not normally a drinker, she was encouraged to imbibe to celebrate the occasion. Shortly, she began experiencing "odd sensations." These continued with nausea, vomiting, confusion, depression, and a full-blown seizure.

The woman was hospitalized, but the doctors were puzzled because the woman's lab tests showed no reason for her convulsions while she continued to become more critically ill. Only when her boyfriend told the physician that she was taking Flagyl and had drunk several glasses of wine did the answer come. The woman hadn't recalled hearing her doctor give any warnings about drinking alcohol while on the medication, "but even if he had," she added, "who really listens to those things?" Luckily, she recovered.

Notes: This drug acts much like Antabuse, given alcoholics to stop their drinking. Severe behavior and emotional problems may also result if taken with alcohol.

The effects of Warfarin and other anticlotting drugs are increased.

Name: Insulin. *Other*: Iletin, Insular.

Toxicity: 5.

Form: Insulin is the water-soluble hormone of the Langhans islets of the pancreas. Although insulin is administered both orally and by injection, the tablets (usually orinase) are generally given to adults with late-onset diabetes in conjunction with diet restrictions. Diabetes mellitus, the most common version, is controlled by diet and injected insulin.

A clear liquid, injectable insulin is measured in units, not milliliters. Many patients are on a sliding scale depending on their morning sugar test. The amount varies with each type of insulin. The types are *lente* or *crystalline*. Insulin injections are given under the skin (subcutaneously) into the calf, abdomen, or buttocks and not in the muscle.

Effects and Symptoms: Symptoms of high blood sugar (hyperglycemia) indicating the body needs more insulin are increased urination, loss of appetite, thirst, bad breath, and dry skin later leading to chills, coma, and death if not taken care of. Death is rare in this case, and high blood sugar is less dangerous than hypoglycemia in which too much insulin is given.

Insulin overdosage or "insulin shock" causes hypoglycemia resulting in fatigue, reddening of the face, sensation of hunger, nervousness, rapid heartbeat, nausea, vomiting, chills, sweating, tachycardia, shallow breathing, hypotension, shock, coma, and death.

Reaction Time: A short time after injection—to several days.

Antidotes and Treatments: Administration of glucose (sugar). Orange juice or candy bars are good examples. This will keep the insulin temporarily bound up and lessen the symptoms.

Case Histories: Most recall the famous case of Klaus von Bulow who supposedly put his wealthy wife into an insulin coma.

Another recent case is an AIDS patient who was mistakenly given a large dose of insulin. He was not diabetic. He went into a coma, and while the insulin coma did not kill him, it weakened him enough so that within four days he died of an AIDS-related tumor.

In May 1957, Ken Barlow, a male nurse, asked a neighbor to call the doctor to his home. His wife, Elizabeth, had died in the bath, he said. When the doctor arrived, Barlow told him that his wife had been ill all evening and had vomited in bed about 9:30 p.m. She had decided to have a bath, and he had gone to bed and dozed off to sleep after changing the sheets. When he woke at 11 p.m., he found that his wife was not beside him and hurried to the bathroom. There he found his wife had apparently drowned, and despite frantic attempts to pull her out and revive her with artificial respiration, he had been unable to do so.

The doctor found the body lying in the empty bath, on her right side. Barlow had pulled the plug. She had apparently vomited, and though there were no signs of violence on the body, the eyes were dilated. The doctor called the police and Barlow repeated his story.

The police noted that although Barlow claimed to have made "frantic efforts" to save his wife, his pajamas were still dry and there was no sign of splashing on the bathroom floor. Then a detective noted there was water in the crooks of Mrs. Barlow's elbows, which threw doubt on the artificial respiration story. Since to do artificial respiration he would have needed to turn her slightly or at least move her arms out of the way, the water found in the crooks of her elbow indicated that artificial respiration was probably not done as the husband had said, that in fact the body had not been moved since her attack and death.

Two hypodermic syringes were found in the kitchen, which Barlow explained by saying he had been treating himself for a carbuncle with penicillin. The syringes did have some penicillin in the needles and the coroners could find no trace of drugs in the woman's body. However, with the aid of a hand lens, they went over every inch of her skin, looking for marks of injection. With her freckles it was difficult. Finally, they found two telltale puncture marks on the right buttock and another two in the fold of skin under the left buttock. An incision showed characteristic inflammation, suggesting an injection had been given a short time before death. But what? The dilation of eyes, vomiting, sweating, and weakness described hypoglycemia — a deficiency of blood sugar and characteristic of insulin shock. An exam of the heart showed an average sugar level. Since there were no prescribed tests for detecting insulin in the body tissues, the police were at a loss.

Forensic experts noted that high levels of sugar in the heart had been found in cases of violent death and felt that Mrs. Barlow could not have died violently, since her blood sugar level was normal. Biochemical research had shown this increased sugar level in victims who died violently was due to the liver trying the assist survival by discharging a heavy dose of sugar into the bloodstream moments before death.

However, the experts found another way to trip up Barlow. Until that time, it had been common belief among doctors and nurses that insulin disappeared very quickly from the body. But new research came up to prove them wrong. The acidic conditions preserved the insulin, and the formation of lactic acid in the muscles after death had prevented the insulin breakdown.

On July 29, 1957, Barlow was arrested and charged with murdering his wife. He confessed to having given her a dose of ergonovine to induce an abortion but not to the insulin. The defense stated that in her moment of fear, realizing she was slipping into the water, her pancreas had released an incredible dose of insulin — 15,000 units. Barlow was found guilty. It later came out his first wife had died in 1933. Cause of her death had never been explained.

Notes: Oral insulin tablets such as Diabinese, Orinase, or Tolinase are sometimes given to diabetics with mild cases of the illness. These people usually find they have diabetes as adults and not as children. Childhood diabetes almost always requires injected insulin.

Alcohol should be avoided as the increased sugar can lead to problems. Periods of heavy exercise and missing meals may lead to low blood sugar. Those who vomit or have a high fever will need to have their insulin needs reevaluated.

All oral antidiabetic drugs interfere with clotting drugs.

Drugs in the beta-adrenergic class such as propranolol will greatly increase the effects of these diabetic drugs and lower the blood sugar—even to a lethal level. Other drugs such as aspirin and adrenal hormones, epinephrine, oral contraceptives, and diuretics can decrease effectiveness so that even though the victim is taking the insulin properly, he or she could still go into diabetic shock and coma. Someone in a diabetic coma has acetone-smelling breath.

Postmortem specimens of brain, liver, or kidney have not shown significant amounts of insulin either in normal subjects or victims of overdose, but in several instances tissue from the site of injection has been analyzed and the results used to prove administration of an overdose.

Name: Lomotil. *Scientific Name*: Diphenoxylate plus atropine.
Toxicity: 4.
Form: This antidiarrheal agent can be administered orally as a liquid or a tablet.
Effects and Symptoms: The atropine in the drug is partially responsible for some of the symptoms. There is a sudden high fever, a flushed appearance, and rapid breathing. The second phase of symptoms includes abdominal discomfort, severe constipation, swelling of gums, retention of fluid, lethargy, depression, tingling sensations, restlessness, progressive central nervous system depression with pinpoint pupils, cyanosis, severe respiratory depression, seizures, and coma. The drug may be excreted in the urine up to ninety-six hours later.
Reaction Time: A half hour.
Antidotes and Treatments: Gastric lavage and naloxone administration are used for overdoses.
Notes: Numerous cases of poisoning and fatalities have been reported. The drug has a small amount of atropine in it and is not addicting at normal doses, but can be at higher doses. Sedation increases when taken with tranquilizers, alcohol, or narcotics. If

taken with MAO inhibitors, excessive rise in blood pressure may result.

Name: Norflex. *Scientific Name*: Orphenadrine citrate. *Other*: Disipal, distalene, orpadrex, tega-flex, Ex-otag.

Toxicity: 4.

Form: Practically odorless, Norflex is sparingly soluble in water and slightly soluble in alcohol. A white, crystalline powder, it has a bitter taste. It can be administered orally or by injection.

Effects and Symptoms: The drug possesses anticholinergic actions and is used for relief of muscle pain. Adverse reactions include dryness of mouth, pupil dilation, blurred vision, tachycardia, weakness, nausea, vomiting, headache, dizziness, and drowsiness. Coma, convulsions, and cardiac arrest frequently occur in acute poisoning.

Reaction Time: Symptoms start within a half hour, but it takes from three to six hours for coma and heart failure.

Antidotes and Treatments: Treated as atropine poisoning, the drug must be removed from the stomach immediately since within thirty minutes it will be nearly all absorbed. Convulsions are usually managed with Valium since barbiturates will dangerously slow the respiratory and cardiac systems.

Notes: First found in 1951, it works as a sedative and has an anticholingeric effect to quiet the jerking nerves in Parkinsonlike symptoms. It's primary use is in Parkinson's disease and to control the side effects of psychiatric drugs. Also used as a muscle relaxant. Mentioned in the literature from the Hemlock Society as one of the best ways for "helping yourself or a loved one over," the drug can be bought over-the-counter in Mexico and is readily available in Holland. A bitter taste is often hidden by orange juice. Barbiturates deepen the coma.

Of course, if someone is a member of the Hemlock Society, it indicates they or someone they love might be terminally ill and they might be contemplating suicide. This would allay suspicions that the victim had been murdered.

Name: Phenergan. *Scientific Name*: Promethazine hydrochloride. *Other*: Compazine (prochlorperazine), Sparine (promazine).

Toxicity: 4.

Form: Found as an injectable, pill, or suppository, Phenergan is used to relieve nausea and sedate, as well as in pre- and postoperative situations and as an adjunct to painkillers.

Effects and Symptoms: Symptoms include drowsiness, confusion, ringing in ears, diplopia, blurred vision, insomnia, dizziness, head-ache, dilated pupils, nightmares, hysteria, agitation, and mental and physical abilities impaired. Extrapyramidal symptoms such as drool-ing, excess salivation, unsteady gait, dry mouth, and slurred speech can occur as well as rapid heartbeat and slowed breathing, hyperex-citability, respiratory depression, seizures, catatoniclike states, and increased or severely lowered blood pressure. Sometimes the ad-ministration of this drug can confuse the doctors and hide other central nervous system problems, brain disease, or Reyes syndrome.

Reaction Time: Within ten minutes.

Antidotes and Treatments: Symptoms are treated as they occur.

Notes: The drug reacts negatively to and increases the effects of other central nervous system depressants such as alcohol, barbitu-rates, and narcotics. Patients with liver or heart disease are espe-cially prone to problems when given this drug.

If given intraarterially, there is likelihood of arterospasm and possibly gangrene setting in, which would perhaps require an ampu-tation. Taken with MAO inhibitors, extrapyramidal symptoms are increased.

Name: Quinine. *Other*: Quinacrine, chloroquine, Atabrine, Plaque-nil.

Toxicity: 5.

Form: Administered by ingestion or injection, Quinine is used for treatment of malaria.

Effects and Symptoms: It depresses the functions in all the cells, especially the heart. The kidney, liver, and nervous system may also be affected.

Progressive ringing in the ears, blurring of vision, weakness, fall of blood pressure, hemoglobin in the urine, oliguria, and cardiac irregularities occur. Injection or ingestion of large doses causes sud-den onset of cardiac depression. Convulsions and respiratory arrest can also occur.

Reaction Time: Immediate.

Antidotes and Treatments: Remove swallowed drug by gastric lavage.

Name: Reglan. *Scientific Name*: Metoclopramide.

Toxicity: 2.

Form: Usually administered orally, it may also be found in injectable forms. Used to relieve symptoms of stomach and intestinal inflammation as well as associated vomiting, Reglan is often taken with cancer chemotherapy.

Effects and Symptoms: Symptoms include restlessness, drowsiness, laziness, inability to sleep, nausea, bowel disturbances, depression, and involuntary muscle movements.

Reaction Time: A half hour or more.

Antidotes and Treatments: Artificial respiration is maintained and atropine is given slowly. Recovery can be immediate if treatment is started soon after the drug is taken.

Notes: Reglan is interesting mainly because it decreases the absorption of drugs like digoxin from the stomach. Because it retards food digestion, insulin may begin to act before the food has left the stomach, causing hypoglycemia and resultant insulin shock. Naturally, this is especially bad if one is diabetic or is being given insulin for other purposes.

Those with stomach or intestinal problems, epilepsy, or seizures might have bad reactions.

Name: Tagamet. *Scientific Name*: Cimetidine.

Toxicity: 5.

Form: Used to treat ulcers, Tagamet decreases the flow of stomach acid. It can be given orally or intravenously.

Effects and Symptoms: Diarrhea, headache, fatigue, dizziness, muscle pain, rash, confusion, delirium, low blood pressure, and ulcer perforation on withdrawal. Also, liver and kidney damage can occur, resulting in renal failure.

Reaction Time: Fifteen to thirty minutes.

Antidotes and Treatments: Remove overdose via gastric lavage and activated charcoal. Respiration is maintained and atropine is sometimes used.

Notes: The activity of anticlotting drugs may be increased, causing someone to bleed to death. Sedatives and sleeping drugs also increase their action combined with Tagamet.

Name: Thyrolar. *Scientific Name*: Liotrix. *Other*: Euthroid, Synthroid, Cytomel, Proloid, Levothroid, thyroxine, thyroglobulin, liothyronine, levothyroxine.

Toxicity: 4.

Form: Given as replacement therapy for underactive thyroid, it is found in pill form.

Effects and Symptoms: If the medication brings the thyroid up to normal range, then there are no side effects. If overdoses occur, nervousness, tremor in hands, weakness, sensitivity to heat, reduced sweating, overactivity, weight loss, pounding heartbeat, bulging eyeballs, headache, nausea, abdominal pain, diarrhea, high blood pressure, and heart failure are possible.

Reaction Time: Twenty minutes to a half-hour.

Antidotes and Treatments: Symptoms are treated as they occur.

Notes: These drugs should be used carefully with people who have had previous heart problems. Anticlotting drugs, digitalis preparations, and tricyclic antidepressants will have their effects increased. On the other hand, if the patient is taking barbiturates, the effect of the barbiturates will be decreased. Aspirin and phenytoin (Dilantin) also increase the effects of Thyrolar.

Name: Air embolism.

Toxicity: 5.

Form: Given by syringe, air stops the heart by blocking blood vessels.

Effects and Symptoms: A small amount of injected air, while not killing the patient, can make the victim very sick, causing them to go berserk, lose control of their bladder and bowel, and want very much to die. But in and of itself, this small amount does not kill.

Air going into the heart contracts and compresses it, blocking the vascular system so that oxygen can't get through.

The presence of air can cause death either by cutting off the blood supply to a vital part, like the heart, or by lodging in the brain and causing death in coma by the cutting off of the blood supply and oxygen. If it goes into the heart, a froth would form, blocking the heart.

Reaction Time: A few minutes.

Case Histories: A forensic pathologist told one author that when he opened a victim's heart after death, he found air bubbles in the heart and in pockets of the veins. It was obvious then how the man had died. Air embolisms can be detected in the body after death.

In Dorothy Sayer's *Unnatural Death*, a woman was suspected of killing a number of people since she was the only one who had the motive and opportunity, but all the deaths were attributed to heart failure. Lord Peter Wimsey discovered that she injected air bubbles into the arteries and stopped the circulation. As Lord Peter found out, the syringe would have been quite a good-sized one.

Notes: Air is technically not a drug but it is related to medicine, and usually we picture the villain sneaking into our hero's room to inject his IV with a syringe filled with air. This can be done and it will kill, but a small amount of air does not cause death. This is a myth. One would need a large-sized syringe to kill a victim. The average syringe seen in the movies would not be enough to kill.

Air usually enters the body during operations on the neck or during an attempt to inject air into the chest during a test. Sometimes the needle accidentally hits a vein and the air goes into the blood instead.

Air emboli can also be confused with other types of emboli (clots) that accomplish the same thing: impeding the flow of blood to the heart and oxygen to the cells, causing death.

E I G H T

PESTICIDES

Mr. Pugh
Here is your arsenic, dear.
And your weedkiller biscuit,
I've throttled your parakeet,
I've spat in the vases,
I've put cheese in the mouseholes.
Here's your . . . [door creaks open]
tea, dear.

— Dylan Thomas
Under Milkwood

For a long time, the farmer was relatively defenseless in his struggle against pests, only having at his disposal insecticides of vegetable origin — nicotine, pyrethrum, and finally rotenone.

Most farms, both here and abroad, now use toxic chemical pesticides and herbicides to control parasites on animals and crops and to destroy unwanted weeds. Simple though highly dangerous chemicals, as arsenic, had been sparsely used for many years, and only in the last twenty years have they been replaced by a large number of chemical compounds stemming from the discovery of DDT, which was first used extensively in World War II. Many of these new products work by inhibiting the enzyme cholinesterase, which helps to regulate the amount of acetylcholine in the body.

Acetylcholine is needed to send messages from one nerve synapse to another and then to the brain. When the acetylcholine from the nerve synapse builds up during such a blockage, the symptoms experienced are increased secretions, gastrointestinal cramping, diarrhea, vomiting, twitching, difficult breathing, and loss of muscle strength, which can result in respiratory arrest.

As with any poison, children, the ill, and the aged are more susceptible. A nine-year-old child died after playing in a recently sprayed field. Within a few hours after exposure, he vomited, and then his face, arms, and chest swelled. The insecticide had destroyed his lung tissue.

This chapter covers both pesticides—which kill insects, rodents, weeds, and all other pests—and insecticides, which deal only with insects.

Pesticides fall into two groups—those that coat the outside of the crop and those absorbed by the roots, stems, or leaves into the plant itself—and take in six major types:

Minerals—fuel oil, kerosene, sulfur, and borax—some of the oldest and still-used insecticides.

Botanicals—nicotine, pyrethrin, and rotenone, which were in use before 1900 and are still the favorites because they leave no toxic residue.

Chlorinated hydrocarbons—DDT, lindane, and chlordane were the most widely used insecticides from the 1940s through the 1960s. Environmental contamination has caused severe restrictions in the use of this group.

Organophosphates—malathion and diazinon have generally replaced the chlorinated hydrocarbons because they control resistant insects, are biodegradable, and do not, manufacturers say, contaminate the environment.

Carbamates—carbaryl and propoxur, a relatively new class of contact insecticides that supplement the organophosphates.

Fumigants—including such well-known materials as naphthalene and paradichloro.

Benzene (moth crystals), and other toxic materials such as methyl bromide or hydrogen cyanide.

Almost all the substances in this chapter can be absorbed by ingestion, by inhalation, or through skin absorption. Such chemicals as DDT, which is stored in the fatty tissues, build up so that chronic conditions are more often the case. Most acute or fatal poisonings are observed only when large quantities are accidentally or intentionally ingested or inhaled.

Many of the chemicals researched cause cancer in chronic cases, but since cancer is not a sure killer and since there's no guarantee that everyone exposed will get cancer, those insecticides have been eliminated from these lists as have those that do not kill humans within a reasonable time.

Botanically Derived Pesticides

Name: Nicotine. *Other*: Beta-pyridyl-*a*-methyl pyrrolidine.
Toxicity: 6.
Form: A pale-yellow to dark-brown liquid with a slightly fishy odor when warm, nicotine boils at 266 degrees C. It poisons by inhalation, skin absorption, ingestion, or eye contact.
Effects and Symptoms: Nicotine stimulates and then depresses the brain and spinal cord. Skeletal muscles, including the diaphragm, are paralyzed.

Initial burning of the mouth, throat, and stomach is followed rapidly by nausea, vomiting, diarrhea, confusion, twitching, disturbances in hearing and vision, headache, dizziness, breathing difficulty, rapid heartbeat, incoherence, convulsions, slowing respiration, cardiac irregularity, coma, and death. Death usually results from respiratory failure due to paralysis of the muscles.
Reaction Time: Death occurs within five minutes to four hours.
Antidotes and Treatments: Nicotine on the skin must be thoroughly washed off. If ingested, encourage vomiting and use activated charcoal to absorb excess nicotine in the system, and use gastric lavage to get rid of ingested poison. Atropine is given in maximum doses to control hyperactivity, and Valium is used to control convulsions.
Case Histories: A woman living in England in 1940 mixed nicotine with her husband's aftershave lotion. He liberally applied it to his face and body and died quickly.

In 1968, another woman did in her wealthy but elderly sister by mixing the residue of several cigarette butts into a jug of water, straining it, and placing the poisoned water at her sister's bedside. Although the sister died, the killer was caught.

In *Bilbao Looking Glass*, Charlotte MacLeod killed off her victim by putting nicotine in a martini, which the victim drank in one gulp without noticing the poison. Ingestion, however, is not as effective as skin absorption.

A jealous dentist in Ed McBain's *Poison* used nicotine twice to do in his victims. Obtaining the chemical from a lab which was doing tests on cigarette-stained teeth, he put some in one victim's bottle of scotch and hid more in the temporary crown covering his second patient's root canal, making sure the crown had a thin spot that could be worn away by normal chewing or brushing.

Notes: Slow poisoning is possible, though a smoker will have a higher tolerance. Nicotine has the distinction of being the oldest insecticide in current use. It was first employed as a concentrated tobacco juice, but it is little used nowadays except for special purposes — notably against rose-aphids.

Name: Pyrethrum. *Other*: Pyrethrum flowers, pyrethrum extract, pyrethrins, dalmatian insect powder.

Toxicity: 4.

Form: Pyrethrum is a powder extracted from the head of a chrysanthemum cultivated in Kenya and Zaire. Pyrethrum is a neurotoxin. While inhalation causes the most toxic reaction, pyrethrum also reacts through ingestion and skin absorption.

Effects and Symptoms: Dermatitis is the first symptom, followed by hyperexcitability, loss of coordination, tremors, nausea, vomiting, diarrhea, convulsions, and muscular paralysis, leading to respiratory paralysis and death. A lesser dose produces headache, digestive troubles, and loss of sensation in lips and tongue.

Reaction Time: Within a half-hour the skin turns red at the site of contact and affected area burns and itches. The cheeks rapidly swell as the symptoms progress. Once removed from exposure, the victim's symptoms may take two days to two weeks to subside.

Antidotes and Treatments: Remove from exposure. Treat symptoms.

Notes: Although one of the oldest insecticides known to man, pyrethrum is now seldom used because it has been replaced by more toxic insecticides. This is being listed because of its historical importance.

Name: Rotenone. *Other*: Derrin, derris, nicouline, tubatoxin.

Toxicity: 4.

Form: A white, odorless crystal derived from the derris root, rotenone is an insecticide. It is also found as a lotion for chiggers and an emulsion for scabies. It is much more toxic when inhaled; but while ingestion can also cause problems, it will seldom lead to death. Contact with skin will prove a mild irritant.

Effects and Symptoms: Rotenone affects the nervous system. Inhalation causes numbness of the mouth, nausea, vomiting, abdominal pain, muscle tremors, incoordination, convulsions, and stupor.

Chronic exposure leads to kidney and liver damage.

Reaction Time: Skin irritation occurs immediately; other symptoms follow within a few hours.

Antidotes and Treatments: Symptomatic.

Notes: Because the plant grows in Africa and is inconvenient to secure, use has declined. Once thought to be harmless, it's now known to be five times as toxic as pyrethrum.

Name: Sodium fluoroacetate. *Other*: Compound 1080, fluoroacetic acid, sodium salt, Fratol, sodium monofluoroacetate, sodium fluoroacetate.

Toxicity: 6.

Form: A fine white powder, fluoroacetate has no smell or taste. Water-soluble, it was at one time used as a rodenticide, but because it was easily transferred to foodstuffs, fluoroacetate is no longer used. The dust can be inhaled and the powder or solution ingested.

Effects and Symptoms: The chemical blocks cellular metabolism, affecting all body cells, especially those of the central nervous system.

Symptoms include vomiting, irregular breathing, auditory hallucinations, numbness of the face, facial twitching, anxiety, irregular cardiac activity, convulsions, and coma. Death is from respiratory failure due to pulmonary edema or ventricular fibrillation.

Reaction Time: Within minutes up to six hours.

Antidotes and Treatments: Convulsions disappear with injection of calcium gluconate but reappear later. Symptoms are treated as they appear.

Notes: A horse died from drinking a pail of water with only a few drops of fluoroacetate added. Dogs fed with the horse flesh also died. Fluoroacetic acid is no longer sold in United States but fluoroacetamide is still available.

It is suspected that fluoroacetate poisoned drinking water during World War II.

Other insecticides: Cyanides and hydrocyanic acid itself are still used to treat seeds, despite potentially serious consequences.

Synthetic Pesticides

Name: Aldrin. *Other*: 1,2,3,4,10,10-Hexachloro-1,4,4a,5,8,8a-hexahydro-1,4,5,6-di-methanonnaphthalene; HHDN (ISO); aldrine, octalene; compound 118.

Toxicity: 5.

Form: A white, crystalline, odorless solid, aldrin is used as a dust to control grubs and wire worms and as a spray against caterpillars. It is insoluble in water. Aldrin is most toxic when ingested or inhaled, but *chronic* skin absorption can prove fatal.

Effects and Symptoms: The central nervous system is depressed and renal damage occurs. Causing similar symptoms to DDT, aldrin produces headaches, dizziness, nausea, vomiting, malaise, convulsions, coma, bloody urine, respiratory failure, and death.

Reaction Time: One to four hours. It often takes six hours for maximum symptoms to occur. Recovery is likely if convulsions are delayed more than one hour.

Antidotes and Treatments: The whole body must be decontaminated. In case of severe exposure, an amyl nitrate pearl is broken and held before the victim's nostrils for fifteen to thirty seconds of every minute until sodium nitrite is administered. However, the injection of nitrite and thio-sulfate can cause methemoglobinemia, which inhibits the flow of oxygenated blood to the brain, so oxygen is often used as an additional therapy.

Notes: Aldrin, an extreme disaster hazard, is the most toxic of the insecticides used for flies, mosquitoes, and field insects. It is two to four times as toxic in animals as chlordane. Use of aldrin and dieldrin was banned in 1974 by the EPA as being unsafe. However, brands imported from Europe are still used for termites.

Dogs who ate the flesh of cows that had died from poisoning by DDT's cousin, aldrin, soon died themselves. Combining DDT or other insecticides with other solvents makes the mixture far more poisonous.

Previous liver injury enhances possibility of toxic exposure.

Similar in reaction to aldrin are chlordane, chlordecone, endrin, heptachlor, mirex, thiodan, and toxaphene, all part of the same family of chlorinated hydrocarbons.

Name: Benzene hexachloride. *Other*: Gammahexane; 1,2,3,4,5,6-hexachlorocyclohexane; lindane, streunex; BHC; DBH; HCCH; HCH; 666. *Trade Name*: Gammexane, Benzahex, Chemhex, Gamexan, Gamoxol, Hexadon, Pecusanol, Pultox, Vermaxan.

Toxicity: 4. The lindane compound is slightly more toxic.

Form: A white crystalline, wettable powder, emulsion, dust, and solution in organic solvents, benzene hexachloride and lindane are extremely toxic when ingested and moderately toxic when inhaled or absorbed by the skin. Soluble in oily or fatty solutions but not in water, it has an unpleasant, moldy odor and is especially dangerous to ingest after a fatty meal.

Benzene hexachloride is used extensively in veterinary medicine since it's better against ticks and fleas than DDT.

Effects and Symptoms: Causing liver necrosis and kidney damage, it also affects the central nervous system.

Skin absorption, which causes contact dermatitis, and inhalation produce moderate irritation including headache and nausea.

When ingested, symptoms start with irritation of mucous membranes that come into direct contact with the substance, leading to vomiting, diarrhea, and severe convulsions. Death may follow from pulmonary edema.

Reaction Time: Thirty minutes to three hours and up. Reaction may be delayed up to six hours.

Antidotes and Treatments: Treat symptomatically.

Notes: Disease has appeared in people who've eaten bread contaminated with HCH, and in suckling infants whose mothers ate the bread.

Benzene hexachloride is expelled from the body fairly quickly, making chronic poisoning almost impossible.

Name: Chlordane. *Other*: 1,2,4,5,6,7,8,8 octachloro-4,7-methano-3a,4,7,7a-tetrahydroindane; chlordan octachlorotetrahydro methano indane. *Trade Name*: Velsicol 1068, 1068, Octa-Klor, Ortho-Klor, CD-68, Dowklor, Toxichlor.

Toxicity: 6.

Form: Chlordane is a colorless to amber, odorless, viscous liquid used as a bait for mole crickets. Found as powders, dust, emulsion concentrates, and concentrated solutions in oil, it is also water and fat soluble.

Effects and Symptoms: Chlordane stores in the brain, fatty tissue, and liver. Typically, the poisoning is characterized by the onset of violent convulsions within one-half hour to three hours and either death or recovery within a few days. Other symptoms include petechial hemorrhages (small red dots); hepatic damage; and congestion in the brain, lung, spinal cord, and heart, all leading to eventual death.

Reaction Time: The first interval of four to twelve hours is the most dangerous. Death may take as long as twenty days but usually happens within three.

Antidotes and Treatments: Recovery is questionable if convulsions are protracted. Activated charcoal and syrup of ipecac will sometimes help. Anticonvulsants such as Valium are given. Do not give stimulants like epinephrine as they sometimes induce ventricular fibrillation (heart attack).

Case Histories: One victim receiving an accidental skin application of a 25 percent solution developed symptoms within forty minutes and died before medical attention could be obtained.

In another case, two men died following ingestion of a low dose of chlordane. An autopsy showed severe fatty degeneration of the liver caused by chronic alcoholism. In this case, the chlordane was not the direct cause of death, but exacerbated the condition to a fatal conclusion.

In a third case, a man poisoned by chlordane skin contamination went into convulsions within forty minutes and died of respiratory failure before emergency medical aid could arrive.

Notes: Similar to chlordane is heptachlor, which is three times as toxic and is used against cotton parasites.

Name: DDT — Dichlorodiphenyltrichloroethane. *Other*: 1,1,1-Trichloro-2,2-bis(p-chlorophenyl) ethane, chlorophenothane, dicophane. *Trade Name*: Gesarol, Neocid, Trix, Geaspon, Multacid, Lucex, Duolit, Dicophane.

Toxicity: 3.

Form: A white powder or colorless crystal, DDT is insoluble in water but readily dissolvable in oils. Although usually odorless, it might give off a slight aromatic scent. A broad-spectrum insecticide, it builds up in fatty tissue. Eating animals that have consumed DDT or that have eaten others that consumed DDT will poison a human who eats the meat.

DDT can be inhaled, absorbed through skin, or ingested either dry or as a liquid. It penetrates easily through the hard shell of insects, but human exposure is primarily from ingestion of contaminated foods. According to Research Labs in Maryland, the inhalation of dust or contact with the solution is harmless to humans when used in normal concentration, unless that human has on an oily insect repellent that would assist the absorption. If surfaces of contact are large and exposure prolonged, poisoning will occur.

Effects and Symptoms: DDT works chiefly on the central nervous system, causing hyperexcitability, muscle weakness, and convulsions.

Skin contact may lead to eczema. Early acute poisoning produces symptoms of nervous excitability, twitching of eyelids, and generalized tremor, followed by confusion; malaise; headache; numbness of tongue, lips, and face; and vomiting. Twitchings begin in the facial muscles and proceed in increasing intensity to involve all the muscles, strongly affecting the limbs. Attacks take the form of convulsions and resemble strychnine poisoning since they may be started by noise and light stimuli. In severe cases there is pronounced dilation of the pupil. Death occurs from respiratory arrest and ventricular fibrillation (heart attack).

In cases of chronic poisoning symptoms are loss of weight, anorexia, headache, nausea, eye irritation, weakness of muscles, and gradually increasing tremor. Finally, there are convulsions, possible coma, and death.

In autopsy, analysis of blood serum or fat biopsy will not confirm DDT poisoning. Data obtained at an autopsy are therefore not reliable, says Driesbach.

Reaction Time: Depending on amount taken: severe vomiting from thirty minutes to one hour; twitching of eyelids and gastric pain from eight to twelve hours; and death anywhere from one to fifty days.

Antidotes and Treatments: Recovery is questionable if convulsions are protracted. Activated charcoal and syrup of ipecac will sometimes help. Anticonvulsants like Valium are given. Stimulants, such as epinephrine, sometimes induce ventricular fibrillation (heart attack).

Case Histories: A fifty-eight-year-old worker erroneously drank from a bottle of 120 ml of 5 percent DDT. Even though he noticed his mistake and drank one quarter liter of milk and several glasses of beer, within an hour he had severe gastric pain, colic, and vomiting of coffee-ground-like fluid. Vomiting continued every thirty to sixty minutes. Thirty-six hours after the ingestion of the poison, vomiting persisted and spastic cramps in the arms and calves appeared. His last urine was two hours after the absorption of DDT and then anuria followed. Admitted to the hospital on the sixth day after poisoning, the victim's pupils were unequal and there was no reaction to light (indicating brain involvement). Despite transfusions, death followed in a few hours.

Notes: After contamination of the eyes with DDT powder, temporary blindness may occur. There may be gradual sensitization and allergic reactions from people working with DDT.

Most deaths from DDT are complicated by the presence of other insecticides and solvents. A fat biopsy will be needed to determine DDT level, and urine will have a high level of organic chlorine.

Although DDT is supposed to be nontoxic to humans, the opposite has been found true. Cow's milk may contain as much as 25 parts per million and the fat of this cow, eaten by a human, would be enough to cause illness.

Some products similar to but less toxic than DDT are Methoxychlor, Perthane, and TDE (tetrachlorodiphenylethane).

Name: Dieldrin. *Other*: 1, 2, 3, 4, 10, 10-hexachloro-6, 7-epoxy-1,4,4a,5,6,7,8,8a-octanhydro-1,4,5,8-dimethanonaphthalene. *Trade Name*: Compound 497, Octalox, HEOD.

Toxicity: 6.

Form: Dieldrin is a white, odorless crystal found as a spray, powder, or dust. It can be inhaled, ingested, or absorbed through the skin.

Used against potato beetles, corn pests, and rape plant parasites, dieldrin was manufactured by the Shell Chemical Company until the 1974 EPA Fungicide and Rodenticide Act forbade it. It is now being manufactured for use in Holland. It has a high affinity for fat and progressively accumulates in an animal or person until the lethal dose is reached.

Effects and Symptoms: Early symptoms include headache, dizziness, nausea, vomiting, and sweating, followed by hyperexcitability, hyperirritability, convulsions, coma, and death.

Reaction Time: Symptoms may appear from within twenty minutes to twelve hours.

Antidotes and Treatments: Symptomatic.

Notes: A disaster hazard, dieldrin is dangerous when heated to decomposition, emitting highly toxic chloride fumes.

Name: Endrin. *Other*: 1,2,3,4,10-hexachloro-6,7-epoxy-1,4,4a,5,6,7,8,8a-oxtahydro-1,4,5,8-endo-endo-dimethanonaphthalene. *Trade Name*: Compound 269, Experimental Insecticide 269.

Toxicity: 5.

Form: A white, crystalline solid melting at 226 degrees C., endrin is an insecticide, avicide, and rodenticide. It can be inhaled, ingested, or absorbed through eye and skin contact.

Effects and Symptoms: Early symptoms include giddiness, weakness of legs, nausea, confusion, anorexia, insomnia, and lethargy, followed by repeated epileptic convulsions and loss of consciousness, ending in respiratory failure.

Reaction Time: Thirty minutes up to ten hours before first symptoms appear.

Antidotes and Treatments: Symptomatic.

Case Histories: There have been numerous reports of endrin fatalities. A mass poisoning of bread prepared from flour sprayed with endrin killed three people in the Midwest.

Name: Ethylene chlorohydrin. *Other: beta*-chloroethyl alcohol; glycol chlorohydrin; 2-chloroethanol.

Toxicity: 6.

Form: A colorless, flammable liquid with a faint etherlike odor, ethylene chlorohydrin boils at 130 degrees C. It is used in certain pesticides; as a solvent for removal of resins and waxes; in the dyeing and cleaning industry where it removes tar spots; as a cleaning agent for machines; and as a solvent for fabric dyeing. Ethylene chlorohydrin is also found in agriculture as an agent for speeding up sprouting of potatoes and in treating seeds to inhibit biological activity.

Ethylene chlorohydrin poisons by inhalation, skin contact, or ingestion. Under prolonged contact, a teaspoonful of liquid can be fatal. Skin contact is especially hazardous since absence of signs of immediate irritation prevent any warning that the skin has been wet by the substance.

Effects and Symptoms: A neurotoxic agent, it affects the heart and lungs. High vapor concentrations are irritating to eyes, nose, throat, and skin; other symptoms include nausea, vomiting, dizziness, headache, thirst, delirium, low blood pressure, collapse, and unconsciousness. Death may follow from cardiac and respiratory collapse.

Reaction Time: Several minutes to one hour. Inhalation for fifteen minutes is enough to make someone quite ill.

Antidotes and Treatments: Remove from further exposure, give artificial respiration and oxygen. Use gastric lavage if ingested. Combat shock and treat pulmonary edema.

Notes: A disaster hazard when heated, ethylene chlorohydrin emits highly toxic phosgene fumes. When reacting with water or steam, it produces toxic and corrosive fumes and also reacts with oxidizers.

Name: Malathion. *Other*: Diethyl mercaptosuccinate, S-ester with 0,0-dimethyl phosphorodithioate, carbophos. *Trade Name:* Cythion, 4049.

Toxicity: 4.

Form: A colorless to light amber liquid with a characteristic odor, malathion is slightly soluble in water. Used on insect pests that attack fruits, vegetables, and ornamental plants, it also controls household flies, mosquitoes, and lice on farm and livestock animals. While malathion can be ingested, absorbed through the skin, or inhaled, and causes dermatitis and skin sensitization with heavy field use, almost all fatalities reported have involved ingestion.

Found as wetted powders, emulsifiable concentrates, dusts, or aerosols, malathion is incompatible with strong oxidizers.

Effects and Symptoms: Initial symptoms include dermatitis, severe headaches, nosebleeds, nausea, diarrhea, blurred vision, vomiting, pallor, tearing, and excessive salivation, followed by dyspnea, bronchitis, shock, cardiac arrhythmias, and pulmonary edema. Death can result from respiratory failure.

Reaction Time: Immediate to several hours. Even after twenty-four hours, appearing to recover, the victim can still die.

Antidotes and Treatments: Maintenance of respiration is critical since death usually results from muscle weakness—including the muscles of the lungs. Other treatment is symptomatic.

Notes: When malathion and certain other organic phosphates are administered simultaneously, they potentiate each other, making far less needed for a toxic result.

A disaster hazard when heated, it emits highly toxic fumes of phosphorous oxide (with water this turns into phosphoric acid).

Malathion was used recently in a medfly spraying of the San Fernando Valley in Southern California. While officials claimed it was harmless, many people reported toxic reactions.

Closely related to malathion is Sarin, a deadly nerve gas and most widely used in household insecticides and mosquito sprays. Like parathion, it is absorbed through the skin.

Name: Paraquat. *Other*: Methylviologen; 1,1'-Dimethyl-4,4'-bipyridinium dichloride or dimethosulfate; gramoxone; 1,1'-dimethyl-4,4'dipridrium dichloride; 1,1'-Dimethyl-4,4'-bipyridylium chloride.

Toxicity: 6.

Form: A water-soluble, yellow solid herbicide, paraquat is inactivated by contact with clay particles in soil. Paraquat poisons by skin contact, ingestion, and inhalation.

Effects and Symptoms: Skin absorption causes severe skin irritation. Initial symptoms of ingestion include burning mouth and throat, vomiting, abdominal pain, diarrhea, ulceration of tongue, and fever. After two or three days, liver and kidney toxicity develop showing as jaundice and oliguria. This is followed by tachycardia, respiratory distress, cyanosis, and fatal lung damage. Paraquat turns the victim's urine blue.

Reaction Time: Two to five days for first symptoms; five to eight days for final ones.

Antidotes and Treatments: Care must be taken as paraquat may be corrosive to the esophagus. Treatment is symptomatic.

Case Histories: There are numerous reports of fatal accidental and suicidal ingestion by humans. One victim ingested approximately 114 ml of a 20-percent solution and another took only a mouthful. The former died in seven days, the latter died after fifteen.

In the late sixties and early seventies, the United States Government inadvertently caused numerous poisonings by spraying illegal marijuana fields with paraquat in an attempt to kill the weed. These fields were harvested and the weed smoked by unsuspecting victims, who got more kick than they'd anticipated. Many people died as a result.

Notes: Paraquat is produced in a 30-percent concentrate aqueous solution and is not sold in regular garden supply shops. It's the less toxic diquat, which is half as lethal as paraquat, that is used as a general defoliant.

Name: Parathion. *Other*: 0,0-Diethyl 0-p-nitrophenyl phosphorothioate, 0,0-Diethyl 0-p-nitrophenyl thiophosphate. *Trade Name:* Akron, Alkron, Compound 3422, DNTP, DPP, Niran, Amer Cyan 3422, Bay E-605, Bladan, Folidol E605, Genihion, Paradust, Paraflow, Paraspray, Parawet, Penphos, Phos-kil, Thiophos, Vapophor.

Toxicity: 6.

Form: Parathion is a brown or yellowish liquid used as an acaracide and an insecticide.

Parathion, also a nerve gas, is fatal upon skin contact. It absorbs through the lungs as well. The victim in question dies a torturous death with tremors, muscle spasms, and convulsions.

Effects and Symptoms: A cholinesterase-inhibiting insecticide, parathion destroys the enzyme that keeps the nerves and muscles functioning well. The symptoms include contraction of the pupils, headache, photophobia, spasm, abdominal pain, muscle weakness, involuntary twitching, diarrhea, convulsions, nosebleeds, nausea, dermatitis, loss of sphincter control, heart block, paralysis, respiratory difficulty, and pulmonary edema. Death can result from respiratory failure. Laboratory blood studies of cholinesterase would show it markedly reduced.

After exposure, when the cholinesterase level is drastically low, the victim can still recover if given time. However, should another small dose of the poison be given at this time, before recovery is complete, the victim will most likely die.

Reaction Time: Thirty to sixty minutes to a maximum of twelve hours.

Antidotes and Treatments: Symptomatic, although atropine is given in a dose ten times the amount usually considered safe. The victim is kept on heavy atropine for forty-eight hours.

Case Histories: A chemist swallowed a small amount of malathion and parathion mixture and was paralyzed instantaneously, dying before he could take the antidote he'd prepared beforehand.

In another case, two children died after handling an empty bag that had once contained parathion and malathion.

In yet another case, two children died after eating potatoes fried in fat contaminated with parathion. Traces of parathion in what appeared to be empty bottles also killed children.

Notes: The majority of parathion poisonings seem to occur when spraying against the wind, cleaning airplanes used for the spraying, or gathering vegetables and fruit that have been sprayed.

Poisoning has been observed in factory workers who probably absorbed the material through their skin. Common in rural areas, an increasing number of suicide and murder reports in Germany, Belgium, and France have centered on this product.

Chlorthion, an equally dangerous pesticide and close relative of parathion, has been confused with nose drops. Even though absorption is not apparent for several hours, death can occur after eleven hours.

Sarin, another relative of parathion, and a highly toxic nerve gas itself, can kill a man in fifteen minutes with only a small drop on the skin. The liquid does not injure the skin but penetrates rapidly. Sarin is also dangerous when heated and gives off toxic fumes. Reacting with water or steam, corrosive and toxic fumes result.

Name: TEPP. *Other*: Tetraethyl pyrophosphate. *Trade Name*: Tetron, NIFOS, TEP, Vapotone, Fovex, Hesamite Nifos-T.

Toxicity: 6.

Form: In its pure state, TEPP is a colorless, odorless liquid. In the crude state, TEPP is amber-toned. Both varieties are used as an aphicide and acaricide.

Effects and Symptoms: A cholinesterase inhibitor, TEPP destroys

198 / Deadly Doses

the enzyme. If the victim has not fully recovered, an additional dose can be fatal. Small doses at frequent intervals are addictive, similar to parathion.

After inhalation, respiratory and eye problems are the first to appear. These include eye pain, impaired vision, tearing, headache, pinpoint pupils, loss of depth perception, cramps, excessive sweating, chest pain, dyspnea, cyanosis, anorexia, vomiting, diarrhea, twitching, paralysis, loss of reflexes and sphincter control. Cheyne-Stokes respiration, convulsions, low blood pressure, and death.

Reaction Time: Fifteen minutes to four hours; may be delayed up to twelve hours. Death usually occurs within twenty-four hours.

Antidotes and Treatments: Same as parathion.

Notes: Skin absorption is greater at higher temperatures and increased by previous skin irritation. TEPP is absorbed by all routes, including unbroken skin.

Name: Toxaphene. *Other*: Octachlorocamphene, polychlorocamphene; chlorinated camphene. *Trade Name:* Synthetic 3956, Strobane, Alltox, Geniphene, Toxakil, Toxadust.

Toxicity: 5.

Form: A yellow, waxy solid with a pleasant piny odor, toxaphene is an insecticide that is soluble in fatty substances and insoluble in water. Toxaphene is used against rape-plant parasites. Most fatal cases occur from accidental ingestion when the solutions are left in unlabeled containers. Poisoning, however, can also occur from inhalation and skin absorption.

Effects and Symptoms: Affecting the central nervous system, toxaphene causes convulsions, vomiting, auditory hallucinations, congestion in brain and lungs, respiratory failure, coma, and death.

Reaction Time: Symptoms begin within four hours; death occurs from four to twenty-four hours.

Case Histories: One family was fatally poisoned after eating greens contaminated with toxaphene.

A nine-month-old child died after being exposed to cotton dusting.

Notes: Numerous human deaths have been reported from toxaphene poisoning. A disaster hazard, it emits highly toxic chloride fumes. Its toxicity is four times as great as that of DDT.

Name: Vacor. *Other*: N-3 pyridylmethyl-N'-p-nitrophenyl urea-PNU. *Trade Name:* VACOR Rat Killer, DLP-787 2% Bait, DLP-787-10% House Mouse Tracking Powder.

Toxicity: 5.

Form: The rat killer is yellow and resembles corn meal; the mouse powder is a pale light-green powder. Most reported deaths are the result of suicidal ingestion. Ingestion in small amounts requires repeated doses to become toxic.

Effects and Symptoms: The main effect is destruction of the beta islet cells (insulin-producing cells) of the pancreas causing hypoglycemia and hypotension. The many symptoms include twitching, low blood pressure, polyuria, thirst, diabetes, nausea, vomiting, diffuse abdominal pain, lightheadedness, chest pain, weakness, blurred vision, numbness of legs, lethargy, ataxia, constipation, impaired intellect, disturbed balance, delirium, collapse, coma, respiratory failure, and death.

If the victim recovers, the diabetes developed is permanent.

Reaction Time: Within thirty minutes.

Antidotes and Treatments: Remove with syrup of ipecac, inject nicotinamide within thirty minutes, and treat hyperglycemia with insulin. Other treatments are symptomatic.

Notes: Containing a warfarinlike anticoagulant, Vacor has more serious effects on humans than on rats. While the poison was supposed to have been banned in the United States, and was withdrawn from the shelves in June 1979, professional exterminators can still use Vacor. It was formerly marketed in 39-gram packets and is available elsewhere in the world.

N I N E

INDUSTRIAL POISONS

"She's not dead yet, but she soon will be."
— Louisa May Merrifield
Convicted poisoner
England 1953
The Murderer's Who's Who

Prior to 1950, industrial poisons were primarily limited to organic materials. But as industry expanded and more products were needed, newer by-products and poisons were created. Often the deadly nature of the chemicals took years to discover because death took the form of slow-acting cancer.

Besides poisoning people individually, many of these chemicals can be used to kill en masse as the disastrous factory explosion in Bhopal, India proved. The combined vapors in the air were more fatal than the large plant fire. What a perfect terrorist story.

Because the symptoms of industrial poisoning vary so greatly, the treatment for such is usually symptomatic. Unless otherwise stated in the listings, it should be understood that antidotes and treatments are symptom-oriented.

Acids

Most acids have a similar corrosive effect. Since they are treated in the same way, they have been grouped together here. Acids vary in strength, depending on the concentration within the solution. Acids are used in production of fertilizers, dyes, artificial silk, electroplating, tanning, soap refining, and metal cleaning. Some are produced as by-products of other chemical reactions.

Name: Hydrochloric acid, chlorine gas (not to be confused with the solution found in pools), osmic acid, ethyl chlorocarbonate, and chloroacetylchloride are just a few of the more corrosive and toxic acids, all of which have similar symptoms and treatments.

Toxicity: 6.

Form: Acids can be found in both liquid and gaseous states. As a gas, it is colorless and nonflammable. Soluble in water, it is often found as a solution.

Acids can be swallowed; however, a fatal dose would be very difficult to get down because the corrosive action also closes up the throat. Skin absorption (usually total immersion) or breathing in gaseous vapors are the most likely methods to produce fatal results. Do remember that corrosion hurts a lot, and your character would be immediately warned that something is wrong and take action against it, unless your villain prevents it.

Effects and Symptoms: Highly corrosive to skin and eyes and mucous membranes, acid produces burns, ulcerations, and scarring, destroying any tissue it comes into contact with.

Eye contact may result in reduced vision or blindness. Redness and peeling of skin may be seen as well as burns and scarring. The irritating effects of the vapors may produce an inflammation of the throat, tongue, and lungs. When acid fumes are inhaled, the victim experiences coughing, choking, headaches, dizziness, and weakness. After six to eight hours, the victim will feel a tightness in the chest, followed by gasping for air, foaming at the mouth, and turning blue. The blood pressure will be low and the pulse will be high. Pulmonary edema can develop, followed by death.

Severe burning pain is the principal symptom when swallowed. Vomiting and dark, bloody diarrhea will occur along with a steep drop in blood pressure. Brownish or yellowish stains sometimes appear around or in the mouth. The back of the throat can swell and suffocate the victim. Later peritonitis (an inflammation of the stomach lining, which can occur from the acid-caused rupture) can set in with rigid abdomen and fever. This disease process, in and of itself, is almost always fatal unless medical attention is given immediately. Ingestion may cause death from the esophageal or gastric necrosis.

Corrosion and irritation are the primary findings in an autopsy. Brown and black stains are found wherever the acid had contact. Thick coffee-colored blood is often found in the stomach.

Reaction Time: Immediate to several hours.

Antidotes and Treatments: Acid should be diluted. A mild alkali, such as milk, is sometimes used, if it can be quickly obtained, to neutralize the acid. Symptomatic treatment for burns follow.

Case Histories: Industrial workers have been known to fall into vats of acid and either die or become hideously disfigured. This occurs frequently enough that "scare films" showing the gory results of these accidents are shown to chemical workers in much the same way high school driver education students are shown films of highway accidents. Your villain might be inspired by one of these films.

Notes: If the victim recovers, the flesh will be permanently scarred. A good reason for revenge.

Other Industrial Chemicals

Name: Acrylamide, propenamide, acrylic amide, acrylamide monomer.

Toxicity: 5.

Form: Found as a flakelike crystal, it melts at a relatively low heat and should be kept in a dark, cool spot. It also dissolves easily in water. It can be inhaled, swallowed, or absorbed through the skin.

A fairly potent toxin, acrylamide is used to make polyacrylamide, which while not toxic, is in turn used to stabilize soil, to make jet chromatography (a process used to identify unknown chemical substances), to clear and treat water for drinking, and also as a strengthener in the paper-making process.

Effects and Symptoms: Acrylamide is a neurotoxin affecting the nervous system as well as the eyes and skin.

The most obvious sign of acrylamide poisoning is peeling and redness of skin on the victim's hands and sometimes feet. There is numbness in the lower limbs, and both palms and feet are sweaty. Also included are drunken stumbling and weak or absent reflexes. Victims can lose their ability to identify their position without using their sight. The killer, too, might be left with peeling hands.

Reaction Time: The effects are delayed after initial exposure, which can be useful if time is needed to establish as alibi.

Case Histories: Some years ago, a La Jolla, California chemist, angry with his coworkers, put acrylamide in the coffee filters of the office coffee pot. Although none of them died, many exceptionally intelligent chemists suffered severe brain damage. The guilty chemist was found out and is currently serving time for his deed.

Notes: Acrylamide causes severe brain damage, which is only sometimes reversible.

Name: Aniline.

Toxicity: 5.

Form: Aniline is found in printing, stamp-pad and cloth-marking inks, as well as paints, paint removers, and dyes. Aniline can be absorbed through the skin as a powder, liquid, or gas. It can also be swallowed.

Effects and Symptoms: Aniline changes the hemoglobin to methemoglobin and thus interferes with oxygen transportation in the central nervous system.

Symptoms progress from cyanosis (blue coloration of the skin and lips), headaches, shallow respiration, dizziness, confusion, a drop in blood pressure, lethargy, and stupor to convulsions, coma, another drop in blood pressure, and death. An autopsy will show chocolate-colored blood (methemoglobin); damage to the kidneys, liver, and spleen; and red pinprick spots on the organs. Sometimes the bladder shows little ulcers with decayed tissue in them.

Reaction Time: The first symptoms appear within one to two hours. Aniline works fairly slowly, depending on the dose.

Antidotes and Treatments: Methylene blue dye is sometimes given to reverse the effect on the red blood cells, but if that doesn't work, dialysis or transfusion might be necessary.

Notes: Infants have been known to die from wearing diapers that had been marked with aniline ink and not first washed. Of course, the dye can mark the killer as well as the victim. Dyes like these often get under the fingernails, and while they appear to wash off, traces usually remain.

Name: Antimony. *Other*: Antimony regulus, tartar emetic, and stibium.

Toxicity: 6.

Form: Antimony is a silvery-white soft metal that does not dissolve in water. Tartar emetic, a white powder, has been hidden with food, but there is a slight bitter taste. As a gas, antimony is also called stibine, which is a colorless and odorless gas released when metals containing antimony come into contact with acids.

Many chemicals and commonly used items contain antimony. It's used in alloys, typesetting metals, foil, batteries, ceramics, glass, enamels, glazes, explosives, safety matches, and ant paste. Ant paste is what the Victorian poisoners bought at the chemist (pharmacy). Antimony is also an element in the periodic table.

Effects and Symptoms: Topically, it's a skin irritant. Lesions causing intense itching appear on exposed moist areas of the body, but rarely on the face. While this is not fatal, it is a good clue as to who might have been into the antimony.

The clinical picture is similar to arsenic poison. Poisonings in which antimony were suspected were historically diagnosed as "gastric fever" because the symptoms include nausea, frequent vomiting, dehydration, and severe diarrhea with mucus and later blood. Also seen are slow, shallow respiration; pulmonary congestion; coma; and sometimes death due to circulatory or respiratory failure. Inhalation of stibine can also cause weak pulse, jaundice, anemia from the destruction of the red blood cells, and generalized weakness.

Chronic poisoning is very similar to chronic arsenic poisoning and presents the additional symptoms of dry throat, headache, sleeplessness, loss of appetite, and dizziness.

The autopsy may show damage to the liver and other organs. The gastrointestinal tract may also show congestion and swelling.

Reaction Time: Thirty minutes to several hours.

Antidotes and Treatments: Treatment is similar to that for arsenic poisoning—the stomach is pumped and the victim is sometimes given dimercaprol, the generic name for BAL, a drug used to promote the excretion of arsenic, gold, and mercury in the case of poisoning. But it must be given within an hour or two of the poison in order to neutralize it. The *Physician's Desk Reference* says, "Use is of questionable value in poisoning caused by other heavy metals such as antimony and bismuth. It should not be used in iron, cadmium, or selenium poisoning because the resulting dimercaprol-metal complexes are more toxic than the metal alone, especially to the kidneys."

Case Histories: At the turn of the nineteenth century, George Chapman, née Severin Klosowski, lived in London with a married woman, Isabella Spink, although he was married to another woman in America. He used Isabella's money to set himself up as a landlord, and within a few months, she became ill and died. Chapman hired barmaid Bessie Taylor to assist him with his duties. On Bessie's death, the physicians became puzzled. Not until the death of Maud Marsh, whose mother called foul play, were the bodies exhumed and antimony found in all three. Police at the time suspected Chapman might have been involved in the Jack-the-Ripper murders — having given up the knife because of fear of detection — and turned to poisoning instead.

Dr. Edmund Pritchard of Glasgow impregnated a servant girl. He killed her when she insisted on money. He then became involved with a second girl, whom he promised to marry as soon as his wife died. Dr. Pritchard then murdered his mother-in-law, who suspected he was trying to slowly murder her daughter. At the final illness of both women, Dr. Pritchard had the audacity to ask Dr. Patterson, another physician, to verify his "diagnosis" of gastric distress and asked that it be written up as "gastric fever." Bold as most villains are, he kissed his wife while she lay in the coffin. The letter that brought him to suspicion was thought to have been written by Dr. Patterson. Before Dr. Pritchard's death, he first tried to blame the servant. Later, he made three confessions.

Notes: Tartar emetic (antimony potassium tartrate) has historically rivaled arsenic as a poisoner's favorite. In fact, several well-known Victorian murderers, Dr. Edmund Pritchard for one, combined the two drugs. Catherine de Médicis used it in France, as did the Borgias in Italy. Unlike metallic antimony, most of the antimony compounds are extremely toxic.

Name: Benzene. *Other*: Benzol, phenyl hydride, coal naphtha, phene, cyclohexatriene.

Toxicity: 4.

Form: A pleasant-smelling, colorless liquid at 80 degrees C., it becomes a vapor at 26 degrees C. It's used in motor fuels and as a solvent for fats, inks, oils, paints, plastics, and rubber. It is also used as a component of other chemicals. The writer might find its highly flammable nature an additional plus — if the villain smokes, setting a trap might be difficult or dangerous.

The vapor can be breathed and can occasionally be absorbed by direct contact with the skin. An abrasion or lesion will facilitate absorption. The poison can also be ingested.

Effects and Symptoms: Affecting the central nervous system, only a light exposure of benzene is needed to cause weakness, dizziness, euphoria, headache, nausea, and vomiting. This is followed by tightness in the chest and staggering. Continued exposure causes blurred vision, tremors, shallow respiration, and heart palpitations, which can result in a heart attack, paralysis, convulsions, spasms, violent delirium, and unconsciousness.

Chronic poisoning is insidious. Symptoms start with fatigue, headache, loss of appetite, and nausea. Blood studies will show anemia. Lab tests find it difficult to distinguish between aplastic anemia and bone-marrow failure due to benzene poisoning.

Skin contact will reveal redness, scaling, and cracking — always a good clue.

Reaction Time: Immediate upon inhalation, a little longer upon ingestion.

Antidotes and Treatments: As with all poisonous vapors, the victim should be removed from contaminated air immediately and given artificial respiration. Convulsions or spasms are treated with Valium. While epinephrine or ephedrine can trigger heart attacks and are contraindicated, the writer may want to use this on the victim.

Notes: A pattern of apparent drunken behavior due to benzene called the "benzol jag" consists of unsteady gait, euphoria, and confusion. This occurs after a small amount of inhalation. Many people chronically exposed to benzene later develop leukemia.

Name: Cadmium.

Toxicity: 4.

Form: Cadmium is used for plating metals and in the manufacture of alloys and silver. It alloys with mercury in dental cement and is used in the manufacturing of fluorescent lamps and in jewelry, as well as by the automobile and aircraft industries. Various compounds are also found in glazes, paints, insecticides, and in wide use in the photographic industry.

A bluish-white metal, it will not dissolve in water but does dissolve in acid. It is found as a by-product of zinc, copper, and lead ore. Cadmium plating is soluble in acid foods such as fruit juices and vinegar. So if the victim wants tomato juice . . .

When products containing cadmium are heated to above its melting point (321 degrees C.), deadly cadmium fumes are released.

Cadmium can be ingested or the fumes inhaled. The fumes are by far more deadly since swallowed cadmium causes immediate vomiting, making ingestion of a fatal dose nearly impossible.

Effects and Symptoms: Cadmium damages all cells of the body but especially the respiratory system.

The earliest symptoms from inhaled fumes, occurring several hours after exposure, include a slight irritation of the upper respiratory tract, which can be followed over the next few hours with coughing, chest pain, sweating, and chills. At this point many victims believe they have the flu. Eight to twenty-four hours later, they develop painful breathing, more pain in the chest, hypertension, generalized weakness, pulmonary edema, and possible emphysema. If the patient recovers, lung problems will persist.

Ingesting the poison causes immediate nausea, vomiting, diarrhea, headache, increased salivation, muscle aches, stomach pain, shock (a drastic fall in blood pressure), and renal failure.

Chronic poisoning includes weight loss, anemia, irritability, yellow-stained teeth, and a loss of the sense of smell.

Autopsy reveals severe liver and kidney damage. Lung tissue is scarred, fluid might be present from edema, and emphysema can be seen.

Reaction Time: With inhalation, there is a latent period of several hours before symptoms begin. If the victim survives for four days, there is a probability of recovery. Complete recovery, however, will take up to six months.

Antidotes and Treatments: Allay gastric irritation with milk or beaten eggs every four hours. Treat pulmonary edema and other symptoms as liver damage and renal failure. Calcium disodium edetate given (IV) intravenously or (IM) intramuscularly appears effective. Do not give dimercaprol as it can aggravate the situation.

Notes: Once absorbed, the cadmium has a long half-life and stays in the body for a number of years.

Early chest X-rays may look like bronchial pneumonia so victims may not necessarily realize they are being poisoned. At least ten fatalities have occurred with exposure to the fumes.

Heavy smoking appears to increase the toxic effects of the poison.

Name: Carbon monoxide.

Toxicity: 5.

Form: Carbon monoxide is inhaled. This odorless gas is the result of incomplete burning of carbon materials. Not only can't victims smell it, but its effects make victims so drowsy, they are unable to do anything once they realize something is wrong.

An unvented gas heater can make a small room dangerous in minutes. The exhaust from gasoline engines can be 3 to 7 percent carbon monoxide. Tobacco smoke is 4 percent carbon monoxide.

People breathe carbon monoxide all the time, and every time they do, they diminish the number of red blood cells carrying oxygen to their bodies and in addition make it harder for the blood cells left to release the oxygen they contain. When a carbon monoxide atom hooks onto a red blood cell, the cell continues to carry it until it dies. With continued exposure, the contaminated cells continue to build up until the victim suffocates. However, the body makes new blood cells all the time; so once the exposure is over, the victim should recover physically, although brain damage can occur. Studies show that carbon monoxide poisoning is a common suicide method.

Effects and Symptoms: Unlike oxygen atoms, which hook up with red blood cells and let go when they arrive where they are needed, carbon monoxide atoms hook up with a red blood cell, displace the oxygen atom, and hang on permanently. With enough red blood cells unable to carry oxygen to the tissues, the body suffocates.

One of the greatest dangers of carbon monoxide poisoning is that the victim is unaware of being suffocated because the symptoms progress as the blood saturates. The victim will first feel a slight headache and shortness of breath. Continued exposure will make the headache worse and cause nausea, irritability, heavier breathing, chest pain, confusion, impaired judgment, and fainting from exertion. Increased concentrations of the gas and continued exposure will cause respiratory failure, unconsciousness, and death.

The autopsy will reveal microscopic hemorrhages and dead tissues throughout the body, as well as congestion and swelling of the brain, liver, kidneys, and spleen. The skin looks flushed, and the blood is often a bright cherry red.

Reaction Time: The time depends on the concentration of the gas and the activity level of the victim. Fairly heavy concentrations can cause death within one hour.

Antidotes and Treatments: The victim must first be removed from exposure. Then 100-percent oxygen is given until there are enough red blood cells. Treat symptomatically.

Case Histories: In one nearly fatal case the victim described the lightheaded feeling as if his cares were floating away. He "fell asleep" (lost consciousness) soon after.

Depression-era screen star Thelma Todd died of carbon monoxide poisoning when her lover locked her in her garage while she was drunk and running her car's engine. She failed to turn off the ignition and suffocated.

In Harry Kellerman's *Saturday the Rabbi Went Hungry*, the fictional victim died when he passed out from drinking too much. The villain left him in the garage with the car engine running.

In Robin Cook's *Coma*, the villain fed carbon monoxide to patients via the operating room oxygen line during surgery.

Notes: A person who smokes twenty cigarettes a day has at least 6 percent of his or her red blood cells saturated with carbon monoxide.

Name: Carbon tetrachloride.

Toxicity: 6.

Form: Carbon tetrachloride is a colorless, nonflammable liquid with a distinctive odor. It can be inhaled, absorbed through the skin, or swallowed.

This industrial solvent is an extremely dangerous chemical. Used in the manufacture of fluorocarbons, it is also employed as a dry-cleaning agent and occasionally in fire extinguishers. Some household supplies still include carbon tet as a spot remover. The chemical has a very low boiling point (76.7 degrees C.), and when heated it decomposes to form phosgene gas and hydrochloric acid.

Effects and Symptoms: Carbon tetrachloride attacks the central nervous system, predominately the liver and kidneys.

The first symptoms are abdominal pain, nausea, vomiting, dizziness, and confusion. This is followed by unconsciousness, shallow breathing, slow or irregular pulse, and blood pressure dropping. If victims survive these symptoms, they can suffer mild nausea, anorexia, or nothing at all. Further symptoms might be seen between one day and two weeks. This is when liver or kidney damage becomes obvious. Liver damage may cause jaundice. Kidney damage shows up as a decrease in urine output, swelling, sudden weight gain, and uremia. Death often results from kidney failure if immediate steps are not taken to start dialysis. Coma and liver or kidney damage can all appear independently or can all occur at the same time.

While the flesh of most corpses will look somewhat jaundiced, in dead black people the discoloration is often not that apparent. In such cases, physicians check for a yellowish tinge in the whites of their eyes.

Reaction Time: Almost immediate.

Antidotes and Treatments: When inhaled, the first step is to administer artificial respiration until the victim regains consciousness. Any clothing contaminated with the chemical should be removed. Treatment is symptomatic. Stimulants are not given as they can induce a heart attack. If the urine output is adequate, fluids are given to keep it going; diuretics are not recommended. A diet high in carbohydrates can help to restore liver function.

Notes: The mouth will have a sick sweetish taste. Workers are warned not to drink alcohol around carbon tet since that intensifies the effect of the poison. If the victim has drunk alcohol at the same time, damage to all of the organs is increased.

In the 1950s, it was used as a solvent for cleaning airplane motors.

Name: Dimethyl sulfate. *Other*: Sulfuric acid dimethyl ester, methyl sulfate, DMS.

Toxicity: 6.

Form: A colorless, odorless, oily liquid with a boiling point of 188 degrees C., dimethyl sulfate is only slightly soluble in water but readily dissolves in organic solvents. It can be ingested, inhaled, or absorbed by skin or eye contact.

Used in manufacturing dyes, drugs, perfumes, and pesticides, most poisonings come from leakage of liquid and vapors from the apparatus. If alcohol is present, the poisoning can be worse.

Effects and Symptoms: Topically, the chemical exerts a strong corrosive effect after a latency period of four to five hours. Immediate effects of vapor exposure produce tearing; runny nose; swelling of mouth, lips, and throat tissues; sore throat; hoarseness; dyspnea; cyanosis; and death. Eye irritation causes conjunctivitis (pink eye), perforation of the nasal septum through the sinuses (much like one might see in a cocaine habit) and permanent vision problems. Liver and kidney damage may also occur.

Ingestion causes respiratory distress and bronchitis within six to twelve hours. Cerebral edema and other central nervous system effects such as drowsiness, temporary blindness, heart irregularities, and nerve irritation occur before possible convulsions and death. Pulmonary edema is usually the cause of death.

Reaction Time: Exposure produces no immediate effects except for nasal and eye irritation. There is a latent period of up to ten hours before the onset of symptoms. Death may occur in three to four days or be delayed for several weeks.

Antidotes and Treatments: Oxygen is given for pulmonary problems and hydrocortisone is used to reduce injury. Other symptoms are treated as they appear.

Case Histories: A poisoning occurred when dimethyl vapors escaped from a factory transmission belt. One worker had started a distillation test just moments before, and the freed fumes went directly into his face. He suffered nausea and burning of the eyes. Eleven hours later, he died from symptoms of suffocation.

A little boy suffocated from sulfuric acid fumes in 1979 in Los Angeles, California. A local chemical company had accidently spilled the dimethyl sulfate into a cesspool, which sent the fumes into the boy's bathroom, where he had been locked by his mother as punishment. The mother later sued the company.

Notes: Workers who enter contaminated areas must wear positive-pressure airline-hose masks or self-contained breathing apparatus. Canister-type gas masks are not safe.

Name: Ethylene chlorohydrin. *Other*: Glycol chlorohydrin, 2-chloroethanol, *beta*-chloroethyl alcohol.

Toxicity: 6.

Form: Ethylene chlorohydrin is a colorless liquid that smells like ether. The highly toxic chemical can be inhaled, absorbed, or ingested. When heated, it emits phosgene, a deadly gas (see page 219). Ethylene chlorohydrin will react with water or steam to produce toxic and corrosive fumes.

This highly dangerous chemical is used in both industry and agriculture. Used to make indigo dye and novocaine, the chemical is also found as a solvent to clean machines and remove tar from clothing, and is used to speed up the germination of potatoes and other seeds.

Effects and Symptoms: A narcotic poison, the chemical affects the liver, spleen, and lungs. Initial symptoms may be slight. After several hours, symptoms include nausea, vomiting, headache, abdominal pain, excitability, dizziness, delirium, slowed breathing, a drop in blood pressure, muscle twitching, cyanosis, and coma, with death from respiratory and circulatory failure.

The autopsy shows infiltration of the chemical into the fatty part of the liver, swelling of the brain, and congestion and swelling in the lungs. The heart valves are damaged and dilated. The spleen is congested, and the kidneys are swollen.

Reaction Time: Symptoms will usually begin between one and four hours.

Antidotes and Treatments: Remove from further exposure; give CPR and oxygen; combat shock and treat pulmonary edema. Gastric lavage to remove ingested poison or use syrup of ipecac.

Notes: The chemical readily penetrates the skin and most rubber gloves.

Frostbite can occur from handling the chemical's container — an indication of who might have been around the chemical.

Survival for 18 hours after poisoning has always been followed by complete recovery.

Name: Formaldehyde. *Other*: Formalin, methanol, formic aldehyde, oxomethane, oxymethylene, methylene oxide, methyl aldehyde.

Toxicity: 6.

Form: Formaldehyde is a colorless gas with a strong and unpleasant odor. The chemical is more commonly found as formalin, a solution made of 40 percent formaldehyde, water, and sometimes methanol.

Formaldehyde is most dangerous when inhaled or ingested in solution. Absorption through the skin is less severe.

The chemical is more common than most people realize. It's used as a disinfectant, an antiseptic, as the adhesive in plywood and particle board, as sizing on new fabrics, and is even in some explosives. The odor in new furniture and new cars is formaldehyde.

Effects and Symptoms: Formaldehyde attacks the respiratory system. Upon ingestion, tearing and severe abdominal pain is immediate, followed by collapse, loss of consciousness, and shutdown of the liver. Vomiting and diarrhea can also occur. Circulatory failure is the actual cause of death. Breathing formaldehyde irritates the respiratory tract and the eyes.

Inhalation for prolonged periods of time causes pulmonary edema and death.

Contact with the skin may cause irritations and lesions.

The principal findings of an autopsy are decayed and shrunken mucous membranes, along with possible liver, kidney, heart, and brain damage.

Reaction Time: Ingesting formaldehyde causes an immediate reaction. Within thirty minutes of exposure to the gas, symptoms become pronounced.

Antidotes and Treatments: Milk, activated charcoal, or tap water are given to dilute and inactivate the poison — any organic material will inactivate formaldehyde. Afterward, the victim is treated for shock and liver shutdown.

Case Histories: One woman placed formalin in an old lemonade bottle on the garage shelf and conveniently forgot to warn her husband, who drank it and died.

Notes: Paper and cloth containing formaldehyde can cause allergic skin reactions in some people.

It is also a potential explosion hazard. The higher the concentration of formaldehyde or methanol content the lower the flash point. It will easily catch fire.

Name: Hydrogen sulfide. *Other*: Hydrosulfuric acid, sulfureted hydrogen.

Toxicity: 6.

Form: A gas, hydrogen sulfide is inhaled. It is an irritant and an asphyxiant.

Hydrogen sulfide occurs whenever vegetable matter or animal matter undergoes putrefaction. Heavier than air, the gas can be found in manure pits, sewers, and other places where it can easily reach fatal concentrations. Large quantities may also develop in the drains of sugar factories, tanneries, and gelatin factories. Poisoning also occurs in coal mines. Hydrogen sulfide is found, too, as a by-product in numerous chemical processes at places such as blast furnaces and petroleum refineries.

Effects and Symptoms: Hydrogen sulfide has anoxic effects (reduces the body's oxygen supply). Talk about taking your breath away! It directly damages the cells of the nervous system and paralyzes the respiratory system.

A small amount of vapor inhaled causes eye and nasal irritation and sensory loss. Hydrogen sulfide has a distinct rotten-egg odor even with very little in the air. Symptoms are gradually progressive starting with a painful pink eye, appearance of halo around lights, headache, nausea, rawness in throat, cough, dizziness, drowsiness, and pulmonary edema. Very high concentrations cause immediate coma with death quickly following.

If death is delayed twenty-four to forty-eight hours, pulmonary edema and congestion of the lungs are found. A rotten-egg odor is noticeable at autopsy.

Reaction Time: Immediate. Death usually occurs in thirty to sixty minutes.

Antidotes and Treatments: Removal from exposure and giving oxygen are the only known treatments. Stimulants can cause more heart problems and so are not given. Amyl or sodium nitrite can sometimes be used to bind up the sulfide in the tissues and remove it.

Strict bed rest and reduction of sensory input are necessary if the patient is to survive. For hydrogen sulfide, those who survive four days will probably recover, although for several months they will experience lack of initiative, fatigue, headache, and loss of memory and equilibrium.

Case Histories: In one emergency room, three people were rushed in with severe symptoms. The poisoning had occurred in a manure pit. First the husband descended into the pit and lost consciousness because of the high concentration of poisonous gas. His wife and a neighbor, coming to his rescue, suffered the same fate. A fourth person pulled all three out with the aid of a hook. Two of the three victims died.

Name: Lead and lead compounds. *Other*: Plumbum.

Toxicity: 5.

Form: As a disaster hazard, lead creates highly toxic fumes when heated that react vigorously with oxidizing materials. The dust, when exposed to heat or flame, makes it a moderate explosive hazard.

Aside from the many compounds containing lead, the metal itself is blue-gray, very malleable, and heavy. There are over eighty-five known lead compounds, all which are poisonous to one degree or the other. The most dangerous of these are lead carbonate, lead monoxide, and lead sulfate. Lead arsenate is extremely toxic due to the arsenic present. Lead tetraethyl poisons by direct contact to the *intact* skin.

Lead and lead compounds are common air contaminants in the form of dust, fumes, mists, or vapors, often coming into contact with the skin. While it is not absorbed through intact skin, it is often ingested after inhalation—inhaled residue from the upper respiratory tract may be swallowed. Lead dust can also be introduced into the body on food, tobacco, fingers, or anything going into the mouth. Lead compounds in solution can also be injected.

Most people connect lead with peeling house paint and the poisoning of children. Besides paint pigment, lead or lead compounds are also used in toys, enameling, pottery glazes, alloys, solders, rubber, some gasoline, ammunition, ink, leaded glass, battery plates, piping, roof sheeting and guttering, as well as for opalescent coating on plastic beads. Lead dust is found in shooting galleries and in the occasional bad batch of moonshine when the still's lead lining is improperly constructed. The ingestion of acidic foods stored or cooked in leaded pewter pots (pewter being an alloy) can, over a period of time, poison.

Lead is a cumulative poison since it remains in the bones for as long as thirty-two years and in the kidneys for seven.

Effects and Symptoms: Lead works on the brain and the peripheral nervous system.

Chronic poisoning causes a number of symptoms including a blue lead line on the gums, vomiting, wasting away, and other nervous system symptoms. Acute poisoning causes a metallic taste in the mouth, abdominal pain, vomiting, diarrhea, black stools, oliguria, collapse, and coma.

When large amounts are taken in, the central nervous system is affected, leading to severe headache, convulsions, coma, delirium, and possibly death.

Lead arsenate is a white, heavy powder with arseniclike qualities that is found in some insecticides and veterinary tapeworm medicines. It leads to arsenic intoxication with symptoms including stomach pain, appetite loss, constipation, tiredness, weakness, nervousness, and loss of sensation in the limbs.

An autopsy of an acute poisoning will reveal inflamed mucous membranes in the gastrointestinal tract and damage in the liver area. Chronic poisoning shows cerebral edema and damage to the nerve and muscle cells.

Reaction Time: Onset of symptoms is often abrupt. Death usually occurs only after long-term, high-level exposure but can also be rapid and acute depending on the compound involved.

Antidotes and Treatments: Stomach pumping can remove some of the lead. The cerebral edema is treated with mannitol or prednisolone. Dimercaprol and calcium disodium edetate are given as antidotes, followed by penicillamine.

Case Histories: Paint chips fell into a victim's coffee cup every morning, slowly poisoning him until he was finally committed to the state mental hospital. Only then was the lead discovered in his body.

Recently, the Los Angeles water system was found to have a substantial quantity of lead form the old lead pipes, and pregnant women were urged to drink bottled water.

Notes: Lead poisoning is one of the most common occupational diseases. Inhalation is the quickest way for the poison to reach the body.

The severe brain damage caused by lead poisoning might just be the thing needed in a story where the villain wants to take control of a relative's estate.

Name: Mercury. *Other*: Quicksilver, mercury vapor, mercury liquid, and mercury salts. There are also over one hundred fifteen known mercury compounds. Some of these are mercuric chloride and the mercurial diuretics such as mersalyl, meralluride, and mercumatilin.

Toxicity: 5.

Form: Mercury is a silvery, mobile liquid that beads up easily. Usually breathed as a vapor, mercury can also be ingested or absorbed by the skin. Ingested metallic mercury is not as toxic as mercuric vapor or salts, since it's not well absorbed into the body. Mercuric salts, such as mercuric chloride, can be fatal even in small doses. An injection of metallic mercury or a mercuric salt solution also causes death.

Mercury boils at 40 degrees C and becomes a deadly vapor. Besides in thermometers, mercury is also found in dental work, where minute amounts are used in tooth fillings. Mercury is also used in explosives, lamps, electrical apparatus, batteries, paints, and felts.

Foods prepared from seed grains treated with organic mercury fungicides have caused poisoning. Eating fish that have ingested mercury discharged from industry can also cause poisoning. This probably won't be fatal unless it builds up, but it's a good distraction for the killer.

Effects and Symptoms: Mercury vapor goes immediately to the brain and lung cells. Acute poisoning from mercury vapor attacks the respiratory system, although chronic poisoning damages the central nervous system.

Soluble mercuric salts, such as mercuric chloride, are toxic to all cells, and high concentrations can damage the kidneys. Symptoms of mercuric salt poisoning occur in the gastrointestinal tract and include liver and kidney damage. Ingesting a mercuric salt will cause a metallic taste, thirst, severe abdominal pain, vomiting, and bloody diarrhea. Mucus shreds and blood may be vomited or voided for several weeks. Between one day and two weeks after ingestion, the kidneys will fail, causing death.

Inhaling a high concentration of mercury vapor causes almost immediate metallic taste, upset stomach, salivation, dyspnea, coughing, fever, nausea, vomiting, and diarrhea. The bronchial tubes start decaying, and pneumonia sets in along with pulmonary edema. Death is also due to ventricular fibrillation. The effects of breathing high concentrations of some volatile compounds can mimic the symptoms of drunkenness, followed by a metallic taste in the mouth, diarrhea, and sometimes fatal convulsions.

Injections of organic mercurial diuretics have caused depressions and heart irregularities as well as anaphylaxis. Injection of organic mercurial compounds also shows up as hives progressing to weeping dermatitis, anemia, diarrhea, liver damage, and renal failure.

Inhalation or skin contact of mercury vapor, dusts, or organic vapors or skin absorption of mercury or mercury compounds has variable symptoms including mental depression, insomnia, instability, weight loss, anorexia, headache, anxiety, hallucinations, pain in extremities, a blue line on the gums, loosening of teeth, and tremors.

More chronic poisonings, either by ingestion or inhalation, will produce variable symptoms, including gingivitis with loosened teeth, excess salivation, increased irritability, and muscle tremors. Rarely will one person exhibit all four symptoms.

Extensive exposure to mercury vapor will cause characteristic psychosis, which can lead to suicide. Because of the tenseness and excitability mercury poisoning causes, the victim will often use sleeping pills. The fictional killer may want to encourage this—a few more pills may not be noticed.

Reaction Time: Inhalation reactions are immediate, while ingestion takes ten to thirty minutes. Chronic poisoning may take several weeks to years.

Antidotes and Treatments: Dimercaprol is administered in addition to symptomatic treatment.

Case Histories: One lab worker, seeking revenge on his immediate superior, placed a mercuric compound in the overhead fluorescent lamps of the supervisor's office. When heated to a vapor, the inhaled mercury fumes slowly drove the man insane. Committed to a hospital and freed of the gas, the victim made a satisfactory recovery. But returning to work, he was once again exposed and the symptoms returned. Not wanting a life of insanity, the supervisor shot himself.

Fatal mercury intoxication occurred abruptly in a middle-aged woman who had worked for twenty years as a dental assistant. The amalgams she regularly handled contained 40 percent mercury compound.

Notes: Straight metallic mercury is not absorbed into the system when ingested, and so is not toxic. Therefore, decorating a birthday cake with mercury balls will not work.

Soluble inorganic mercury salts are the most toxic of the mercury compounds. Organic mercurials were formerly used medicinally.

In the 1800s, the hatting industry was also well known for its use of mercury in shaping felt hats. The Mad Hatter of *Alice in Wonderland* fame was not entirely fictional. Many hatters went insane from breathing mercury fumes.

Name: Phenol. *Other*: Carbolic acid; phenic acid, phenylic acid, phenyl hydroxide; hydroxybenzene, oxybenzene.

Toxicity: 5.

Form: A white, crystalline substance that turns pink or red if not completely pure, phenol has a burning taste and a distinct aromatic, acrid odor; it melts at 41 degrees C. and is soluble in water. It is used in production of fertilizers, paints, paint removers, textiles, drugs, and perfumes. Phenol is also found in the tanning, dye, and, agricultural industries.

Inhalation of mist or vapor; skin absorption of mist, vapor, or liquid; ingestion; and skin or eye contact are all equally deadly. Phenol penetrates deeply and is readily absorbed by all surfaces of the body.

Effects and Symptoms: Phenol has a marked corrosive effect on any tissue. Coming in contact with eyes can cause blindness. Contact with skin, which can occur at low vapor concentrations, causes no immediate pain but a whitening of the exposed area. Later intense burning is followed by gangrene. Symptoms develop rapidly with serious consequences, including paleness, weakness, sweating, high fever, ringing in ears, shock, cyanosis, excitement, frothing of nose and mouth, coma, dark-colored urine, kidney damage, and death.

Ingestion of lethal amounts causes severe burns of mouth and throat; marked abdominal pain; nausea; corrosion of lips, mouth, esophagus, and stomach with possible perforation; cyanosis; muscular weakness; collapse; coma; and death. Tremor, convulsions, and twitching have also occurred.

Concentrated phenol solutions cause swelling of the eye tissue and, in some cases, loss of vision.

If used medicinally for weight loss, the chronic symptoms are skin eruptions, neuritis, liver and kidney damage, and cataract formation.

Reaction Time: Thirty minutes to several hours.

Antidotes and Treatments: In treatment of ingested poison, milk, olive oil, or vegetable oil can be given followed by repeated gastric lavage. Mineral oil and alcohol are contraindicated since they increase the gastric absorption of phenol, but their use is still suggested in some medical texts. Castor oil dissolves phenols and retards their absorption, hastening their removal. This is followed by a saline enema. For skin contact, after washing for fifteen minutes, castor oil is applied as a surface solvent.

Case Histories: An antimildew agent containing pentachlorophenol was used in the last rinsing of diapers and nursery linens until discovery of the fever and "sweating syndrome" it caused. There were two deaths and severe intoxication in nine other infants in a Chicago day care center.

Notes: Danger is greatest in hot weather when loss of body heat is impaired. Phenol can be detected in blood and urine.

Dinitrophenol was formerly used medically as a metabolic stimulator for weight reduction.

Phenol is used in making creosotes (wood or coal tar); phenol derivatives are used in making disinfectants, antiseptics, caustics, germicides, surface anesthetics, and preservatives.

Name: Phosgene. *Other*: Carbon oxychloride, carbonyl chloride.

Toxicity: 6.

Form: Phosgene is a gas, which in low concentrations smells like hay but is very pungent in larger concentrations. Phosgene is inhaled or absorbed through the skin.

While phosgene is used in making dyes and other chemicals, it's better known for its involvement in accidents. If one of several compounds is overheated—including carbon tetrachloride, chloroform, and methylene chloride—phosgene will result. Some solvents, paint removers, and nonflammable dry-cleaning fluids become extremely dangerous in the presence of fire or heat for this reason.

Effects and Symptoms: After inhalation, phosgene reacts with the body's internal moisture to become hydrochloric acid and carbon monoxide. When the gas reaches the lungs, the tissues expand into abscesses and further degeneration continues to occur.

Symptoms start as a burning sensation in the throat, tightness in the chest, dyspnea, cyanosis, followed by severe pulmonary edema and death from respiratory and circulatory failure.

The autopsy shows extended damage to the trachea bronchial tubes, and pneumonia with hemorrhages.

Reaction Time: Symptoms can start any time up to twenty-four hours after exposure. The victim usually dies within thirty-six hours.

Antidotes and Treatments: The victim is removed from further exposure, and if necessary, given artificial respiration. Oxygen is given as soon as possible. Cortisone acetate is given to prevent more injury to the tissues, then the victim is treated for pulmonary edema.

Notes: There may be no immediate warning that a dangerous level of the gas is being breathed.

The symptoms of phosgene poisoning are similar to those of Legionnaire's disease. The Environmental Protection Agency believes phosgene might actually have caused the disease.

Name: Phosphorus (white or yellow). *Other:* Phosphide, phosphine.

Toxicity: 6.

Form: The cubic crystals range from colorless to yellow, darkening on exposure to light. The waxy, fat-soluble and water-insoluble, highly toxic yellow phosphorus ignites in the air to form white fumes and a greenish light. Phosphorus melts at 44 degrees C. Phosphides, used in rat poisons, may release phosphine gas on contact with water.

The red, granular, nonabsorbed form of phosphorus is nontoxic. Red phosphorus can sometimes be contained with the yellow, causing toxic effects. However, white phosphorus turns red in sunlight and is dangerously reactive in air. If combustion occurs in a confined space, it will remove oxygen and render the area unfit to support life.

Inhalation of the vapor, fumes, or mist is most dangerous, but contact with the skin and eyes or ingestion can also cause severe problems or death.

Phosphorus is used in the manufacture of explosives, smoke bombs, pyrotechnics, artificial fertilizers, rodenticides, and gas analysis. Therefore the magician might have it among his bag of tricks and a farmer might find it on his shelf.

Effects and Symptoms: Contact with the chemical causes tissue destruction, attacking the liver, lungs, and eyes. Chronic contact destroys the jaw bone, a condition called "phossy-jaw."

Any exposure above two parts per million in the air will cause a decrease in red blood cells, skin irritation, and nerve and testicular degeneration. This latter is a great clue!

Ingestion of yellow phosphorus is followed within two hours by nausea, vomiting, diarrhea, heart irregularities, and a garlic odor on the breath and excretions. The breath and excreta may appear to smoke. Death in coma or cardiac arrest may occur in the first twenty-four to forty-eight hours.

The victim may appear to improve for one or two days; then the symptoms will return more severe that before — with liver tenderness and enlargement, jaundice, muscle spasms, scanty urine, and hypoglycemia. Death may occur as late as three weeks after poisoning.

Phosphide ingestion causes jaundice, dyspnea, pulmonary edema, and cyanosis. Death occurs within one week.

Yellow phosphorus ignites spontaneously in air. If it dries on skin, it will cause second- and third-degree burns.

When the vapor is inhaled, symptoms show within forty-eight hours, including nausea, vomiting, fatigue, coughing, jaundice, double vision, tremors, uneven gait, numbness in limbs, fall of blood pressure, dyspnea, pulmonary edema, collapse, heart irregularities, convulsions, and coma. Kidney damage can appear after several days. Death may occur anywhere from four days to two weeks after inhalation.

In chronic poisoning, the first sign often is a toothache, followed by swelling of the jaw, and then necrosis of the jaw bone. Other symptoms are weakness, weight loss, loss of appetite, anemia, and spontaneous fractures. Anyone who has dental problems or poor dental hygiene is at risk for the chemical poison.

Autopsy findings include jaundice; necrosis of liver, kidney, and heart; and hemorrhages in the intestinal tract.

Reaction Time: Symptoms begin within two hours and may continue for one to three weeks before death. Death in coma or cardiac arrest may occur in first twenty-four to forty-eight hours, or symptoms improve for one to two days and then return.

Antidotes and Treatments: Remove from exposure. Remove ingested material with gastric lavage or induce emesis. Use copious amounts of water to remove from skin or eyes. Treat pulmonary edema, shock, and give calcium gluconate to maintain serum calcium. Treat liver failure. Treat jaw necrosis by surgical excision of infected bone.

Case Histories: A forty-two-year-old San Francisco physician, J. Milton Bowers, was married three times in fifteen years. All three wives died unexpectedly. The demise of his third wife, in 1885, led to murder charges.

Grief-stricken, he appeared at the grave of Cecelia, to whom he had been married for three years. Ill for two months, she had supposedly died of a liver abscess. But an anonymous letter suggested there was more to Mrs. Bowers's end. At the exhumation, her hastily buried body was found to contain phosphorus. Bowers's brother-in-law, Henry Benhayon, gave evidence against Bowers, and the widower was accused of first-degree murder. During the appeal, Benhayon was found dead, along with three suicide notes and a bottle of potassium cyanide pills. In the notes, Benhayon confessed to killing Mrs. Bowers.

Meanwhile, the police learned that John Dimmig, who had recently purchased a bottle of potassium cyanide, had visited Benhayon shortly before his death. Bowers and Dimmig were indicted for murder, but the jury acquitted them on circumstantial evidence. Bowers returned to his medical practice and married a fourth time.

In a more recent case, Louisa May Merrifield and her husband, Alfred, worked as housekeepers for the elderly Mrs. Sarah Ann Ricketts in Blackpool, England. Mrs. Ricketts complained that she wasn't getting enough to eat. Louisa reportedly boasted to a friend that her employer had left her a sum of money, saying, "She's not dead yet, but she will soon be." An autopsy showed Mrs. Ricketts died of phosphorus poisoning, taken in the form of rat poison, on April 14, 1953. Although no poison was found during a search of the grounds, Louisa was found guilty and hanged.

When a young man committed suicide by taking phosphorus, the ECG changes mimicked those associated with acute myocardial infarction, leading police to believe, at first, that he had had a fatal heart attack.

Notes: Special clothing is used for working with phosphorus. Workers must bathe on leaving work, and dental exams are made frequently.

Phosphorus was at one time used for the production of matches but has long since been replaced due to its chronic toxicity. In the Old West, matches were called lucifers.

A fire, explosion, and disaster hazard emitting highly toxic fumes, phosphorus also ignites spontaneously in air when it mixes with oxidizers.

Name: Tetrachloroethane. *Other:* Acetylene tetrachloride. sym-tetrachloroethane, perchloroethylene, 1,1,2,2-tetrachloroethane.

Toxicity: 6.

Form: A heavy, clear liquid with a chloroformlike odor, tetrachloroethane vaporizes easily. The sweetish odor is detectable with only a small amount. Most toxic when ingested, it can also be harmful when inhaled or absorbed by the skin during prolonged or repeated contact. Used in the manufacture of artificial silk, leather, and pearls, tetrachloroethane is also a solvent, a fumigant, and a drycleaning agent.

Effects and Symptoms: Tetrachloroethane acts like a narcotic and also seriously damages the liver and kidneys.

Eyes, nose, and throat irritation are the first signs. This is followed by vomiting, nausea, drowsiness, an attitude of irresponsibility, and an appearance resembling alcoholic intoxication. When inhaled, the chemical acts as an anesthetic. Symptoms of fatal intoxication also include fullness in the head, mental confusion, headache, and stupefaction. After one to four hours, the victim becomes cyanotic and goes into a coma.

Repeated or prolonged use to skin will cause dermatitis — sometimes blistering the skin.

Upon ingestion, it causes irritation of the gastrointestinal tract, diarrhea, and bloody stools, as well as abdominal pain, anorexia, and jaundice. The jaundice often progresses to delirium, convulsions, coma, and death.

An autopsy reveals a severely atrophied liver, except in the case of immediate death. Then the only traces may be congestion of the lungs, kidneys, brain, and gastrointestinal tract. The corpse can be jaundiced in the case of a slower death.

Reaction Time: The first symptoms can be immediate. Mild symptoms of liver and kidneys damage can continue up to three months, then suddenly become serious and cause death.

Antidotes and Treatments: See carbon tetrachloride.

Notes: A disaster hazard when heated to decomposition, it emits highly toxic chloride fumes. Its popularity as a solvent has decreased because less toxic solvents are replacing it.

Name: Trinitrotluene. *Other*: TNT, a-trinitrotoluol, sym-trinitro-toluol, 2,4,6-trinitroltolune, 1-methyl-2,4,6-trinitrolune, sym-trini-trotoluene, triton.

Toxicity: 6.

Form: TNT is a solid, colorless, or pale yellow crystal. It explodes when heated to 240 degrees C or when shocked. When combined with oxidizers, TNT becomes even more explosive. When heated to decomposition, it emits highly toxic fumes of nitro oxide.

Inhalation and ingestion of TNT are much more toxic than skin absorption, but prolonged contact will cause dermatitis.

Effects and Symptoms: Exposure of a small amount destroys red blood cells.

Sneezing, coughing, and sore throat start the symptoms after dust or vapor inhalation. Skin, hair, and nails of exposed workers may be stained yellow. Other symptoms include jaundice, rash, cyanosis, pallor, muscle pains, nausea, loss of appetite, anemia, and kidney failure resulting in oliguria or anuria. Severe cases show delirium, convulsions, and coma.

The first symptom of chronic poisoning is gastrointestinal disorders followed by cardiac irregularities and renal failure.

Reaction Time: First symptoms begin within several hours, and death can occur within two to four days.

Case Histories: In the 1960s, a young radical making a bomb carelessly forgot to use gloves and absorbed a little too much TNT. He was brought into the emergency room, where he died of kidney failure.

Notes: This was the invention that inspired Alfred Nobel to start his Peace Prize. It is relatively stable for an explosive.

Deaths from aplastic anemia and toxic hepatitis were reported up until the 1950s, after which industry safety practices tightened.

Soap with 10 percent potassium sulfite will turn red in contact with TNT and can be used as an indicator of its removal from the skin.

T E N

STREET DRUGS

This is drugs (butter sizzling in hot pan).
This is your brain on drugs (egg frying).
Any questions?

— Television commercial
for the federal antidrug
program.

The majority of drugs listed in this chapter were originally developed for therapeutic purposes, but now, with the exception of cocaine and morphine, these drugs are used almost solely for abuse. Some popular, easily abused drugs, such as barbiturates and tranquilizers, are still actively used for medical purposes.

Only a tiny amount of pure heroin, cocaine, or PCP is needed to kill, but most street drugs are cut with fillers. The few times pure drugs do get on the street, fatalities occur quickly. Mixtures with PCP and other harmful fillers can also kill. Since most street drugs are cut, if a victim has a known drug habit it would be simple to murder someone by administering pure drug as was done in the recent Clint Eastwood movie *Dead Pool*, where the addict was forced to inhale a synthetic drug combined with the heroin, to make it seem as if the victim had taken an accidental overdose.

The local police or drug dependency center may provide a more current list of street names for cocaine and other addictive drugs.

Name: Ethyl alcohol. *Other*: Ethanol, grain alcohol, methyl carbinol, spirit of wine.
Toxicity: 3.
Form: Ethyl alcohol is found in a liquid or gaseous state and is used as a solvent, an antiseptic, a chemical intermediate, and most popularly as a beverage. In its pure state, ethyl alcohol is a clear, colorless, fragrant liquid with a burning taste. While not considered a true street drug, ethyl alcohol is a drug of abuse; and as an alcoholic beverage, it has myriad forms, including wines, beers, liquors, and liqueurs. Its industrial uses include gaseous vapors, but while industrial vapors can intoxicate by inhalation, most ethyl alcohol is ingested.

When alcohol is denatured by the addition of a substance like methanol (wood alcohol), which makes the liquid unfit for consumption and hazardous to imbibe, its chemical composition is altered and it has several industrial uses.

While it is difficult to think of wine or beer as potentially lethal, most people are familiar with the slow death alcoholics sometimes bring on themselves from liver damage; yet drinking too much alcohol too quickly can bring on hallucinations, psychosis, coma, and death.

The tastes of various alcoholic beverages differ, and so does the proof—the percentage of alcohol (e.g., 100-proof bourbon contains 50 percent alcohol). [The proof can vary from 3.2-proof beer, which is sold in some states for the twilight ages of eighteen to twenty-one and can often be found at supermarkets and convenience stores, to 12-proof beer; 12- to 40-proof wine and fortified wine; 80- to 100-proof vodka, whiskey, gin, rum, and other spirits; and some rums at 151 proof.] To determine the percent of alcohol in a given alcoholic beverage, divide the proof by two. The higher the proof, the quicker the reaction. Liquors can be mixed to hide the taste and strength of the alcohol. A fruit-flavored Mai Tai of 151-proof rum, a Long Island iced tea, or a pitcher of sangria can be deceptive in potency. The maximum, of course, is 200 proof, which is 100-percent alcohol; but absolute alcohol is never found in commercial liquor. Used primarily by industry, it can be added to beverages to enhance the alcohol content.

Depressants, sleeping pills, tranquilizers, and other medications are dangerous when mixed with alcohol. Although the combination is not always fatal, a permanent coma may result. A fictional villain might dupe a victim on medication into drinking an alcoholic beverage laced with additional medication.

Effects and Symptoms: Alcohol depresses the central nervous system and can be used as an anesthetic, but the amount needed is perilously close to a fatal dose. Symptoms vary with the drinker and the amount consumed. The height and weight of the imbiber affects how much alcohol needs to be consumed before inebriation occurs.

Someone mildly inebriated may stumble slightly, experience a relaxation of inhibitions, and react more slowly than usual. Pupils are almost always dilated, even in bright light where they'd normally be constricted, and speech is deliberate. Other symptoms are loquacity, impairment of judgment, and slight drowsiness. This stage is usually considered tipsy.

Someone moderately inebriated shows increased symptoms and slightly slurred speech and may or may not pass a breathalizer test.

Large amounts of consumed alcohol will cause nausea, vomiting, vertigo, excessive sweating, ataxia, acidosis, dyspnea, complete incoordination, blurred or even double vision, circulatory collapse, hallucinations, convulsions, unconsciousness, and coma. Death occurs when the drinker has consumed too much too fast. A quart of bourbon ingested over a twenty-four-hour period would metabolize and be eliminated by the body; the same amount consumed in less than two hours would have deleterious effects.

A commonly overlooked complication of alcohol consumption is hypoglycemia. Alcohol changes to sugar in the body, overloading the system and causing most of the sugar to be eliminated, creating a hypoglycemic condition that could lead to brain damage, convulsions, and death.

In industrial situations, where alcohol vapors are inhaled, irritation of the eyes and nose is present along with drowsiness and headache.

Chronic poisoning symptoms from alcohol ingestion include anorexia, weight loss, diarrhea, cirrhosis of the liver, optic atrophy, mental deterioration, acute alcoholic mania (delirium tremens or DTs), and alcoholic psychosis (Korsakoff's syndrome).

Reaction Time: Fatalities occur when large amounts of alcohol are consumed within an hour or less.

Antidotes and Treatments: In an acute poisoning, the physician will pump the stomach and possibly give some activated charcoal to absorb the alcohol. Sodium bicarbonate is used to neutralize the alcohol.

A drug often given to help alcoholics overcome their addiction is Antabuse. Working on a principle of behavior-modification, the drug causes a drinker to vomit violently if any form of alcohol is imbibed. If enough Antabuse and alcoholic beverage are consumed, the victim might vomit violently enough to die of dehydration or go into convulsions severe enough to kill. Chances are, however, that medical help would be sought before this.

Case Histories: Recently, a depressed overweight woman drank a liter of bourbon within an hour's time and suffered a psychotic episode. Thinking the woman friend who had come to rush her to the hospital was the husband who had just left her, the drunken woman attacked her friend with intent to kill.

Notes: Most ethyl alcohol fatalities occur during the practice of chugalugging at parties, university fraternity rushes, or initiations where the victim tries to consume as much beer, wine, or whiskey in one gulp or one breath as possible. It would be very easy for someone well versed in the psychology of peer pressure to trick an eager pledge or sheltered innocent into downing too much too fast, with fatal results appearing to be a prank.

Alcohol enhances the effects of some anticoagulants, antihistamines, hypnotics, sedatives, tranquilizers, insulin, and antidepressants. Some of these chemical substances, such as barbiturates and carbon monoxide, produce the same "drunken" reaction as alcohol.

Antabuse and alcohol combined could be a good red herring to make victims think they are coming down with stomach flu.

Name: Amphetamine. *Street Name*: Beans, bennies, black beauties, black mollies, copilots, crank, crossroads, crystal, dexies, double-cross, go-fast, hearts, meth, mini-bennies, pep pills, speed, rosas, roses, thrusters, truck drivers, uppers, wake-ups, whites. *Trade Name:* Aktedron, Benzedrine, Elastonon, Orthedrine, Phenamine, Phenedrine.

Toxicity: 5.

Form: Amphetamine is a white powder or a colorless liquid. Most frequently taken orally, in pill or capsule form, it can also be injected when in solution. A form of amphetamine called methamphetamine, but better known on the street as "speed" or "meth," is usually injected intravenously, although speed also comes in oral doses.

Amphetamines once gave women energy when dieting. They

were also used to treat Parkinson's disease and Parkinsonlike symptoms, mental depression, alcohol withdrawal, premenstrual tension, and hyperactivity in children. Now, amphetamines are strictly controlled and seldom prescribed because of serious withdrawal problems and dangerous side effects.

Effects and Symptoms: Amphetamines stimulate muscle and gland cells innervated by the sympathetic nervous system. They can also stimulate the central nervous system. Used as an appetite suppressant for many years, they have since been banned for this use by the FDA. Toxic reactions include insomnia, restlessness, tremors, palpitations, nausea, vomiting, diarrhea, anorexia, delirium, hallucinations, euphoria, nervousness, confusion, irritability, short temper, and depression. More severe reactions include cyanosis, sweating, convulsions, coma, and cerebral hemorrhages. Moderate overdoses are followed by fatigue, mental depression, and a rise in blood pressure.

Chronic users often become paranoid and can develop hyperpyrexia (a sudden high fever) precipitated by strenuous exercise.

Reaction Time: An oral dose will start to take effect between half an hour and an hour, and last between four to twenty-four hours.

Antidotes and Treatments: The patient should be kept quiet in darkened surroundings to avoid overstimulation and possible heart failure. Valium will slow the heart flutter and rapid heartbeat. If the victim is conscious, the stomach might be pumped and other reactions treated symptomatically.

Case Histories: The California Highway Patrol estimated that as many as 5 percent of all truckers are driving under the influence of "go fast" and other amphetamines. In September 1988, the California Highway Patrol cracked a ring of drug runners who were selling amphetamines from their eighteen-wheel trucks to other truckers, using citizen-band radios to communicate.

Notes: Addicts frequently become anorexic, and the appetite can remain suppressed for up to eight weeks after the drugs have been terminated. Amphetamines can be emotionally and physically addicting. If someone has hypertension, an overdose might cause a stroke and coma, leading to death.

Name: Cocaine. *Other*: Methyl benzoylecgonine, benzoylmethylecgonine. *Street Name*: Big C, blanco, blow, C, coca, coke, crack, champagne drug, flake, girl, heaven dust, lady, mujer, nose candy, paradise, perico, polvo, rock, snow, white.

Toxicity: 5.

Form: A colorless to white crystal or a white or off-white powder, cocaine is a poisonous and habit-forming alkaloid. Mixed with baking soda to make a paste, then dried, it becomes rock cocaine or "crack," as it is know on the street. Crack resembles chunks of dirty rock-candy sugar.

Cocaine can be absorbed through the mucous membranes or skin abrasions, or be inhaled, ingested, injected, or smoked in the form of crack. Smoking cocaine through a liquid or mixed with ether is an extremely explosive method called freebasing.

Cocaine is also widely used in nasal surgery as an anesthetic to constrict the blood vessels and prevent excessive bleeding. But before breaking into the local hospital pharmacy, keep in mind that the amount of cocaine used in such a solution is extremely small.

Effects and Symptoms: Cocaine first stimulates, then depresses the central nervous system.

Ingestion is the least toxic means of cocaine poisoning, while intravenous injection is the most potent. Crack and freebasing produce the fastest, most intense highs.

The symptoms in an acute poisoning are hyperactivity, dilated pupils, hallucinations, fast heartbeat, abdominal pain, vomiting, numbness, muscular spasms, in some cases irregular respiration, convulsions, coma, and heart failure. Cocaine affects people differently. Addicts can be hyperactive or lethargic. They are prone to paranoia, weight loss, the sniffles, and reddened noses.

Chronic symptoms include mental deterioration, confusion, hallucinations, psychotic and paranoid behavior, weight loss, severe character changes, and possible perforation of the nasal septum.

Reaction Time: Cocaine can be absorbed immediately from any site. Death usually occurs a few minutes to a half hour after a fatal dose, but may be delayed between one to three hours. Death due to hypersensitivity may also be immediate.

Antidotes and Treatments: If the cocaine has been ingested, activated charcoal and gastric lavage often help to rid the poison from the body. Washing the mucous membranes or skin can also delay absorption if done quickly enough. After injection, a tourniquet or ice pack may help slow absorption. Efforts to remove the drug after thirty minutes are probably useless. Symptoms are treated as they occur.

Case Histories: Probably the best known case of cocaine abuse involves comedian Richard Pryor, who set himself afire while free-basing and was lucky to have survived.

Actor Stacy Keach had trouble with cocaine on the set of *Mike Hammer*. He was then jailed by British customs authorities for possession of coke.

Recently in Southern California, a group of seven-year-olds were rushed to the hospital when one of them shared a hunk of her mother's rock cocaine with the other children thinking it was rock candy. Fortunately, none of the children suffered anything worse than stomach problems.

In Janet Dailey's recent novel, *The Glory Game*, about the fast-paced world of polo, the heroine's brother dies in an explosion caused while freebasing. During the story, Dailey made it seem as if the victim had been murdered before the explosion. He hadn't, but this could always be used as a red herring.

Notes: No matter what its form, cocaine is extremely addictive.

Cocaine is an alkaloid of the coca plant (*Erythroxylon coca*) that grows in the Andes Mountains of South America. For centuries, natives have chewed the leaves and used them to tell fortunes. Mixed with lime and chewed by the Peruvian Indians as early as the sixth century, it was an essential part of the Inca religion. Cocaine was thought to be a gift of Manco Cepac, the royal son of the Sun God.

Fatalities have occurred when ingested plastic bags or rubber balloons containing cocaine being smuggled through customs have broken.

Until 1903, cocaine was part of the "up" in Coca-Cola. Once the company became aware of the dangers of the drug, they substituted caffeine for it.

Of all the drugs in the United States, cocaine is considered the largest producer of illicit income.

Name: Heroin. *Other*: Diacetyl morphine, diamorphine. *Street Name*: H, horse, stuff, smack, junk, TNT, white junk, noise, dujie, snow, harry, shit, crap, Mexican brown, Persian brown, rufus, and dana.

Toxicity: 6.

Form: A poisonous, habit-forming drug, heroin is usually a white, odorless, bitter crystal or crystalline powder; however, the substance varies in color from brown to white, depending on where it has been processed. Mexican heroin tends to be brown, whereas Middle Eastern is white.

There are numerous ways to intake heroin: the drug can be sniffed or snorted by placing it in the nostrils and inhaling it like snuff. It can be smoked when the end of a cigarette is dipped in heroin powder and lighted (this is called ack-ack). In another form, called chasing the dragon or playing the organ, heroin is mixed with barbiturates. The drug is lighted and the smoke inhaled. Subcutaneous injection is called skin popping, while intravenous injection is termed mainlining. Those only occasionally using the drug are said to be chipping, and those who dissolve hydrochloride salt in ether and evaporate the ether to collect the drug as a base are freebasing. Heroin is generally injected into the veins or sometimes just under the skin. It is also sniffed.

Effects and Symptoms: Heroin depresses the central nervous system, creating a feeling of euphoria.

If conscious, the victim of an overdose exhibits such symptoms as pinpoint pupils; slow, shallow respiration; disturbed vision; restlessness; cramps in extremities; cyanosis; weak pulse; very low blood pressure; coma; and death from respiratory paralysis.

Heroin acts more on the respiratory system than morphine and codeine, making it more toxic. Heroin leaves no distinctive signs in the autopsy though it would be recognizable in a blood analysis. Scars, called tracks, are left from frequent injection.

Reaction Time: The victim will feel an immediate "rush" upon intravenous injection. In the case of an overdose, death occurs within a few minutes. If the drug is sniffed or injected subcutaneously, however, death may take anywhere from two to four hours.

Antidotes and Treatments: Naloxone, a drug that binds up addictive drugs, is often given to rid the body of the heroin. Other treatment is symptomatic.

Case Histories: Comic actor John Belushi died of a heroin overdose as he mixed several drugs at once.

Rock singer Janis Joplin died of the side effects of an overdose.

Former Los Angeles County coroner Thomas Noguchi, M.D., believes that these and many other heroin deaths result from unexpectedly pure heroin.

Notes: Derived from the opium poppy, heroin is often processed in Turkey. Currently the Middle East is the world's primary heroin source. Ironically, heroin was invented to cure morphine addiction.

The discoverers didn't realize that heroin's addictive powers were four times stronger than morphine's until their patients became hooked on heroin. As of yet, there is no legal or approved medical use for heroin in the United States, though a few experimental places are using minute amounts to control cancer pain. In British hospices, heroin is an accepted painkiller. Being stronger than morphine, it produces longer, more satisfactory relief from pain with a smaller dose.

Television and movies all too often show street-wise cops moistening the end of their fingers, dipping them into suspicious white powder, and tasting it. Real police know this is nonsense. The amount of fillers in street drugs often makes it impossible to taste the drug. Furthermore, there is always the possibility that the powder contains something lethal and that one taste could be the cop's last. The police never taste substances, but instead wait for the lab to test it chemically. The finger-dipping act is Hollywood's dramatic license.

Name: Opium. *Scientific Name*: Papaver somniferum. *Other*: Gum opium, poppy seed.

Toxicity: 5.

Form: Opium is a gummy substance found in the fruit and juices of the opium poppy. Illicitly smoked or chewed, it can also be drunk. In liquid form, the syrup is usually thick and very sweet. Combined with other drugs, it becomes paregoric, laudanum, or other such medications.The opium itself contains morphine, codeine, thebaine, papaverine, and narcotine.

Effects and Symptoms: Opium depresses the central nervous system.Opium exhibits similar symptoms to heroin and morphine, including nausea; vomiting; constipation; pinpoint pupils; slow, shallow respiration; weak pulse; very low or very high blood pressure; itching of skin; dry mouth; dehydration that may become severe, producing cardiovascular irregularities; loss of sense of time and space; euphoria; elevated pain threshold; imaginary freedom from anxiety; cardiovascular depression; general unresponsiveness; deep coma; respiratory failure; and death. Pupils may dilate as death approaches.

Reaction Time: Fatal reaction occurs two to four hours after ingestion or inhalation.

Antidotes and Treatments: Similar to the treatment of any central nervous system depressant, vital signs must be maintained and monitored. Other treatment is symptomatic.

Case Histories: Critics are still arguing about whether or not "The Rime of the Ancient Mariner" and other works by Samuel Taylor Coleridge were the products of opium dreams. In any case, it is fairly certain that the drug contributed to the poet's death.

Lewis Carroll was said to be high on opium while creating his stories of *Alice*, and the caterpillar's hookah was purportedly filled with the drug.

Agatha Christie's *By the Pricking of My Thumbs* used morphine so one of the characters wouldn't tell what she knew. In *Sad Cypress*, two characters were murdered by morphine ingestion.

In the film *The Last Emperor*, Emperor Pu Yi's wife became an opium addict.

Notes: Cultivated since 200 B.C. for its painkilling and somnambulistic effects, opium was exploited in China and used in Chinatowns all over the world. Victorian-era use of the drug was especially heavy. The opium dens were smoky places where addicts lay about in stupor. These were romanticized or sensationalized in many novels of the time. Laudanum, a form of the drug, was used by Victorian- and Edwardian-era physicians in treating feminine "hysteria" and "the vapors."

Popular reforms in the early twentieth century resulted in the abolition of many patent medicines that contained opium. One of these, called Mother's Helper, turned countless children into opium addicts. Today, most drug abusers prefer its narcotic offspring: morphine, codeine, heroin, Dilaudid, Percodan, and Darvon.

Name: LSD. *Other*: Lysergic acid diethylamide, lysergide. *Street Name*: Acid, blotter acid, California sunshine, haze, microdots, paper acid, purple haze, sunshine, wedges, window panes.

Toxicity: 2.

Form: LSD is usually found as a clear liquid. The drug of the flower children of the sixties and early seventies, LSD brings to mind hippies, sugar cubes, hallucinations, and people throwing themselves off buildings. A synthetic derivative of ergot, it is considered a psychosis-inducing or hallucinogenic drug.

LSD can be injected or ingested. A common method of ingestion was LSD-soaked sugar cubes.

Effects and Symptoms: LSD works on the brain, producing hallucinations. Scientists are not clear how the drug works. Although

LSD's hallucinations can be hazardous, the drug itself is not deadly. The danger arises from what the victim does while hallucinating.

Besides hallucinations, other symptoms may include hyperexcitability, tremors, prolonged mental dissociation, exaggerated reflexes, psychopathic personality disorders, convulsions, and coma. There is an increased homicidal or suicidal risk.

Occurrences have been reported by habitual users of "flashback" reaction years after the last dose has been taken.

Reaction Time: Within twenty minutes after ingestion.

Antidotes and Treatments: Valium usually controls the hyperactivity or convulsions. The coma is treated similar to a barbiturate coma.

Case Histories: LSD flowed like water in Jacqueline Susann's *Once Is Not Enough.* The Beatles' song "Lucy in the Sky with Diamonds" is said to be about LSD, though the Beatles claim the inspiration was a picture done by Julian Lennon.

In the sixties and seventies, many people were the subject of party pranks where LSD-laced punch or spiked drinks sent the victims onto bad trips.

Name: Marijuana. *Scientific Name*: *Cannibis sativa. Other*: Cannabin resin, Indian hemp, Indian canabis, hashish, guaza, marihuana. *Street Name*: Pot, grass, bush, boo, dope, shit, maryjane, and tea.

Toxicity: 3.

Form: A resinous, bitter, greenish-black mass, dried marijuana leaves can be mistaken for oregano. A narcotic analgesic, it is also a sedative. Grown all over the world, it's not unusual to find it in someone's window flower garden or backyard. Traditionally marijuana is baked into brownies or cookies for ingestion. It's possible to see the leaves and stems in the finished cake, although a hungry victim might miss this and eat the brownies anyway.

In addition, hashish is also found as an oil. Hashish is a concentrated resin from the plant's flower that is fried into a brownish-black cake, and is often called "hash."

Both marijuana and hashish are smoked. Bongs, or water pipes, bowls, and pipes are popular variations on the handrolled cigarettes and are sold in a variety of "head shops."

Effects and Symptoms: Marijuana reacts the same as LSD, often producing mild to severe hallucinations. The drug can be habit forming.

Symptoms include widely dilated pupils, reddened eyes,

blurred vision, euphoria, delirium, increased pulse rate, lethargy, distorted depth perception, hallucinations, memory loss, uncontrolled laughter, drowsiness, weakness, stiffness, and loss of consciousness. Bizarre thought patterns may occur and cause schizophrenic episodes. Many psychiatric patients began their mental history with a schizophrenic break brought on by a bad trip. An overdose can cause coma and death. While marijuana is not usually deadly, deaths can result from ingested overdoses or accidents occurring while the victim is under its influence. Heavy, chronic use usually takes its toll in psychological effects as increased anxiety, paranoia, and phobias. Users can also experience lung cancer and emphysema, loss of fertility, and an increase of abnormal sperm cells, which can cause genetic defects in children.

Reaction Time: Marijuana's effects start shortly after smoke is inhaled and lasts from one and a half to four hours. Ingested effects start within two hours but last longer.

Antidotes and Treatments: Treated symptomatically.

Case Histories: A chocoholic UCLA student unknowingly downed six large marijuana-laced brownies and ended up in the hospital in a coma. The physicians projected that had she eaten more, she would probably have died.

Notes: As with DDT, marijuana stays in the body for long periods of time, usually between six weeks and six months. The user's body can still be feeling the drug's effects without the user feeling high or impaired. Like LSD, negative effects can occur years after the initial experience.

Early American settlers called the plant "loco weed," because animals that ate it reacted strangely.

A relatively recent phenomenon involves a practice called wall hits. The user hyperventilates while crouched down and backed up against a wall, then takes a hit from a bong and slowly slides up the wall. Someone else pushes the user's chest in while the user inhales. This has led to collapsed ribs and death.

Cigarettes made from marijuana are called reefers, doobies, numbers, smoke, or joints.

Research shows marijuana's active chemical, THC, has possible uses against epilepsy, glaucoma, and high blood pressure, as well as in preventing the nausea associated with chemotherapy.

Name: Phencyclidine. *Other*: Sernyl. *Street Name*: Angel dust, angel hair, angel mist, animal tranquilizer, busy bee, Cadillac, CJ, crystal,

crystal joints, cyclone, DOA, dust, elephant tranquilizer, embalming fluid, goon, gorilla biscuits, hog, hog dust, horse tranquilizer, jet fuel, Kay Jay, KJ, killer weed, kristal joint, KW, magic mist, mint dew, mint weed, mist, monkey dust, PCP, peace, peace pill, peace weed, pits, rocket fuel, scuffle, Selma, sheets, Sherman, snorts, soma, stardust, supergrass, superkools, superweed, sufer, T, TAC, TIC, tranks, whack, whacky weed, wobble weed, zombie dust.

Toxicity: 6.

Form: PCP is most frequently found as crystals or granules. It's also found as a white powder, liquid, tablet, or leaf mixture, and sometimes contained in a capsule. PCP can be ingested, smoked, or snorted and occasionally is injected intravenously. The powder form is usually the purest. When sold as a leaf mixture, it is often combined with oregano, parsley, or mint and rolled into a joint.

Effects and Symptoms: Although classed as a stimulant, PCP both excites and depresses the central nervous system.

Small doses will cause hyperactivity; rigidity; numbness in fingers and toes; visual, auditory, and tactile illusions; delusions, especially of being God, the devil, or an animal; eyes crossing; lack of coordination; lack of sensation; hypertension; ataxic gait; facial grimaces; anxiety; outright hostility; feeling of inebriation, disorientation; prominent body image distortions; amnesia of the experience; lack of pain perception; delusions of superhuman strength and invulnerability; and wild movements. Stupor or coma follows medium to large doses. In addition, the victim has a high fever, muscle rigidity, increased salivation, and seizures. Large doses also cause high blood pressure, convulsions, decreased or absent reflexes, grand mal seizures, renal failure, apnea, and respiratory arrest, which is a major cause of death.

Reaction Time: Fairly rapid, especially if smoked.

Antidotes and Treatments: Ammonium chloride is sometimes given to help remove the PCP from the central nervous system and to work against the convulsions and respiratory problems. Other symptoms are treated as they occur.

Notes: Symptoms can persist over several days, as the drug excretes itself into the stomach, and is then reabsorbed through the intestines.

As an analgesic and a short-acting intravenous anesthetic agent, PCP was first developed in 1957. The side effects were found to be so toxic in humans that the drug was switched over to veterinary purposes under the trade name of Sernyl or Sernylan.

PCP became popular as a street drug in the late sixties and soon was mixed with THC, LSD, psilocybin, or mescaline. PCP is sprinkled onto parsley or marijuana for recreational smoking. Mixed with amphetamines, methampethamines, benzocaine, or procaine it can be deadly.

Users have been known to snap handcuffs and, unarmed, attack large groups of people or police. The loss of fear leads victims to try such bizarre actions as stopping a train by standing in front of it, grossly mutilating themselves and others, or jumping from windows or cliffs. One woman fried her baby in cooking oil.

E L E V E N

CREATING YOUR OWN POISON

Nervously, he waited in the sterile hospital. Finally the doctor entered. "Well? The flu?" The doctor shook her head. "Something worse. You have radium chloride poisoning." He stared at her. "Where did I—?" "I don't know. There's something else." "Yeah?" "There's no antidote. You have forty-eight hours to live!"

—Paraphrased from the film
remake *D.O.A.*

Put away the chemistry set. The point of this chapter is not to formulate a real poison but to create a fictional one. As part of the research for this book, an attempt was made to identify the poison used by Umberto Eco in his book, *The Name of the Rose*. After exhaustive checking, it was concluded that Signor Eco had made up a poison to suit his own purposes. None could be found historically to match all the characteristics of his poison.

But why make one up?

There are many reasons an author might want to create a fictional poison. A novel set in the future might need something unheard-of to maintain believability. Perhaps an exceptionally fast-acting poison is needed to move the plot, and the antagonist has no acceptable access to those that actually exist. Often an obscure but distinctive poison can highlight the exceptional knowledge of a superior detective. Sometimes, a fictional poison can simply be more fun.

Whatever the reason, if the writer decides to create a fictional poison, two factors should be kept in mind at all times: 1) the writer should use the poison with the authority of someone who has done the research in describing a genuine poison; and 2) the writer should always be consistent. Even if the poison is an extremely bizarre toxin from planet Alpha that reacts differently in each person it contaminates, the poison should be consistent in its inconsistency.

The poison's level of toxicity will depend entirely on what sort of mayhem the writer has in mind. When creating a romantic suspense novel in which the heroine slowly wastes away before an antidote is discovered, a moderately toxic poison will do. On the other hand, if the villain is merely trying to scare off the hero, a mild poison that will injure sooner than kill is more appropriate. Most poison-oriented mystery-story plots, however, depend on slipping something deadly to an unwitting victim.

Creating a fictional poison's name can be tricky. Of course, knowledge of chemistry helps, but anyone conversant with chemicals should be able to find a suitable genuine poison. For stories set in past times, the simpler the name the better. Multisyllabic chemical names should be avoided for stories set prior to the 1930s, since those names were not commonly known then. Even now, people are more likely to use familiar names, such as TNT instead of the cumbersome but chemically correct trinitrotoluene.

Reading a chemical list can help. Study the names and how their syllables are put together, then try breaking them apart and putting them with other syllables. Check to make sure the new arrangement of syllables does not already exist. If it sounds good, use it.

Common chemical prefixes, for example, are bi-, tri-, and di-, and three common chemicals are chlorine, methanol, and acetate. Now, let's put them together. Start with "tri." Add "chlor" from chlorine and attach an "o." Next, hook on the "meth" from methanol, and end it with "ate" from acetate. Voila: Trichloromethate. Keep in mind, however, that too long a name can be a real nuisance to read over and over again.

Knowing how a fictional or genuine poison affects the human body—even though it may rarely be discussed in the story itself—can make it easier to tell how the toxin will react in any given circumstance.

If a poison is supposed to be a combination of real chemicals, then it's important to know how those elements work, since the fictional poison will be an offshoot of them. In the remake of the movie *D.O.A.*, this principle did not work. Radium Chloride, as the name of the film's created poison suggests, would make the concoction part radium and part chloride. Any form of radium will most likely cause radiation sickness, which will usually cause nausea, vomiting, hair loss, dry skin, diarrhea, internal bleeding, infections, incontinence, dehydration, high fever, wasting away, and coma before death. These symptoms can occur anywhere from twenty-four hours to several weeks after ingestion, depending on the amount of exposure. Chloride, as a gas or an acid, would probably cause internal burning, stricture of the throat, inability to swallow, and other problems. Nowhere in the feature film did the victim exhibit any of the above symptoms or indicate that radiation sickness was part of his disease. For many people, that aspect alone destroyed the enjoyment of the movie.

Certain primary effects of poisons also cause secondary symptoms.

Corrosion, or caustic action, is chemical destruction—usually by mere contact—as with an acid such as hydrochloric acid or an alkali such as lye. On humans, the action leaves slow-healing burns that often become permanent scar tissue unless the victim dies. The initial symptom following ingestion is burning pain, then vomiting, uncontrollable diarrhea, and blood-stained feces.

Cytotoxicity means cell poisoning. Translated into symptoms, this is destruction and death of cells—cells in the human body. Red blood cells are affected by carbon monoxide, which starves them of oxygen and leads to tissue anoxia. The body then takes on a blue tinge (cyanosis) from lack of sufficient oxygen, and everything shuts down.

Aniline will also cause cell poisoning, since it will turn the red blood cells into methemoglobin; mercuric salts attack the kidney-tissue cells, causing renal failure; the neurotoxin curare affects the nerve cells, bringing about a total collapse of cell communication and death.

Functional poisons work on the central nervous system, short-circuiting the body's functions as a whole. Depressants, such as barbiturates and alcohol, interfere with the communications between the brain, heart, and lungs, slowing their functions down and bringing about coma, paralysis, and possibly death.

Arsenic and some pesticides work by blocking the production of vital enzymes, which in turn prevent the body from functioning.

The primary effects of each specific poison can also cause secondary effects that relate directly to the vital body functions—respiration, circulation, and excretion. When breathing stops for a period of five minutes or more, the heart usually ceases and the brain cells die. When the kidneys and/or liver fail, the body cannot excrete its wastes (including the poison), and death occurs unless extraordinary measures—kidney dialysis, artificial respiration, or cardiopulmonary resuscitation (CPR)—are taken to keep the patient alive.

After choosing which primary and secondary effects the fictional poison will produce, decide how the poison will be administered; then make everything else reflect that. A solid toxin can be swallowed when mixed with food or dissolved in a liquid. As a liquid, the toxin can also be injected or absorbed through the skin. Many liquids become gases when heated, but a victim must be in a closed environment for most gases to take effect.

There are many means of administering a poison to a victim. Perhaps a rough pin-prick from the sharp, toxin-coated tip of a specially prepared photographer's tripod can open the way for a potent poison to enter the bloodstream. Many spy and jungle stories include the mysterious poisoned blowgun dart, such as in the film *Young Sherlock Holmes*.

While the fiction writer can be truly creative when it comes to inventing symptoms, it is important to remember—or learn—how the body works. Substances that kill quickly after being ingested may not affect the lungs. And inhalation may not cause stomach ulcers, although it might cause nausea and vomiting. Most ingested poisons cause nausea, vomiting, and either constipation or diarrhea, although diarrhea is much more common.

The interior-design maxim of form follows function definitely applies when determining what form a fictional poison should take. If the poison is to be dropped into the victim's scotch and soda, it had better be a tasteless liquid or powder that dissolves easily.

When using a fictional poison that produces an unusual reaction or has unique properties—such as the fava bean, which is toxic only to those of Mediterranean descent, or digitalis, which can kill those with a good heart but will help someone with a bad heart—the writer should set up the reader in advance.

In a true case history, members of a family in Chicago tried to murder their elderly aunt by slipping small amounts of arsenic in the old woman's food. To their amazement and frustration, the aunt grew stronger with each dose. They finally put aside the poison and shot her. An autopsy showed that the aunt was one of those rare people who need arsenic supplements to live. Ironically, the old woman, who had never told anyone about the enzyme-deficiency that forced her to take daily doses of prescribed arsenic, had become depressed. Deciding to commit suicide, she stopped taking her medication. Her family's attempted poisoning only served to strengthen her physical condition.

Most antidotes and treatments for toxins are symptomatic, involving removal of the poison and treating the symptoms as they arise. There are poisons, however, that have specific antidotes or unusual treatments. For example, only a few poisons can be deactivated by chemical reactions with other drugs. Antibiotics kill bacteria, but not viruses, much to the annoyance of those suffering from the common cold who insist on a penicillin shot. Steroids build up and heal tissue but present a multitude of side effects. Analgesics, such as aspirin, kill pain. Aspirin also slows the clotting of blood and in large quantities may assist the victim in bleeding to death.

If the writer chooses to use a fictional poison causing a reaction that mimics natural death, there should be some clue to alert the investigator to foul play. If the victim dies of what appears to be a massive heart attack, there should be some minor clue—such as a strange odor to the breath, a blue tinge to the gumline, clumps of hair falling out, a skin rash, or burned palms—to ultimately call attention to the murder.

Administration and reaction time for the fictional poison are crucial. Skin absorption usually has the slowest reaction time, while inhalation and injection work the quickest. Although intravenous injection works even more rapidly than an intramuscular shot, few untrained people have the expertise to hit the vein. Of course, if the victim happens to be unconscious and hooked up to an IV, there's no problem.

Few poisons kill instantaneously or within a few minutes; even cyanide, which is extremely fast acting, takes about fifteen minutes after ingestion to work. A highly lethal gas that destroys liver cells with one whiff may take several hours before death occurs. A corrosive liquid, such as lye or phenol, may burn the digestive system on the way down, but will take several hours or more to destroy vital organs.

For credibility's sake, the writer should keep realistic reaction times in mind when setting the killer's alibi, planting clues, or saving the victim. Researching poisons, anatomy, physiology, and chemical reactions will add that touch of believability so necessary to a good murder mystery.

Appendix A

Poisons by Methods of Administration

Administration is how the poison gets into your character's system. If your villain has a wonderful way to trap an unsuspecting hero in a closed room, all the poisons under *breathed* might be of use. Membrane absorption is different from skin absorption. Vaginal, rectal, and nasal passages are all membranes, as well as under the tongue. These areas absorb medications and other toxins much more rapidly than skin.

Poison

Breathed

Acid	Isopropanol
Acrylamide	Lead
Aldrin	Malathion
Ammonia	Marijuana
Arsenic	Mercury
Atropine	Methanol
Barium	Nicotine
Benzene	Nitroglycerin
Benzene hexachloride	Nitrous oxide
Bronchial tube relaxers	Opium
Cadmium	Paraquat
Carbon monoxide	Parathion
Carbon tetrachloride	PCP
Chloramine-T	Petroleum distillates
Cocaine	Phenol
Cyanide	Phosgene
DDT	Phosphorus
Dieldrin	Propane
Dimethyl sulfate	Pyrethrum
Endrin	Rotenone
Ether	Stibine
Ethyl alcohol	TEPP
Ethylene chlorohydrin	Tetrachloroethane
Formaldehyde	Toxaphene
Heroin	Trichloroethane
Hydrogen sulfide	Trinitrotoluene
	Turpentine

Injected

Adder	Brown recluse
Amphetamines	Caffeine
Anectine	Calcium
Atropine	Camphor
Barbiturates	Catapres
Beaked sea snake	Cinchophen
Black widow	Cobra
Blue-ringed octopus	Cocaine

Codeine
Cottonmouth
Curare
Digitoxin
Elavil
Epinephrine
Fer-de-lance
Geography cone
Gila monster
Haldol
Heroin
Insulin
Iodine
Ipecac
Jellyfish
Lasix
Lead
Lithium
LSD
Mercury
Monoamine oxidase (MAO)
  inhibitors
Morphine
Nitroglycerin
Norflex
Paral
Pavulon

PCP
Percodan
Permitial
Phenergan
Physostigmine
Portuguese man-of-war
Potassium
Preludin
Procainamide
Procaine
Quaalude
Quinidine
Rattlesnake
Reglan
Scorpionfish
Scorpions
Sea anemones
Sodium
Sodium azide
Stelazine
Stingray
Stonefish
Tagamet
Thorazine
Tubarine
Valium
Warfarin

Membrane absorption

Arsenic
Atropine
Barbiturates
Boric acid
Caffeine
Cocaine
Epinephrine

Haldol
Nitroglycerin
Phenergan
Physostigmine
Potassium permanganate
Thorazine

Skin absorption

Acid
Acrylamide
Aldrin
Aniline
Antimony
Aspirin
Benzene
Benzene hexachloride
Boric acid
Camphor
Cantharidin
Carbon tetrachloride
Cationic detergents
Chloramine-T

Chlordane
Cobra
Cyanide
DDT
Dieldrin
Dimethyl sulfate
Endrin
Ethylene chlorohydrin
Iodine
Isopropanol
Lead
Malathion
Mercury
Methanol

Monkshood
Nicotine
Nitroglycerin
Paraquat
Phenol
Phosgene
Phosphorus

Procaine
Propane
Pyrethrum
Silver nitrate
Sodium azide
Tetrachloroethane
Toxaphene
Trinitrotoluene

Swallowed

Acid
Acrylamide
Akee
Aldomet
Aldrin
Alkalies
Amanita
Ammonia
Amphetamines
Aniline
Antimony
Arsenic
Aspirin
Atophan
Atropine
Baneberry
Barbados nut
Barbiturates
Barium
Belladonna
Benzene
Benzene hexachloride
Betel nut seed
Bivalve shellfish
Black hellebore
Black locust
Bloodroot
Boric acid
Botulism
Bromates
Bryony
Cadmium
Caffeine
Calcium
Camphor
Cantharidin
Carbon tetrachloride
Cassava
Castor bean
Catapres
Cationic detergents
Celandine

Chloral hydrate
Chloramine-T
Chlordane
Cinchona bark
Cinchophen
Codeine
Colocynth
Columbine
Corn cockle
Cortinarius
Croton oil
Cuckoopint
Cyanide
Dalmane
Daphne
DDT
Death camas
Depakene
Dieldrin
Digitoxin
Dilantin
Dimethyl sulfate
Dog mercury
Dyphylline
Elavil
Elderberry
Endrin
Epinephrine
Ergot
Ether
Ethinamate
Ethyl alcohol
Ethylene chlorohydrin
False hellebore
Fly agaric
Fool's parsley
Formaldehyde
Foxglove
Galerinas
Grounsel
Gyromitra

Hemlock
Horse chestnut
Hydrangea
Inderal
Indian tobacco
Inocybe
Insulin
Iodine
Ipecac
Isopropanol
Jimsonweed
Larkspur
Lasix
Lead
Librax
Lily of the valley
Lithium
Lomotil
LSD
Malathion
Mandrake
Marijuana
Meadow saffron
Mercury
Methanol
Minipress
Monkshood
Monoamine oxidase (MAO)
  inhibitors
Moonseed
Morphine
Mountain laurel
Naphthalene
Narcissus
Nicotine
Nitroglycerin
Norflex
Norpramine
Oleander
Opium
Panther mushroom
Paral
Paraquat
Parathion
Paternoster pea
PCP
Percodan
Permitial

Haldol
Petroleum distillates
Phenergan
Phenol
Phosphorus
Physostigmine
Poinsettia
Pokeweed
Potassium
Potassium permanganate
Potato
Preludin
Privet
Pufferfish
Pyrethrum
Quaalude
Quinidine
Reglan
Rhododendron
Rhubarb
Savin
Silver nitrate
Sinequan
Sodium
Sodium azide
Sodium fluoroacetate
Sodium thiocyanate
Spindle tree
Star of Bethlehem
Stelazine
Strychnine
Tagamet
Tanghin
Tansy
TEPP
Tetrachloroethane
Thorazine
Thyrolar
Toxaphene
Trichloroethane
Trinitrotoluene
Turpentine
Tylenol
Vacor
Valium
Warfarin
Water hemlock
White snakeroot
Yellow jasmine
Yew

Appendix B

Poisons by Form

A poison can be found in almost as many different forms as there are poisons. Of particular interest to the mystery writer might be those that are colorless, or the poison that has a pleasant odor.

Form	Poison
amber liquid	Chlordane
aromatic liquid	Paral
batteries	Alkalies
bluish grey metal	Lead
bluish white metal	Cadmium
bluish black powder	Iodine
brown liquid	Nicotine Parathion
brown powder	Heroin
clear	Tetrachloroethane
clear liquid	Insulin LSD
colorless	TEPP
colorless crystal powder	Strychnine
colorless gas	Formaldehyde
colorless liquid	Amphetamines Benzene Carbon tetrachloride Chloral hydrate Chlordane Codeine Depakene Dimethyl sulfate Ethylene chlorohydrin Procaine Trichloroethane
colorless powder	Morphine
colorless solid	Trinitrotoluene
creams	Cationic detergents
crystal	Acrylamide Aldrin Phosphorus
dust	Aldrin Dieldrin
fish	Bivalve shellfish

	Blue-ringed octopus
	Geography cone
	Jellyfish
	Portuguese man-of-war
	Pufferfish
	Scorpionfish
	Sea anemones
	Stingray
	Stonefish
fungus	Ergot
gas	Acid
	Ammonia
	Aniline
	Arsenic
	Atropine
	Carbon monoxide
	Cyanide
	Hydrogen sulfide
	Isopropanol
	Nitrous oxide
	Parathion
	Phosgene
	Propane
	Stibine
gel	Procaine
germ	Botulism
grey metal	Arsenic
gum	Opium
insect	Scorpions
liquid	Acid
	Adder
	Aldomet
	Ammonia
	Aniline
	Atropine
	Beaked sea snake
	Cobra
	Cottonmouth
	Cyanide
	Digitoxin
	Ether
	Ethyl alcohol
	Fer-de-lance
	Gila monster
	Haldol
	Ipecac
	Isopropanol
	Lasix
	Lomotil
	Methanol
	Norpramine

Opium
Permitial
Petroleum distillates
Phenergan
Propane
Rattlesnake
Silver nitrate
Stelazine
TEPP
Tetrachloroethane
Turpentine

mushroom	Amanita
	Cortinarius
	Fly agaric
	Galerinas
	Gyromitra
	Inocybe
	Panther mushroom
odorless	Aldrin
	Anectine
	Chlordane
	Codeine
	Dieldrin
	Rotenone
	Sodium fluoroacetate
	TEPP
odorless liquid	Dimethyl sulfate
pill	Aldomet
	Amphetamines
	Aspirin
	Atropine
	Dalmane
	Digitoxin
	Dyphylline
	Haldol
	Lasix
	Librax
	Lomotil
	Norpramine
	Persantine
	Phenergan
	Stelazine
	Thorazine
	Thyrolar
plant	Akee
	Baneberry
	Barbados nut
	Belladonna
	Betel nut seed
	Black hellebore
	Black locust
	Bloodroot

Bryony
Cassava
Castor bean
Celandine
Cinchona bark
Colocynth
Columbine
Corn cockle
Croton oil
Cuckoopint
Curare
Daphne
Death camas
Dog mercury
Elderberry
False hellebore
Fool's parsley
Foxglove
Grounsel
Hemlock
Horse chestnut
Hydrangea
Indian tobacco
Jimsonweed
Larkspur
Lily of the valley
Mandrake
Marijuana
Meadow saffron
Monkshood
Moonseed
Mountain laurel
Narcissus
Oleander
Paternoster pea
Poinsettia
Pokeweed
Potato
Privet
Rhododendron
Rhubarb
Savin
Spindle tree
Star of Bethlehem
Tanghin
Tansy
Water hemlock
White snakeroot
Yellow jasmine
Yew

pleasant odor	Benzene
	Camphor
powder	Aniline

	Benzene hexachloride
	Chlordane
	Dieldrin
	Malathion
	Parathion
	Pyrethrum
red capsules	Chloral hydrate
salt	Atropine
	Barium
	Silver nitrate
	Sodium azide
	Tubarine
silvery liquid	Mercury
silvery white metal	Antimony
soaps	Alkalies
solid	Chloramine-T
solution	Benzene hexachloride
	Bromates
	Cationic detergents
	Chloramine-T
	Chlordane
	Formaldehyde
	Iodine
	Malathion
	Paraquat
spider	Black widow
	Brown recluse
spray	Aldrin
	Dieldrin
	Malathion
strong odor	Formaldehyde
suppository	Phenergan
	Thorazine
syrup	Dyphylline
	Thorazine
tasteless	Cantharidin
	Sodium fluoroacetate
vapor	Ethyl alcohol
violet crystal	Potassium permanganate
waxy yellow solid	Toxaphene
white	Aldrin
white crystal	Benzene hexachloride
	Dieldrin
	Phenol
	Rotenone
white crystalline powder	Catapres
white crystalline solid	Minipress

	Naphthalene
white powder	Amphetamines
	Anectine
	Antimony
	Arsenic
	Aspirin
	Cantharidin
	Cocaine
	DDT
	Heroin
	Morphine
	PCP
	Preludin
	Sodium fluoroacetate
	Tylenol
white solid	Boric acid
	Cyanide
	Endrin
yellow liquid	Nicotine

Appendix C

Poisons by the Symptoms They Cause

The vast majority of poisons cause several symptoms in varying degrees of severity. Some poisons will generate some twitching; quite a few cause full convulsions. Some poisons will cause violent vomiting as opposed to just vomiting. The severity of the symptom is not listed so be sure to read the full information in the main text. Not all symptoms are listed for each poison. Poisons are listed by the most major symptoms. Organization of this section is by body organs and organ function.

Symptoms	Poison
BLOOD	
Anemia	Dilantin; Naphthalene; Rattlesnake; Trinitrotoluene
Bleeding - Slow Clotting Time	Aspirin; Atophan; Depakene; Warfarin
Blood In Urine	See Urine
Blood In Vomit	See Gastrointestinal—Vomit
Hemoptysis	See Lungs—Coughing Up Blood
Hemorrhage	Adder; Atophan; Aspirin; Castor bean; Chlordane; Cinchona bark; Cottonmouth; Cuckoopint; Depakene; Fer-de-lance; Isopropanol; Paternoster pea; Potassium permanganate; Rhubarb; Savin; Warfarin; Vacor
Low Red Blood Count	Carbon monoxide; Ethinamate; Warfarin
BODY TEMPERATURES	
Chills	Adder; Black widow; Bronchial tube relaxers; Brown recluse; Cadmium; Epinephrine; Insulin; Monkshood
Clammy Skin	Arsenic; Bloodroot; Lily of the valley
Hyperthermia or Fever	Adder; Aldomet; Aspirin; Atropine; Belladonna; Bronchial tube relaxers; Brown recluse; Chloral hydrate; Cinchophen; Corn cockle; Dilantin; Epinephrine; Iodine; Lasix; Lomotil; Mercury; Monoamine oxidase (MAO) inhibitors; Naphthalene; Paraquat; PCP; Permitial; Phenol; Portuguese man-of-war; Scorpionfish; Spindle tree; Stelazine
Hypothermia	Chloral hydrate; Norpramine; Permitial; Yellow jasmine
Sweating	Acrylamide; Adder; Amphetamines; Black widow; Bronchial tube relaxers;

Cadmium; Caffeine; Dieldrin; Ethyl
alcohol; Fly agaric; Inocybe; Insulin;
Isopropanol; Monkshood; Oleander;
Panther mushroom; Phenol; Sodium;
Stingray; TEPP

BRAIN

Cerebral Edema	Aspirin; Dimethyl sulfate; Methanol; Nitrous oxide; Potato
Coma	Akcc; Aldrin; Amphetamines; Aniline; Antimony; Arsenic; Aspirin; Atropine; Barbiturates; Belladonna; Boric acid; Bromates; Bryony; Cantharidin; Cassava; Castor bean; Catapres; Cationic detergents; Celedine; Chloral hydrate; Cinchona bark; Cinchophen; Cocaine; Codeine; Columbine; Corn cockle; Cortinarius; Croton oil; Cuckoopint; Daphne; Death camas; Dieldrin; Elavil; Epinephrine; Ergot; Ethyl alcohol; Gyromitra; Haldol; Heroin; Hydrogen sulfide; Inderal; Indian tobacco; Insulin; Isopropanol; Jimsonweed; Lead; Lithium; Lomotil; LSD; Mandrake; Marijuana; Morphine; Nicotine; Nitroglycerin; Norpramine; Opium; Panther mushroom; Paral; Paternoster pea; PCP; Percodan; Permitial; Petroleum distillates; Phenol; Potato; Procaine; Rhododendron; Savin; Silver nitrate; Sinequan; Sodium fluoroacetate; Stelazine; Tetrachloroethane; Thorazine; Toxaphene; Vacor; Valium; Yew
Headache	Acid; Aldomet; Aldrin; Aniline; Arsenic; Barbiturates; Benzene; Bronchial tube relaxers; Cadmium; Camphor; Carbon monoxide; Colocynth; Corn cockle; DDT; Dieldrin; Dyphylline; Elderberry; Ergot; Ethylene chlorohydrin; Foxglove; Galerinas; Hydrogen sulfide; Inderal; Jimsonweed; Lasix; Lily of the valley; Malathion; Methanol; Minipress; Naphthalene; Nicotine; Nitroglycerin; Nitrous oxide; Norflex; Panther mushroom; Parathion; Persantine; Potato; Preludin; Quinidine; Stibine; Tagamet; Tanghin; TEPP; Tetrachloroethane; Thyrolar; Trichloroethane; Yellow jasmine

CARDIOVASCULAR

Bradycardia/Slow heartbeat/ Slow pulse	Black locust; Bloodroot; Carbon tetrachloride; Catapres; Codeine; Curare; Dog Mercury; False hellebore; Fly agaric; Foxglove; Inderal; Larkspur; Lily of the valley; Monkshood; Morphine; Panther mushroom; Physostigmine; Rhododendron; Tanghin; Yellow jasmine
Cardiac Arrest	Air Emboli; Bloodroot; Calcium; Catapres; Cocaine; Elavil; Ergot; Flexeril; Insulin; Norflex; Oleander; Percodan; Potassium; Sodium; Stelazine; Tanghin; Valium
Cardiac Arrhythmias	Barbiturates; Black hellebore; Bloodroot; Caffeine; Dilantin; Elavil; Epinephrine; Ether; Formaldehyde; Foxglove; Inocybe; Ipecac; Nitrous oxide; Norpramine; Phosphorus; Portuguese man-of-war; Sodium fluoroacetate; Stingray; Tanghin; Tylenol
Chest Pain	Cadmium; Carbon monoxide; Ergot; Foxglove; Jellyfish; Monkshood; Portuguese man-of-war; Sea anemone; Tanghin; TEPP; Turpentine; Vacor
Hypertension/ High blood pressure	Amphetamines; Bronchial tube relaxers; Cadmium; Demerol; Monoamine oxidase (MAO) inhibitors; PCP; Preludin; Scorpions; Sinequan; Thyrolar; Yellow jasmine
Hypotension/ Low blood pressure	Acid; Alkalies; Aniline; Anaphylaxis; Arsenic; Barbiturates; Boric acid; Bromates; Cantharidin; Carbon tetrachloride; Catapres; Cationic detergents; Chloral hydrate; Cobra; Curare (*dramatic drop*); Cyanide; Dyphylline; Elavil; Ethylene chlorohydrin; False hellebore; Fly agaric; Haldol; Heroin; Inderal; Insulin; Ipecac; Lasix; Monkshood; Monoamine oxidase (MAO) inhibitors; Nitroglycerin; Norpramine; Opium; Panther mushroom; Paral; Percodan; Permitial; Phenergan; Physostigmine; Procainamide; Procaine; Quinidine; Rhododendron; Scorpions; Sodium azide; Sodium thiocyanate; Stelazine; Stingray; Tagamet; TEPP; Thorazine; Trichloroethane; Turarine; Tylenol; Vacor
Loud Heart Beat	Belladonna; Bronchial tube relaxers;

	Minipress; Thyrolar
Tachycardia or Rapid Heart Beat/Rapid Pulse	Acid; Amphetamines; Atropine; Baneberry; Belladonna; Bromates; Caffeine; Camphor; Cocaine; Cortinarius; Croton oil; Cyanide; Digitoxin; Dyphylline; Elderberry; Epinephrine; Fool's parsley; Foxglove; Halcion; Haldol; Hemlock; Insulin; Ipecac; Marijuana; Minipress; Monoamine oxidase (MAO) inhibitors; Morphine; Nicotine; Norflex; Paral; Paraquat; Paternoster pea; Permitial; Phenergan; Sinequan; Tanghin; Tansy; Thorazine; Turpentine
Weak, thready or irregular pulse	Ammonia; Black locust; Fool's parsley; Hemlock; Heroin; Inocybe; Jimsonweed; Monkshood; Procainamide; Opium; Stibine; Tansy; Turpentine

COLLAPSE

	Adder; Ammonia; Anaphylaxis; Bromates; Cantharidin; Castor bean; Cationic detergents; Chloramine-T; Cinchona bark; Cottonmouth; Ethylene chlorohydrin; Formaldehyde; Haldol; Indian tobacco; Ipecac; Lead; Narcissus; Nicotine; Nitroglycerin; Privet; Procaine; Silver nitrate; Stingray; Vacor

CONVULSIONS/SEIZURES

	Akee; Aldrin; Amphetamines; Aniline; Arsenic; Aspirin; Atropine; Barium; Belladonna; Benzene; Benzene hexachloride; Betel nut seed; Boric acid; Bromates; Bronchial tube relaxers; Bryony; Caffeine; Calcium; Camphor; Cassava; Castor bean; Cationic detergents; Cinchophen; Cobra; Cocaine; Columbine; Cortinarius; Cuckoopint; Cyanide; Daphne; DDT; Dieldrin; Dyphylline; Elavil; Elderberry; Endrin; Epinephrine; Ethyl alcohol; Fool's parsley; Grounsel; Gyromitra; Hydrangea; Inderal; Indian tobacco; Ipecac; Jimsonweed; Lead; Lomotil; LSD; Meadow saffron; Monkshood; Monoamine oxidase (MAO) inhibitors; Moonseed; Mountain laurel; Narcissus; Nicotine; Norpramine; Panther mushroom; Parathion; Paternoster pea; PCP; Permitial; Phenergan;

Physostigmine; Pokeweed; Potato;
Procainamide; Procaine; Pyrethrum;
Quaalude; Ritalin; Rhododendron;
Rotenone; Scorpionfish; Scorpions; Silver
nitrate; Sodium fluoroacetate; Sodium
thiocyanate; Spindle tree; Stelazine;
Stingray; Stonefish; Strychnine; Tansy;
TEPP; Thorazine; Toxaphene;
Turpentine; Water hemlock; Yellow
jasmine; Yew

DEHYDRATION/EDEMA

Dehydration	Amanita; Antimony; Aspirin; Laxatives and purgatives; Opium
Edema	*See Cranial/Pulmonary/Skin — Swelling*

DIABETES OR BLOOD SUGAR

Hyperglycemia	Lasix; Vacor
Hypoglycemia	Akee; Amanita; Dilantin; Inderal; Insulin; Phosphorus

DROWSINESS

Aldomet; Barbados nut; Barbiturates;
Boric acid; Castor bean; Catapres; Chloral
hydrate; Codeine; Dalmane; Demerol;
Dimethyl sulfate; Dog mercury; Elavil;
Flexeril; Haldol; Hydrogen sulfide;
Jimsonweed; Librax; Librium; Mandrake;
Marijuana; Minipress; Morphine; Norflex;
Norpramine; Percodan; Permitial;
Phenergan; Reglan; Sinequan; Stelazine;
Talwin; Tetrachloroethane; Thorazine;
Tylenol; Valium

DRUG INDUCED ANOREXIA

Amphetamines; Arsenic; Boric acid;
Cinchophen; Cocaine; Endrin; Mercury;
Permitial; Preludin; TEPP;
Tetrachloroethane; Thyrolar;
Trinitrotoluene

DRUNKENNESS

Acrylamide; Cassava; Ethyl alcohol;
Isopropanol; Chloral hydrate; PCP;
Tetrachloroethane

EMOTIONAL ABERRATIONS

Aggression	Atropine; Belladonna; PCP; Preludin

Anxiety	Amphetamines; Barium; Bronchial tube relaxers; Camphor; Carbon monoxide; Doridan; Dyphylline; Mercury; Minipress; PCP; Phenergan; Potassium; Sodium fluoroacetate; Thyrolar; Water hemlock; Yellow jasmine
Apathy	Cobra; Lithium
Confusion	Amphetamines; Aniline; Atropine; Barbiturates; Carbon monoxide; Carbon tetrachloride; Chloral hydrate; DDT; Dilantin; Endrin; Inderal; Librax; Lithium; Nicotine; Opium; Phenergan; Preludin; Sodium thiocyanate; Tagamet; Tylenol
Delirium	Atropine; Benzene; Brown recluse; Cinchophen; Corn cockle; Ethylene chlorohydrin; Foxglove; Henbane; Horse chestnut; Inderal; Iodine; Jimsonweed; Lead; Meadow saffron; Panther mushroom; Tagamet; Tanghin; Tetrachloroethane; Vacor; White snakeroot
Depression	Amphetamines; Flagyl; Lomotil; Mountain laurel; Reglan
Disorientation	Camphor; Propane
Euphoria	Amphetamines; Benzene; Halcion; Heroin; LSD; Marijuana; Nitrous Oxide; Opium; Preludin
Excitement	Benzene; Boric acid; Cinchona bark; Codeine; Corn cockle; Cottonmouth; DDT; Dieldrin; Endrin; Epinephrine; Ethylene chlorohydrin; Insulin; Jimsonweed; LSD; Morphine; Naphthalene; Phenol; Procaine; Pyrethrum; Sinequan; Stelazine; Valium; Yellow jasmine; Yew
Hallucinations	Amphetamines; Atropine; Belladonna; Betel nut seed; Bronchial tube relaxers; Cocaine; Doriden; Elavil; Ethyl alcohol; Haldol; Inderal; Lily of the valley; LSD; Marijuana; Mercury; PCP; Preludin; Sinequan; Toxaphene; Valium
Hyperactivity	Cocaine; Cottonmouth; PCP; Preludin; Thyrolar
Irritability	Barbiturates; Carbon monoxide; Cottonmouth; Dieldrin; Lily of the valley; Propane

Lethargy	Aniline; Aspirin; Bromates; Cobra; Doridan; Lithium; Lomotil; Minipress; Potato; Reglan; Vacor
Nightmares	Aldomet; Phenergan
Psychosis	Atropine; Camphor; Cocaine; Depakene; Dilantin; Ergot; Ethyl alcohol; Epinephrine; Halcion; Haldol; LSD; Marijuana; Mercury; Preludin; Sodium thiocyanate
Restlessness	Amphetamines; Aspirin; Black widow; Heroin; Horse chestnut; Lomotil; Lorfan; LSD; Nymorphan; Preludin; Reglan; Water hemlock

EYES

Bulging	Thyrolar
Contracted/pinpoint pupils	Morphine; Opium; Physostigmine; TEPP
Mydriasis/Dilation	Atropine; Belladonna; Bloodroot; Cocaine; Cuckoopint; Doridan; Elavil; Epinephrine; Ethyl alcohol; Heroin; Horse chestnut; Indian tobacco; Jimsonweed; Lily of the valley; Lomotil; Marijuana; Norflex; Norpramine; Parathion; Phenergan; Tansy; Water hemlock; Yellow jasmine; Yew
Red	Dimethyl sulfate; Hydrogen sulfide; Marijuana
Tearing	Dimethyl sulfate; Fly agaric; Formaldehyde; Malathion; Mountain laurel; Panther mushroom; Rhododendron; TEPP

FAINTING

	Alkalies; Cyanide; Librax; Physostigmine; Thorazine; Trichloroethane

FATIGUE

	Boric acid; Endrin; Insulin; Ipecac; Methanol; Monoamine oxidase (MAO) inhibitors; Potato; Preludin; Tagamet; Vacor

GASTROINTESTINAL TRACT

Abdominal or stomach pain	Alkalies; Amanita; Arsenic; Ammonia; Aspirin; Baneberry; Barium; Bloodroot; Bromates; Cantharidin; Carbon tetrachloride; Cassava; Cinchophen;

Cocaine; Cuckoopint; Colocynth; Corn cockle; Daphne; Fool's parsley; Formaldehyde; Hydrangea; Iodine; Isopropanol; Jellyfish; Lead; Lily of the valley; Lomotil; Meadow saffron; Mercury; Methanol; Minipress; Mountain laurel; Paraquat; Parathion; Portuguese man-of-war; Potato; Privet; Rhubarb; Rotenone; Scorpions; Spindle tree; Stibine; Stingray; Tetrachloroethane; Thyrolar; Turpentine; Vacor; Water hemlock; Yew

Black Stool	Lead
Bloating	Barbados nut
Blood in Vomit	*See Vomit*
Bloody Diarrhea	*Also See Diarrhea*; Acid; Amanita; Antimony; Baneberry; Colocynth; Croton oil; Daphne; Fool's parsley; Meadow saffron; Mercury; Moonseed; Oleander; Tetrachloroethane; Warfarin
Constipation	Opium; Percodan; Vacor; White snakeroot
Cramps	Arsenic; Castor bean; Colocynth; Elderberry; Heroin; Panther mushroom; Pokeweed; Scorpions; Stingray; TEPP
Diarrhea	*See Bloody Diarrhea*; Alkalies; Amphetamines; Arsenic; Barbados nut; Barium; Benzene hexachloride; Betel nut seed; Black hellebore; Boric acid; Bromates; Bryony; Cadmium; Cantharidin; Cinchophen; Colombine; Digitoxin; False hellebore; Fly agaric; Formaldehyde; Foxglove; Gyromitra; Hemlock; Horse chestnut; Inderal; Iodine; Lead; Malathion; Mandrake; Minipress; Naphthalene; Nicotine; Panther mushroom; Paraquat; Parathion; Paternoster Pea; Phosphorus; Poinsettia; Pokeweed; Potato; Privet; Pyrethrum; Quinidine; Rhododendron; Silver nitrate; Spindle tree; Tagamet; Tanghin; TEPP; Thyrolar; Turpentine; Water hemlock; Yew
Difficulty Swallowing	Beaked sea snake; Fer-de-lance; Fool's parsley; Meadow saffron; Pavulon; Portuguese man-of-war; Tubarine
Hunger	Insulin

Loss of Appetite	Preludin
Loss of Bowel Control	Air emboli; Parathion; Physostigmine; Reglan; TEPP
Nausea	Akee; Aldrin; Amanita; Amphetamines; Antimony; Arsenic; Baneberry; Barium; Benzene; Bivalve shellfish; Black locust; Black widow; Botulism; Brown recluse; Bryony; Cadmium; Camphor; Cantharidin; Carbon monoxide; Carbon tetrachloride; Cassava; Castor bean; Catapres; Cationic detergents; Celandine; Cinchona bark; Cobra; Columbine; Corn cockle; Cortinarius; Cuckoopint; Daphne; Depakene; Dieldrin; Digitoxin; Dyphylline; Elavil; Elderberry; Endrin; Epinephrine; Ergot; Ethyl alcohol; Ethylene chlorohydrin; False hellebore; Fly agaric; Foxglove; Galerinas; Gila monster; Grounsel; Halcion; Hydrangea; Hydrogen sulfide; Inderal; Indian tobacco; Insulin; Ipecac; Isopropanol; Larkspur; Lasix; Lily of the valley; Malathion; Mercury; Methanol; Minipress; Monkshood; Monoamine oxidase (MAO) inhibitors; Morphine; Mountain laurel; Naphthalene; Narcissus; Nicotine; Norflex; Opium; Panther mushroom; Parathion; Paternoster pea; Percodan; Permitial; Persantine; Phosphorus; Pokeweed; Privet; Pyrethrum; Quaalude; Quinidine; Rattlesnake; Reglan; Rhododendron; Rhubarb; Ritalin; Rotenone; Savin; Stibine; Stingray; Talwin; Tanghin; Tetrachloroethane; Trichloroethane; Trinitrotoluene; Turpentine; Tylenol; Vacor; Water hemlock; White snakeroot; Yew
Vomiting	Acid; Akee; Aldrin; Alkalies; Amanita; Ammonia; Amphetamines; Antimony; Arsenic; Atophan; Baneberry; Barbados nut; Barium; Benzene; Benzene hexachloride; Betel nut seed; Bivalve shellfish; Black hellebore; Black locust; Black widow; Bloodroot; Blue-ringed octopus; Boric acid; Bromates; Bronchial tube relaxers; Brown recluse; Bryony; Cadmium; Caffeine; Camphor; Cantharidin; Carbon tetrachloride; Cassava; Castor bean; Celandine;

Cinchona bark; Cinchophen; Cocaine;
Columbine; Cortinarius; Croton oil;
Cuckoopint; Daphne; DDT; Dieldrin;
Digitoxin; Dog mercury; Dyphylline;
Elderberry; Epinephrine; Ergot; Ethyl
alcohol; Ethylene chlorohydrin; False
hellebore; Formaldehyde; Foxglove;
Grounsel; Gyromitra; Halcion; Hemlock;
Horse chestnut; Inderal; Indian tobacco;
Insulin; Iodine; Ipecac; Larkspur; Lasix;
Lead; Lily of the valley; Malathion;
Mandrake; Meadow saffron; Mercury;
Minipress; Monkshood; Monoamine
oxidase (MAO) inhibitors; Mountain
laurel; Naphthalene; Narcissus; Nicotine;
Nitroglyccrine; Norflex; Oleander;
Opium; Paraquat; Percodan; Petroleum
distillates; Phosphorus; Physostigmine;
Poinsettia; Pokeweed; Potato; Privet;
Pyrethrum; Quaalude; Rattlesnake;
Rhododendron; Rhubarb; Ritalin;
Rotenone; Savin; Silver nitrate; Sodium
fluoroacetate; Spindle tree; Stingray;
Tanghin; TEPP; Toxaphene; Turpentine;
Tylenol; Vacor; Water hemlock; White
snakeroot; Yew

Vomiting blood	Adder; Alkalies; Isopropanol

GENITOURINARY

Lactation	Permitial
Membrane Swelling	Potassium permanganate
Menstrual Upset	Librax
Sexual dysfunction	Aldomet; Elavil
Testicular degeneration	Phosphorus

HAIR

Facial Hair	Clonopin; Dilantin
Loss	Arsenic; Boric acid; Depakene; Minipress

IMPAIRED MOTOR SKILLS

Absent reflexes	Acrylamide; Chloral hydrate; PCP; TEPP
Ataxia	Acrylamide; Aspirin; Benzene; Caffeine; Chloral hydrate; Codeine; Ethyl alcohol; Haldol; Librax; Marijuana; Minipress; Monoamine oxidase (MAO) inhibitors; Morphine; Panther mushroom; PCP; Percodan; Permitial; Phenergan; Phosphorus; Preludin; Pyrethrum;

	Rotenone; Sodium; Tetrachloroethane; Vacor; Valium; Yellow jasmine
Difficulty speaking	Blue-ringed octopus; Codeine; Curare; Chloral hydrate; Ethyl alcohol; Haldol; Lithium; Marijuana; Pufferfish; Thorazine; Yellow jasmine
Disorientation	*See Emotional*
Dizziness/giddiness/vertigo	Acid; Aldomet; Aldrin; Amphetamines; Aniline; Arsenic; Aspirin; Baneberry; Barbados nut; Barbiturates; Benzene; Bloodroot; Bronchial tube relaxers; Camphor; Carbon tetrachloride; Chloral hydrate; Codeine; Cortinarius; Dieldrin; Dilantin; Elderberry; Ethylene chlorohydrin; Fly agaric; Geography cone; Gila monster; Hydrogen sulfide; Jimsonweed; Lasix; Methanol; Monkshood; Morphine; Nicotine; Nitroglycerin; Norflex; Panther mushroom; Percodan; Persantine; Petroleum distillates; Phenergan; Phenol; Preludin; Procaine; Propane; Quinidine; Sinequan; Sodium fluoroacetate; Stingray; Tagamet; Thorazine; Toxaphene; Trichloroethane; Turpentine; Vacor; Valium

IMPAIRED SENSORY FUNCTIONS

Mouth	
Bad/Bitter Taste	Antimony; Arsenic; Bloodroot; Bronchial tube relaxers; Preludin; Strychnine; Tansy
Burning of mouth	Acids; Aspirin; Atropine; Black hellebore; Bloodroot; Bryony; Camphor; Castor bean; Croton oil; Daphne; Hydrochloric acid; Larkspur; Lye; Nicotine; Paraquat; Silver nitrate
Burning of throat	Acids; Arsenic; Daphne; Fool's parsley; Lye; Meadow saffron; Potato
Dry Mouth/Thirst	Amanita; Atropine; Belladonna; Bloodroot; Camphor; Elavil; Ethylene chlorohydrin; Fool's parsley; Haldol; Inderal; Iodine; Jimsonweed; Meadow saffron; Mercury; Monoamine oxidase (MAO) inhibitors; Norflex; Opium; Permitial; Preludin; Rattlesnake; Thorazine; Vacor; Yellow jasmine
Metal Taste	Flagyl; Iodine; Lead; Mercury
Smoking breath	Phosphorus
Sweet taste	Cuckoopint; Horse chestnut

Sore throat	Barbados nut; Corn cockle; Dimethyl sulfate; Hydrogen sulfate
Ears *Deafness*	Bromates
Hearing Loss	Aspirin
Tinnitus	Aspirin; Cinchona bark; Elavil; Endrin; Gila monster; Nicotine
Eyes *Blindness*	Ammonia; Atropine; Hemlock; Jimsonweed; Methanol; Phenol; Propane
Blurred or double vision	Alkalies; Atropine; Beaked sea snake; Belladonna; Benzene; Betel nut seed; Botulism; Cinchona bark; Digitoxin; Dimethyl sulfate; Elavil; Epinephrine; Ethyl alcohol; False hellebore; Fool's parsley; Foxglove; Haldol; Hemlock; Henbane; Heroin; Hydrogen sulfide; Jimsonweed; Lasix; Librax; Malathion; Methanol; Minipress; Monkshood; Nicotine; Norflex; Panther mushroom; Permitial; Phenergan; Tanghin; TEPP; Vacor
Light sensitivity	Atropine; Lasix; Parathion
Nose *Burnt-almond odor*	Cyanide
Garlic Odor	Phosphorus
Touch *Blisters*	Black hellebore; Brown recluse; Cantharidin; Croton oil; Cuckoopint; Jellyfish; Procaine; Savin
Burning	Bloodroot; Croton oil; Jimsonweed; Monkshood; Phosgene; Potassium permanganate; Rhubarb; Tansy
Cold Extremities	Black locust; Ergot; Lily of the valley; Physostigmine
Frostbite	Ethylene chlorohydrin; Propane
Hallucinations	*See Emotional*
Heat Sensitivity	Thyrolar
Numbness/Insensitivity	Acrylamide; Arsenic; Bivalve shellfish; Cocaine; DDT; Ergot; Geography cone; Inderal; Mandrake; Monkshood; PCP; Potassium; Quaaludes; Rattlesnake; Rotenone; Scorpions; Sodium fluoroacetate; Vacor
Tingling	Calcium; Elavil; Lasix; Lomotil; Minipress; Monkshood

INSOMNIA

Amphetamines; Ativan; Bronchial tube relaxers; Caffeine; Dyphylline; Elavil; Endrin; Inderal; Phenergan; Preludin; Reglan

JOINT PAIN

Aldomet; Galerinas

KIDNEY   *See Urine*

Damage

Botulism; Daphne; Dilantin; Galerinas; Methanol; Naphthalene; Phenol; Potassium permanganate; Privet; Rhubarb; Tansy; Tylenol

Failure

Cadmium; Colocynth; Excessive fluid intake; Mercury; Mountain laurel; PCP; Sodium; Turpentine

LIVER

Damage

Arsenic; Botulism; Catapres; Chlordane; Depakene; Dilantin; Ethinamate; Formaldehyde; Methanol; Monoamine oxidase (MAO) inhibitors; Potassium permanganate

Tenderness

Tylenol

LUNGS

Asphyxia/Respiratory Failure

Anectine; Blue-ringed octopus; Bryony; Cantharidin; Cinchona bark; Corn cockle; Ether; Fool's parsley; Geography cone; Gila monster; Heroin; Meadow saffron; Monkshood; Nicotine; Nitroglycerin; Oleander; Opium; Pavulon; Procaine; Star of Bethlehem; Strychnine; Thorazine; Toxaphene; Tubarine; Vacor; Water hemlock

Bronchitis

Dimethyl sulfate; Lead dust; Malathion

Coughing blood/hemoptysis

Aspirin; Castor bean; Warfarin

Coughing

Acid; Ammonia; Cadmium; Hydrogen sulfide; Mercury; Paral; Petroleum distillates; Potassium permanganate; Trinitrotoluene; Turpentine

Dyspnea/Difficulty Breathing

Aldrin; Anaphylaxis; Antimony; Atropine; Barbados nut; Barbiturates; Barium; Belladonna; Betel nut seed; Bivalve shellfish; Bloodroot; Bronchial tube relaxers; Cadmium; Calcium; Camphor; Carbon monoxide; Carbon

	tetrachloride; Cassava; Catapres; Chloral hydrate; Cobra; Cocaine; Codeine; Curare; Death camas; Dimethyl sulfate; Elavil; Elderberry; Ergot; Fer-de-lance; Geography cone; Gila monster; Hemlock; Horse chestnut; Inderal; Insulin; Ipecac; Jellyfish; Larkspur; Lasix; Lomotil; Malathion; Meadow saffron; Mercury; Minipress; Morphine; Mountain laurel; Nicotine; Norpramine; Paral; Parathion; PCP; Percodan; Phenergan; Phosgene; Pokeweed; Potassium; Pufferfish; Physostigmine; Rattlesnake; Rhubarb; Scorpion; Sodium; Sodium fluoroacetate; Star of Bethlehem; Stibine; TEPP; Valium; Water hemlock; Yellow jasmine
Gasping/Hypenea	Acid; Atropine; Belladonna; Benzene; Cinchophen; Cyanide; Epinephrine; Hydrangea; Lomotil
Pulmonary Edema/ Pulmonary Irritation	Ammonia; Aspirin; Antimony; Bronchial tube relaxers; Cadmium; Epinephrine; Formaldehyde; Hydrogen sulfide; Isopropanol; Malathion; Methanol; Parathion; Petroleum distillates; Phosgene; Quaalude; Scorpions; Sodium fluoroacetate; Turpentine
Shallow/Slow Breathing	Aniline; Benzene; Chloral hydrate; Codeine; Heroin; Isopropanol; Morphine; Opium; PCP; Petroleum distillates; Trichloroethane; Turpentine

LYMPHOID SYSTEM

	Dilantin; Messantoin; Rattlesnake

MOUTH

Drooling	Cadmium; Columbine; Death camas; Fly agaric; Haldol; Inocybe; Lily of the valley; Malathion; Mercury; Mountain laurel; Panther mushroom; PCP; Permitial; Phenergan; Rhododendron; Silver nitrate
Foaming at	Acid; Ammonia; Chloramine-T; Phenol; Tansy; Water hemlock
Gum Disease/swelling/ bleeding	Adder; Cobra; Dilantin; Fer-de-lance; Lead; Lomotil; Mercury
Line in gums	Lead; Mercury blue
Lip/Mouth swelling/blisters	Black hellebore; Dimethyl sulfate; Inocybe; Potassium permanganate

Tongue ulcer	Black hellebore; Paraquat; Paternoster pea

MUSCLES

Flaccid	Calcium; Chloral hydrate; Marijuana; Potassium; Percodan; Valium
Leg Cramps	Barbados nut; Potassium
Rigidity	Ammonia; Black widow; Camphor; Haldol; PCP
Spasms	Aldrin; Amphetamines; Benzene; Boric acid; Caffeine; Camphor; Cocaine; DDT; Dieldrin; Dilantin; Elavil; Epinephrine; Lasix; Lithium; LSD; Mercury; Nicotine; Parathion; Permitial; Physostigmine; Pokeweed; Preludin; Procaine; Pyrethrum; Reglan; Rotenone; Scorpions; Sodium fluoroacetate; Sodium thiocyanate; Strychnine; Tansy; TEPP; Thorazine; Thyrolar; Vacor; White snakeroot; Yellow jasmine
Stiffness/Stiff Muscles	Atropine; Black widow; Marijuana; Permitial; Strychnine
Tight Muscles	Barium
Weakness	Acid; Aldomet; Aldrin; Barium; Beaked sea snake; Benzene; Bloodroot; Cadmium; Corn cockle; Cortinarius; Daphne; Death camas; Dieldrin; Endrin; False hellebore; Gila monster; Hemlock; Indian tobacco; Lasix; Lead; Meadow saffron; Minipress; Morphine; Norflex; Parathion; Persantine; Petroleum distillates; Potassium; Phenol; Pokeweed; Rhubarb; Sodium thiocyanate; Stibine; Stingray; Thyrolar; Vacor; Valium; White snakeroot; Yellow jasmine; Yew

NECROSIS/dead tissue

	Acid; Alkalies; Aniline; Benzene mexachloride; Brown recluse; Cantharidin; Cobra; Cottonmouth; Ergot; Ether-chloroform; Iodine; Jellyfish; Mercury; Phenol; Phosphorus; Potassium permanganate; Rattlesnake; Sea anemone; Tylenol

NOSE

Bloody Nose	Malathion; Parathion
Nasal Congestion	Permitial

Runny Nose	Dimethyl sulfate; Mountain laurel

PAIN

Acid; Adder; Alkalies; Ammonia; Beaked sea snake; Brown recluse; Cadmium; Camphor; Cationic detergents; Cinchophen; Cobra; Corn cockle; Fer-de-lance; Gila monster; Hemlock; Jellyfish; Monkshood; Portuguese man-of-war; Scorpionfish; Scorpions; Silver nitrate; Stingray; Stonefish; Tagamet; TEPP; Trinitrotoluene

PARALYSIS

Atropine; Benzene; Blue-ringed octopus; Botulism; Bryony; Calcium; Cobra; Croton oil; Curare; Geography cone; Hemlock; Jimsonweed; Monkshood; Mountain laurel; Narcissus; Parathion; Pavulon; Potassium; Pufferfish; Pyrethrum; Rattlesnake; Rhododendron; Scorpionfish; Sea anemones; Sodium; Stonefish; TEPP

SHOCK

Ammonia; Baneberry; Cadmium; Fer-de-lance; Insulin; Iodine; Lasix; Malathion; Moonseed; Phenol; Portuguese man-of-war; Potassium permanganate; Rattlesnake; Sea anemone; Silver nitrate; Stingray; Yew

SKIN

Bleeding at site	Adder; Black widow; Brown recluse; Cobra; Rattlesnake
Corrosion	Acid; Bromates; Cationic detergents; Cottonmouth; Dimethyl sulfate; Phenol; Potassium permanganate
Dermatitis/skin irritation	Acid; Acrylamide; Aldomet; Antimony; Arsenic; Atropine; Belladonna; Benzene hexachloride; Boric acid; Brown recluse; Cadmium; Cantharidin; Catapres; Croton oil; DDT; Dog mercury; Ethylene chlorohydrin; Formaldehyde; Hydrogen sulfide; Larkspur; Librax; Malathion; Minipress; Narcissus; Paraquat; Parathion; Phosphorus; Pyrethrum; Sodium azide; Tagamet; Tansy; Tetrachloroethane; Trinitrotoluene

Itching	Larkspur; Opium
Swelling	Adder; Anaphylaxis; Blue-ringed octopus; Brown recluse; Cobra; Jellyfish; Rattlesnake; Scorpionfish
Ulceration	Brown recluse

SKIN COLORATION

Black skin	Silver nitrate
Brown stain or color	Acids; Potassium permanganate
Cyanosis/turning blue	Acid; Amanita; Amphetamines; Aniline; Aspirin; Boric acid; Brown recluse; Castor bean; Chloral hydrate; Chloramine-T; Curare; Cyanide; Dimethyl sulfate; Epinephrine; Ether; Ethinamate; Gila monster; Heroin; Hydrangea; Inocybe; Jellyfish; Larkspur; Lomotil; Nitroglycerin; Paral; Paraquat; Phenol; Phosgene; Procaine; TEPP; Tetrachloroethane; Trinitrotoluene
Eccymosis/Bruising	Aspirin; Depakene; Lasix; Warfarin
Flushing/turning red	Ammonia; Atropine; Belladonna; Bronchial tube relaxers; Brown recluse; Cyanide; Inocybe; Insulin; Lily of the valley; Lomotil; Nitrogylcerin; Persantine; Procaine; Pufferfish; Turpentine
Jaundice	Amanita; Arsenic; Atrophan; Carbon tetrachloride; Cortinarius; Elavil; Grounsel; Monoamine oxidase (MAO) inhibitors; Naphthalene; Paraquat; Phosphorus; Stibine; Tetracholorethane; Trinitrotoluene; Tylenol
Pale skin	Malathion; Phenol; Trinitrotoluene; Yew
Red Spots/rash	Aldomet; Arsenic; Bloodroot; Boric acid; Bromates; Chlordane; DDT; Narcissus; Phenurone
Yellow Stain	Indian tobacco; Nicotine; Trinitrotoluene

STUPOR

Aniline; Black locust; Castor bean; Indian tobacco; Inocybe; Iodine; Monoamine oxidase (MAO) inhibitors; PCP; Percodan; Potato; Rotenone

UNCONSCIOUSNESS

Benzene; Camphor; Carbon monoxide; Carbon fumes; Carbon tetrachloride;

Chloral hydrate; Cocaine; Codeine; Cyanide; Dalmane; Endrin; Ether; Ethyl alcohol; Ethylene chlorohydrin; Formaldehyde; Hydrangea; Heroin; Hydrogen sulfide; Inocybe; Marijuana; Minipress; Morphine; Oleander; Opium; Persantine; Petroleum distillates; Stonefish; Trichloroethane; Turpentine; Valium; Vernol

URINE

Anuria/No Urine	Atropine; Belladonna; Black widow; Bromates; Colocynth; Cortinarius; Elavil; Ergot; Iodine; Meadow saffron; Permitial; Rhubarb; Savin; Silver nitrate; Tansy; Trinitrotoluene
Dark Urine	Flagyl; Phenol
Dysuria/painful urination	Barbados nut; Naphthalene; Turpentine
Hematuria/Uremia	Aldrin; Anaphylaxis; Aspirin; Brown recluse; Cantharidin; Carbon tetrachloride; Castor bean; Cortinarius; Dieldrin; Iodine; Mercury; Milontin; Naphthalene; Savin; Turpentine; Warfarin
Oliguria/Urinary Retention	Aspirin; Atropine; Belladonna; Black widow; Bromates; Colocynth; Isopropanol; Lead; Naphthalene; Paraquat; Savin; Trinitrotoluene
Polyuria/Frequent Urine	Lasix; Vacor
Yellow Urine	Atophan

WEIGHT GAIN

Elavil; Mellaril; Carbon tetrachloride; Thorazine

Appendix D

Poisons by the Time in Which They React

The following index is based on the times for when the symptoms first begin to appear. The writer should be aware that some poisons might have effects that are felt immediately, but will cause death somewhat later. This can make an interesting twist in a plot.

Reaction Time	Poison
Instant	Acid
	Alkalies
	Ammonia
	Anectine
	Benzene
	Blue-ringed octopus
	Boric acid
	Bronchial tube relaxers
	Cantharidin
	Carbon tetrachloride
	Chloramine-T
	Cocaine
	Croton oil
	Curare
	Digitoxin
	Epinephrine
	Formaldehyde
	Heroin
	Hydrogen sulfide
	Iodine
	Ipecac
	Larkspur
	Marijuana
	Mercury
	Monoamine oxidase (MAO) inhibitors
	Nitroglycerin
	Pavulon
	Persantine
	Physostigmine
	Portuguese man-of-war
	Procainamide
	Procaine
	Propane
	Scorpionfish
	Sea anemones
	Silver nitrate
	Sodium azide
	Sodium thiocyanate
	Stingray
	Tanghin

	Tetrachloroethane
	Tubarine
1 minute	Arsenic
	Nitrous oxide
1–5 minutes	Caffeine
	Calcium
	Cyanide
	Ether
	Geography cone
	Haldol
	Jellyfish
	Paral
	Potassium
	Potassium permanganate
	Sodium
	Stonefish
	Turpentine
1–20 minutes	Quinidine
	Stelazine
1 minute–2 hours	Monkshood
1 minute–3 hours	Cassava
	Malathion
	Yellow jasmine
3–20 minutes	PCP
3 minutes–6 hours	Antimony
	Phenol
5–20 minutes	Atropine
	Bromates
	Petroleum distillates
5–30 minutes	Catapres
	Mandrake
	Quaalude
5–40 minutes	Morphine
5–60 minutes	Carbon monoxide
	Insulin
5 minutes–4 hours	Nicotine
5 minutes–6 hours	Sodium fluoroacetate
6 minutes	Black locust

10 minutes	Cottonmouth
	Phenergan
10–20 minutes	Dalmane
10–60 minutes	Cationic detergents
	Thorazine
	Valium
10 minutes–4 hours	Pufferfish
15–20 minutes	Barbados nut
	Star of Bethlehem
	Strychnine
15–30 minutes	Barbiturates
	Chloral hydrate
	Cobra
	Ethinamate
	Potato
15–60 minutes	Camphor
	Dilantin
	Lithium
	Rattlesnake
20 minutes	Betel nut seed
	Codeine
	Ethyl alcohol
	False hellebore
	Grounsel
20–30 minutes	Aldomet
	Foxglove
	Thyrolar
	Trichloroethane
20–40 minutes	Adder
	Arsenic
	Isopropanol
	Lily of the valley
	Naphthalene
	Oleander
	Poinsettia
	Privet
	Warfarin
20–60 minutes	Water hemlock
20 minutes–12 hours	Dieldrin
30 minutes	Bivalve shellfish

	Depakene
	Hemlock
	Inderal
	Librax
	Lomotil
	Norflex
	Percodan
	Pyrethrum
	Reglan
	Tagamet
	Vacor
30–60 minutes	Amphetamines
	DDT
	Parathion
	Minipress
30 minutes–3 hours	Benzene hexachloride
	Fly agaric
	Panther mushroom
30 minutes–4 hours	Tylenol
30 minutes–8 hours	Beaked sea snake
30 minutes–12 hours	Endrin
60 minutes	Barium
	Black widow
	Death camas
	Dyphylline
	Elavil
	Inocybe
	Preludin
	Sinequan
	Yew
1–2 hours	Aniline
	Bloodroot
1–3 hours	Gila monster
1–4 hours	Aldrin
	Ethylene chlorohydrin
	Norpramine
1–6 hours	Indian tobacco
1–8 hours	Lasix
2 hours	Phosphorus
	Pokeweed

2–4 hours	Opium
2–5 hours	Bryony
2–6 hours	Meadow saffron
2–8 hours	Brown recluse
2–24 hours	Gyromitra Scorpions
3 hours	Dimethyl sulfate Permitial Rotenone
4 hours	Acrylamide Cadmium Chlordane
4–6 hours	Aspirin
4–24 hours	Toxaphene
6 hours	Akee Rhododendron
6–12 hours	Belladonna Botulism Castor bean Cinchona bark Cinchophen Colocynth Columbine Cuckoopint Dog mercury Elderberry Hydrangea Jimsonweed Moonseed Rhubarb Tansy
6–15 hours	Amanita
6 hours–2 days	Rhubarb
6 hours–3 days	Fool's parsley Mountain laurel Narcissus Paternoster pea White snakeroot

10 hours–3 days	Savin
12–48 hours	Methanol
14 hours	Celandine
24 hours	Phosgene Baneberry
24–28 hours	Horse chestnut
2–5 days	Paraquat
3 days	Atophan Ergot
3–14 days	Galerinas Cortinarius
3 days–3 weeks	Stibine

Appendix E

Poisons by Toxicity Rating

As mentioned before, the toxicity ratings are based on the amount needed to cause a fatal reaction. A rating of one means that tremendous amounts would be needed to kill a victim, therefore it is considered practically nontoxic. A rating of six means only a miniscule amount will kill a healthy adult.

Toxicity	Poison
1	Marijuana
2	Flagyl
	LSD
	Reglan
	Sea anemones
	Tylenol
3	Aldomet
	Ammonia
	Black widow
	Caffeine
	Calcium
	Cortinarius
	DDT
	Ethyl alcohol
	Fly agaric
	Isopropanol
	Librax
	Panther mushroom
	Turpentine
	White snakeroot
4	Acid
	Aspirin
	Benzene
	Benzene hexachloride
	Bloodroot
	Bromates
	Bronchial tube relaxers
	Brown recluse
	Bryony
	Cadmium
	Cationic detergents
	Cinchona bark
	Corn cockle
	Death camas
	Depakene
	Dilantin
	Elderberry

Fool's parsley
Grounsel
Larkspur
Lasix
Lomotil
Malathion
Mandrake
Monoamine oxidase (MAO) inhibitors
Naphthalene
Nitroglycerin
Norflex
Norpramine
Persantine
Petroleum distillates
Phenergan
Poinsettia
Pokeweed
Potassium
Pyrethrum
Rattlesnake
Rhubarb
Rotenone
Sodium
Sodium azide
Spindle tree
Stibine
Stingray
Thyrolar
Warfarin

5

Acrylamide
Akee
Aldrin
Amanita
Amphetamines
Aniline
Arsenic
Baneberry
Barbiturates
Barium
Beaked sea snake
Betel nut seed
Black hellebore
Black locust
Boric acid
Botulism
Camphor
Carbon monoxide
Cassava
Celandine
Chloral hydrate
Cinchophen

Cocaine
Colocynth
Columbine
Cottonmouth
Cuckoopint
Dalmane
Daphne
Digitoxin
Dog mercury
Dyphylline
Elavil
Endrin
Epinephrine
Ergot
Ether
Ethinamate
False hellebore
Fer-de-lance
Formaldehyde
Foxglove
Geography cone
Gyromitra
Haldol
Horse chestnut
Hydrangea
Inderal
Indian tobacco
Inocybe
Insulin
Iodine
Ipecac
Lead
Lithium
Meadow saffron
Mercury
Methanol
Minipress
Moonseed
Mountain laurel
Narcissus
Nitrous oxide
Opium
Paral
Percodan
Permitial
Phenol
Physostigmine
Potassium permanganate
Potato
Preludin
Privet
Procainamide

Quaalude
Scorpionfish
Silver nitrate
Sinequan
Sodium thiocyanate
Stelazine
Tagamet
Tansy
Thorazine
Toxaphene
Trichloroethane
Vacor
Valium
Yellow jasmine

6

Adder
Alkalies
Anectine
Antimony
Atophan
Atropine
Barbados nut
Belladonna
Bivalve shellfish
Blue-ringed octopus
Cantharidin
Carbon tetrachloride
Castor bean
Catapres
Chloramine-T
Chlordane
Cobra
Codeine
Croton oil
Curare
Cyanide
Dieldrin
Dimethyl sulfate
Ethylene chlorohydrin
Gila monster
Hemlock
Heroin
Hydrogen sulfide
Jellyfish
Jimsonweed
Lily of the valley
Monkshood
Morphine
Nicotine
Oleander
Paraquat
Parathion

Paternoster pea
Pavulon
PCP
Phosgene
Phosphorus
Procaine
Pufferfish
Quinidine
Rhododendron
Rhubarb
Savin
Sodium fluoroacetate
Star of Bethlehem
Stonefish
Strychnine
Tanghin
TEPP
Tetrachloroethane
Trinitrotoluene
Tubarine
Water hemlock
Yew

Glossary

ABORTIFACIENT: A substance which induces abortion or labor.

ACETYLCHOLINE: A compound produced by the autonomic nervous system (ANS) to assist transmission of nerve impulses. See Anticholinergics.

ACIDOSIS: A disturbance in the acid-base level of the body in which there is an accumulation of acids. This can happen in diabetes — diabetic acidosis, renal disease, excessive loss of bicarbonate, or intake of acids or acid salts. Impaired liver function can also cause this. Another variety is respiratory acidosis, which comes secondary to breathing problems when someone retains more carbon dioxide than he gives off. Symptoms of respiratory acidosis are light-headedness, fainting, and fast heartbeat. If symptoms continue, the patient can die. Symptoms of metabolic acidosis are apathy, irritability, delirium, and dehydration. Emergency measures must be taken, as both forms can lead to death.

ACUTE: Happening quickly; sudden onset; demanding urgent attention; within minutes, hours, or days.

ALKALOSIS: This is a condition in which the alkalinity (pH) of the body increases beyond normal limits. The two most common types are 1) respiratory alkalosis, usually caused by hyperventilation (breathing too quickly), and which can happen during a crisis, during aspirin poisoning, or because of a lesion of the CNS, and 2) metabolic (cardiac) alkalosis, which results from a loss of acid from the body during heavy vomiting, loss of potassium, or large ingestion of sodium bicarbonate.

ANAPHYLAXIS: Or *anaphylactic shock* happens during an allergic crisis — as with multiple bee stings or drug allergies. The reactions occur swiftly and include increased irritability, a sensation of the throat closing off, difficulty breathing, cyanosis (blue coloring of the skin due to lack of oxygen), sometimes convulsions, unconsciousness, and death. The reaction is due to the contraction of the smooth muscle fibers, and death results from spasm of the muscles in the lung. People who have hay fever, asthma, and hives (urticaria) are thought to be more susceptible to these shock reactions. They can also be caused by badly matched blood transfusions, certain medications, or anything else the body is hypersensitive to.

ANOXIC: "A" means without. Oxic refers to oxygen. This means lack of oxygen or no oxygen.

ANOREXIA: A disease process in which no or limited food is taken in and the patient wastes away, becoming skin and bones. Soon the body cannot support life functions and the patient dies — usually of cardiac complications. Karen Carpenter, the singer, is a famous case.

ANTICHOLINERGIC: Impeding of impulses or action of the nerves. Cholinergic refers to the material produced when the nerves synapse or communicate correctly.

ANTIEMETIC: To prevent vomiting, nausea, or both.

ANTIPYRETIC: An agent used to reduce fever.

ANURIA: The prefix *a-* or *an-* refers to "no" or "nothing." *Uria* means "urine." Anuria refers to a lack of urine output or total failure of the kidneys to produce. A patient who is anuric will soon die.

APHASIA: The inability to express oneself through speech, usually occurring after a stroke or other accident.

APNEA: Cessation of breathing, usually of a temporary nature, as when people have sleep disturbances and stop breathing momentarily during the night.

ATAXIA: Muscular incoordination when voluntary movement is attempted, generally caused by nervous disorders.

ATROPHY: The destruction of muscle or anything through lack of use. Wasting away usually of muscle.

AUTONOMIC NERVOUS SYSTEM (ANS): The part of the nervous system that controls such involuntary bodily functions in the glands, smooth-muscle glands, eyes, intestines, and heart.

BRADYCARDIA: Slow heartbeat.

CARDIAC ARREST: The heart stops; also cardiac collapse.

CARDIOVASCULAR COLLAPSE: The heart stops working and the veins collapse. Blood is no longer pumped through.

CATHARTIC: Anything that contributes to the purgative action of the bowels. Generally several evacuations are produced. Castor oil is one example.

CENTRAL NERVOUS SYSTEM (CNS): The brain, spinal cord, and the nerves controlling voluntary movements.

CHEYNE-STOKES RESPIRATION: Defined by Scottish physician John Cheyne and Irish physician William Stokes in the late eighteenth century as an irregular cycle of breathing that occurs during acute disease of the lungs, heart, or central nervous system. Breathing is at first slow and shallow and then increases in rapidity and depth: then decreases, stopping for ten to twenty seconds before repeating the same pattern. It may occur in heart failure, brain disease, or the final moments of life.

CHOLINESTERASE: An enzyme needed in the body for smooth nerve-muscle function. Also called acetylcholinesterase, it splits acetylcholine into acetic acid and choline. Acetylcholine is released when nerve impulses reach the muscle, where it is split by cholinesterase into its components. Without cholinesterase, the muscle fibers are in constant stimulation, as in the disease—myasthenia gravis.

CHRONIC: Happening over a prolonged period of time—usually over several weeks, months, or years, and sometimes recurring. A person who has chronic arthritic pain will have it come and go.

CLONIC-TONIC CONVULSIONS: An alternation of relaxation and contraction of the muscles; it's a sign of serious nervous system trouble.

COLONIC: A high enema going as far as the intestine. Health faddists swear by it on a regular basis, but its worth is still doubtful. Often people become addicted to them, and their own intestines will no longer move properly without the stimulation provided.

CYANOSIS: A blue tinge of nails, face, and toes from lack of oxygen in the blood.

CYTOTOXIC: Injury or damage to cells. Often the drug will kill the cells. Cancer therapy is cytotoxic for the cancer cells, but sometimes harms good cells as well.

DEPRESSANT: An agent that will depress a bodily function or nerve activity—such as bromide, aconite, or chloral hydrate. A cerebral depressant affects the brain and makes the patient seem slower and dull. Large doses produce sleep or unconsciousness.

DERMATITIS: Skin is red and chapped and may peel. Often the condition can be produced by contact with a plant or medicine. Hairdressers often get contact dermatitis from working with the chemicals in the shop.

DIPLOPIA: Double vision.

DYSPNEA: *Dys* means pain or difficulty, so this would be air hunger or difficult and painful breathing.

ECCHYMOSES: The passage of blood from ruptured blood vessels into the tissue beneath the skin, marked by purple discoloration of the skin commonly known as a black and blue mark.

EDEMA: Edema usually means swelling, but in pulmonary edema, it means the lungs fill with fluid.

EKG — ELECTROCARDIOGRAM: The electrical impulses of the heart measured by machine.

ELECTROLYTE: A solution which conducts electricity or a substance which contains an electrical current. Acids, bases, and salts are common electrolytes.

EMETIC: A substance that encourages vomiting, like syrup of ipecac.

ENTERAL: *Enter* refers to the intestine and enteral means within the intestine or absorbed by the intestine — as in eaten; opposed to parenteral.

EXTRAPYRAMIDAL SYMPTOMS: These symptoms occur mainly from use of psychotropic drugs or drugs that affect the mental state. They include symptoms such as wobbly gait, slurred speech, foaming at the mouth, forgetfulness, drooling, incoordination of muscles, and stiffness.

FATTY INFILTRATION: Increased deposits of fat in the organs that interfere with organ operation. Often found in the liver, kidney, or heart during acute illness.

FLEXOR MUSCLES: Muscles that bend as opposed to muscles that extend.

GASTROENTERITIS: Inflammation of the stomach and bowels causing severe stomach cramps, bloody diarrhea, nausea, and vomiting.

GLYCOSIDES: *Glyco* comes from the root word for "sugar." On hydrolysis, the glycosides that occur abundantly in plants yield one or more sugars (*glycone*) and one or more other compounds called aglycones. Glucose is a commonly occurring sugar. While many glycosides are nontoxic, there are several that are. One of these is the cyanogenetic glycoside that yields hydrocyanic acid or cyanide. Most common of the cyanogenetic compounds is amygdalin, usually found in the rose family and in the seeds of apples and pears, as well as in the stony seeds, bark, leaves, and pits of apricots, bitter almonds, wild cherries, peaches, and plums.

Other glycosides are cardioactive and are characterized by their specific action on the heart muscle. There are perhaps four hundred different types of these. Scrophulariacae, found in foxglove, is one of the most common.

HEMATEMESIS: Vomiting of blood. *Hema* is blood; *emesis* is vomiting.

HEMOLYTIC: *Hemo* refers to the red blood cells and *lytic* is to destroy; therefore, this is the destruction of the red blood cells.

HEPATIC: Liver or associated with liver.

HYPERPYREXIA: Body temperature above 106 degrees F.

HYPERTHERMIA: A fever or any temperature above normal limit. Malignant hyperthermia will sometimes occur during surgery with administration of certain gases. It is a hereditary condition. Prior to an operation, the anesthesiologist should ask if anyone in the patient's family has had this problem. If so, it can be fatal, usually while they're still on the table. However, many people are not aware that family members have suffered from this.

HYPERVENTILATION: *Hyper* refers to anything quicker than normal, and hyperventilation means breathing at a fast rate, as in hysteria.

HYPOTENSION: Low blood pressure — anything below 100/60.

HEMOPTYSIS: Sudden coughing up of blood as in the final death throes or during a TB episode.

HYPOTHERMIA: *Hypo* is anything below normal, so this is any temperature below normal limit. If the body goes into hypothermia when exposed to freezing temperatures, respiration and heart movement slow down to an almost imperceptible rate. A patient can recover with care.

INNERVATE: To stimulate a part of a nerve or an organ and make it respond.

INTENTION TREMOR: A trembling—sometimes barely noticeable, sometimes very noticeable—when the hand purposely reaches out to grab some object or do some job. As in "Every time I write a check to those bastards blackmailing me, my hand trembles."

INTRAMUSCULAR: An IM injection is given into the muscle. The average injection size is 3 ml. This is opposed to subcutaneous (under the skin) and intravenous (into the vein).

INTRAVENOUS (IV): Medication and fluid from a bottle goes directly into the vein. This is very different from an intramuscular injection. An IV is usually given during a major crisis, pre-op (operation), during surgery, and often when a patient is recovering from a major operation or cannot ingest food/fluids.

LEUKOPENIA: An abnormal decrease of white blood cells in the blood. In disease, it means an acute infection.

MONOAMINE OXIDASE INHIBITORS: MAO inhibitors are antidepressants, popular in earlier years, but used less these days because of the dangerous reactions they cause with other drugs.

MYDRIASIS: This is the abnormal dilation of the pupil of the eye.

MYOCARDIAL INFARCTION: Heart attack caused by an embolism.

MYOTONIA: *Myo* means muscle and *tone* refers to the tonic spasm of a muscle. Myotonia is a temporary rigidity that occurs after a muscle contraction.

NECROSIS: Dead and decayed tissue.

NERVINE: Acting as a nerve sedative, or anything that will decrease the irritability of the nerves.

NEUROPATHY: Any disease relating to the nerves, nerve network, or path of the nerves.

NYSTAGMUS: Constant involuntary movement of the eyeball.

OLIGURIA: *Oli* refers to diminished amount and *uria* is urine, so oliguria is a condition whereby a person is not producing the amount of urine necessary to remain healthy.

OLIPNEA: Infrequent respiration.

PARASYMPATHETIC NERVOUS SYSTEM: The control of certain nerves as the vagus, which controls stomach, and the spinal cord.

PARENTERAL: Absorbed outside the intestine, such as by injection.

PARESTHESIA: An abnormal sensation as in numbness, prickling, or tingling of the skin without external cause.

PERCUTANEOUS: *Per* means "through" and *cutaneous* refers to the skin. When something is effected through the skin or as a topical application.

PERISTALSIS: Wavelike muscular contractions that propel contained matter along tubular organs, as in the alimentary canal.

PETECHIAL: Small, red rashlike spots or hemorrhages which appear on the skin or organ.

PITOSIS: The falling or drooping of the eyelid, often seen after a stroke or brain damage.

POLYURIA: Urinating far more frequently than would be considered normal.

PULMONARY: Related to the lung.

PULMONARY EDEMA: Fluid on the lungs. When the lungs don't work properly, fluid from the cells builds up and accumulates in the lungs.

PURGATIVE: Any agent that causes the watery evacuation of the bowels. A cathartic.

PURGE: To evacuate the bowels by means of a cathartic or laxative.

PUTREFACTION: Decomposition of animal matter or other protein usually associated with a horrendous smell and poisonous gas by-products. Decomposition of tissue after death is called autolysis.

RALES: Abnormal sounds from the lungs made by the thickening of mucus in the chest. Known as the death rattle, rales are usually heard just before a person dies.

RENAL: Kidney or associated with the kidney.

RESINS: Resins, found in plants, are amorphous products of a complex chemical nature. Insoluble in water, they are hard, transparent, or translucent. They soften upon heating and finally melt. Often they occur in mixtures with volatile oils, gums, and sugars. Water hemlock and laurel plants are the most infamous of the natural resins.

RESPIRATORY ARREST: The lungs stop and the heart stops immediately afterward from lack of oxygen.

SAPONIN: An unabsorbable glycoside contained in the roots of some plants. These can be mixed to form a watery solution and cause vomiting, diarrhea, and other irritating symptoms if taken internally.

STRIDOR: A harsh, high-pitched sound during inhalation or exhalation.

SUBCUTANEOUS: Under the skin, as in insulin injections.

SYMPATHETIC SYSTEM: A division of the autonomic nervous system which controls the breathing, heart rate, and other nonpurposeful movements within the body that occur without our being acutely aware of them. Also called the parasympathetic nervous system.

TACHYCARDIA: Quickened heartbeat, racing pulse.

TETANIC CONVULSIONS: Spasmlike convulsions associated with the disease process of tetanus. Begins gradually and starts with stiffness of the jaw and locks (lockjaw), it then extends down the spine until the patient is helpless. Muscles of the face contract, voice becomes altered. Muscles of the back and extremities are affected and placed in odd or horrifying shapes from which the patient has much difficulty moving. The convulsions are increased by stimulation of noise or light, and often the patients are kept in a darkened room. The temperature rises to 113 degrees! The pain is great and patient suffers from hunger, lack of sleep, and thirst. It's almost always fatal.

TINNITUS: Ringing in the ears.

VASCULAR or VASO: Vascular refers to veins.

VENTRICULAR FIBRILLATION: Ventricles are chambers in the heart. Fibrillation occurs when the electrical impulses that control the heart go haywire and the heart goes into shock. Commonly known as a heart attack, it's what they call a Code Blue in most hospitals.

Bibliography

Books

Admiraal, P. V. *Justifiable Euthanasia: A Manual for Physicians*. Amsterdam: Netherlands Voluntary Euthanasia Society, 1981.

Arena, Jay M., and Richard H. Drew. *Poisoning*. Springfield, Illinois: Charles C. Thomas, 1963.

Arnold, Happy. *Poisonous Plants of Hawaii*. Rutland, Vermont: Charles E. Tuttle, 1968.

Ballantin, Bryan. *Current Approaches in Toxicology*. Bristol, England: Wright Publishers, 1977.

Bayer, Marc J., Barry H. Rumack, and Lee A. Wanke. *Toxicologic Emergencies*. Bowie, Maryland: Robert J. Brady, 1984.

Beck, Aaron T., Harvey L. Resnick, and Dan J. Lettieri. *The Prediction of Suicide*. Philadelphia: The Charles Press, 1974.

Block, Bradford J. *Signs and Symptoms of Chemical Exposure*. Springfield, Illinois: Charles C. Thomas, 1980.

Boden, Francóis F., and C. F. Cheinisse. *Poisons*. New York: World University Library, McGraw-Hill, 1970.

Browne, George. *Reports of Trials for Murder by Poisoning*. London: Straus, 1883.

Browning, Ethel. *Toxicology and Metabolism of Industrial Solvents*. London: Elsevier, 1965.

Burston, Geoffrey. *Self-Poisoning*. London: Lloyd-Luke Publishers, 1970.

Cassaret, Louis, and John Doull. *Toxicology: the Basic Science of Poisons*. 2d ed. New York: Macmillan, 1980.

Cloudsley-Thompson, John L. *Spiders and Scorpions*. New York: McGraw-Hill, 1980.

Columbia Encyclopedia. 4th ed. New York: J. B. Lippincott, 1975.

Cooley, Lee Morrison. *Pre-Medicated Murder*. Radnor, Pennsylvania: Chilten Books, 1974.

Cooper, Marion, and Anthony W. Johnson. *Poisonous Plants in Britain and Their Effect on Animals and Man*. London: Her Majesty's Stationery Office, 1987.

Cooper, Paulette. *Medical Detectives*. New York: David McKay, 1973.

Cooper, Peter. *Poisoning by Drugs and Chemicals, Plants and Animals*. 3d ed. Chicago: Alchemist Publications, 1974.

Cumming, George. *Management of Acute Poisoning*. Springfield, Illinois: C.V. Mosby, 1961.

Curry, Allan S. *Poison Detection in Human Organs*. Springfield, Illinois: Charles C. Thomas, 1963.

Diechmann, William B. *Signs, Symptoms, and Treatment of Certain Acute Emergencies in Toxicology*. Springfield, Illinois: Charles C. Thomas, 1958.

Department of Justice. *Forensic Pathology, A Handbook*. July 1977.

Driesbach, Robert. *Handbook of Poisoning*. 11th ed. Los Altos, California: Lange Medical Publications, 1983.

Duke, James. *Medicinal Plants of the Bible*. New York: Trade-Medic Books, 1983.

Ellenhorn, Matthew J., and Donald G. Barceloux. *Medical Toxicology*. New York: Elsevier, 1988.

Finkel, Asher J., Alice Hamilton, and Harriet Hardy. *Hamilton and Hardy's Industrial Toxicology*. 4th ed. Boston: John Wright, PSG Inc., 1983.

Forsyth, A. *British Poisonous Plants*. H. M. Stationery Office, Bulletin No. 161, Ministry of Agriculture, Fisheries and Food, 1954.

Freiberg, Marcos, and Jerry G. Wells. *The World of Venomous Animals*. New Jersey: T. F. H. Publishers, 1984.

Goldfrank, Lewis R., et al. *Goldfrank's Toxicological Emergencies*. 3d ed. Norwalk, Connecticut: Appleton-Century-Crofts, 1986.

Goodman, Louis Sanford, and Alfred Gilman. *The Pharmacological Basis of Therapeutics*. 6th ed. New York: Macmillan, 1980.

Gosselin, Robert E., Harold C. Hodge, Roger P. Smith, and Marion N. Gleason. *Clinical Toxicology of Commercial Products*. 4th ed. Baltimore: Williams and Wilkins, 1979.

Graham, James, and David Provins. *The Diagnosis and Treatment of Acute Poisoning*. London: Oxford University Press, 1962.

Guyton, Arther C. *Textbook of Medical Physiology*. 6th ed. Philadelphia: W. B. Saunders, 1981.

Haddad, Lester M., and James F. Winchester. *Clinical Management of Poisoning and Drug Overdose*. Philadelphia: W. B. Saunders, 1983.

Hall, Jay Cameron. *Inside the Crime Lab*. Englewood Cliffs, New Jersey: Prentice-Hall, 1974.

Hanson, William, Jr., ed. *Toxic Emergencies*. New York: Churchill Livingstone, 1984.

Hardin, James W. *Human Poisoning from Native and Cultivated Plants*. Durham, North Carolina: Duke University Press, 1969.

James, Wilma Roberts. *Know Your Poisonous Plants*. Healdsburg, California: Naturegraph Publishers, 1973.

Jensen, Lloyd. *Poisoning Misadventures*. Springfield, Illinois: Charles C. Thomas, 1970.

Kaye, Sidney. *Handbook of Emergency Toxicology*. 5th ed. Springfield, Illinois: Charles C. Thomas, 1988.

Kingsley-Levy, Charles. *Poisonous Plants and Mushrooms of North America*. Lexington, Kentucky: Steven Green Press, 1984.

Lampe, Kenneth F., and Rune Gagerstrom. *Plant Toxicity and Dermatitis*. Baltimore: Livingston, 1968.

Lampe, Kenneth F. *AMA Handbook of Poisoning and Injurious Plants*. Chicago: American Medical Association, Chicago Review Press, 1985.

Le Riche, W. Harding. *A Chemical Feast*. New York: Methuen Publishers, 1982.

Lifflander, Matthew. *Final Treatment — The File on Dr. X.* New York: W. W. Norton, 1979.

The Lippincott Manual of Nursing Practice. Philadelphia: J. B. Lippincott, 1974.

Long, James W. *The Essential Guide to Prescription Drugs*. New York: Harper and Row, 1980.

Loomis, T. A. *Essentials of Toxicology*. Philadelphia: Lea and Febigen, 1968.

Lucas, George, and Herbert William. *Symptoms and Treatment of Acute Poisoning*. Toronto: Clark Irwin Publisher, 1952.

Mair, George. *How to Die with Dignity*. Edinburgh; Scottish Exit, 1980.

Maletzky, B., and P. H. Blachly. *Use of Lithium in Psychiatry*. London: Butterworth's, 1971.

Matthew, H., and A. A. Lawson. *Treatment of Common Acute Poisonings*. Baltimore: Williams and Wilkins, 1967.

McCallum, John D. *Crime Doctor*. Vancouver, B.C.: Gordon Soules Book Publisher, 1978.

The Merck Manual. 13th ed. New Jersey: Merck Sharp and Dohme Research Laboratories, 1980.

Minton, Sherman A., Jr. *Venomous Reptiles.* New York: Scribner's and Sons, 1980.

Moeschlin, Sven. *Poisoning: Diagnosis and Treatment.* New York: Grune and Statton, 1965.

Morton, Julia F. *Plants Poisonous to People in Florida.* Miami: University of Miami Press, 1982.

Muenscher, Walter C. *Poisonous Plants of the United States.* New York: Macmillan Co., 1939.

North, P. *Poisonous Plants and Fungi.* London: Blandford Press, 1967.

Pammel, L. H. *A Manual of Poisonous Plants.* Cedar Rapids, Iowa: Torch Press, 1911.

Physician's Desk Reference. 34th ed. New Jersey: Medical Economics Co., 1980.

Picton, Bernard. *Murder, Suicide, or Accident.* New York: St. Martin's Press, 1971.

Plaidy, Jean. *A Triptych of Poisoners.* London: W. H. Allen, 1968.

Poisonous Plants of U.S. and Canada. New York: Prentice-Hall, 1964.

Polson, C. J., and R. N. Tattersal. *Clinical Toxicology.* 2d ed. London: Pitman, 1969.

Proctor, Nick H., James P. Hughes, and Michael L. Fischman. *Chemical Hazards of the Workplace.* 2d ed. Philadelphia: J. B. Lippincott, 1978.

Regenstein, Lewis. *America, the Poisoned.* Washington, D.C.: Acropolis Books, 1982.

Riley, Dick, and Pam McAllister. *Bedside, Bathtub, and Armchair Companion to Agatha Christie.* New York: Frederick Ungar Publishing, 1978.

St. Aubyn, Giles. *Infamous Victims: Notorious Poisoners and Their Poisons.* London: Constable Publishers, 1971.

Sax, N. Irving. *Dangerous Properties of Industrial Materials.* 4th ed. New York: Van Nostrand Reinhold, 1975.

Schmutz, Erwin M., and Lucretia Hamilton. *Plants That Poison.* Flagstaff, Arizona: Northland Press, 1979.

Silverman, Milton, Phillip Lee, and Mia Leydecker. *Prescription for Death: The Drugging of the Third World.* Los Angeles: University of California Press, 1982.

Sittig, Marshall. *Handbook of Toxic and Hazardous Chemicals.* New Jersey: Noyes Publications, 1981.

Skoutakes, Vasilios A. *Clinical Toxicology of Drugs: Principals and Practice.* Philadelphia: Lea and Febigen, 1982.

Smyth, Frank. *Causes of Death.* New York: Van Nostrand Reinhold, 1980.

Soderman, Harry, and John O'Connell. *Modern Criminal Investigation.* 4th ed. New York: Funk and Wagnalls, 1973.

Stackhouse, John. *Australia's Venomous Wildlife.* New South Wales: Paul Hamlyn, 1970.

Taber, Clarence. *Taber's Medical Dictionary.* 10th ed. Philadelphia: F. A. Davis, 1965.

Thienes, C. H., and T. J. Haley. *Clinical Toxicology.* 4th ed. Philadelphia: Lea and Febigen, 1896.

Thompson, Charles, and John Samuel. *Poisons and Poisoning with Historical Aspects of Some Famous Mysteries.* London: H. Stysen, 1931.

Thorp, Raymond. *Black Widow.* Chapel Hill: University of North Carolina, 1985.

Trainor, D. C. *A Handbook of Industrial Toxicology.* London: Angus & Robertson, 1966.

Trevethick, R. *Environmental and Health Hazards.* New York: Heineman Medical Books, 1973.

Tu, Anthony T., ed. *Plant and Fungal Toxins*. Vol. 1, *Handbook of Natural Toxins*. New York: Marcel Dekker, 1983.
————. *Marine Toxins and Venoms*. Vol. 3, *Handbook of Natural Toxins*. New York: Marcel Dekker, 1988.
————. *Survey of Contemporary Toxicology*. New York: Wiley and Sons, 1980.
Vercourt, Bernard. *Common Poisonous Plants of East Africa*. London: Colliers, 1969.
Von Oettinger, Wolfgang. *Poisoning: A Guide to Clinical Diagnosis and Treatment*. Philadelphia: W. B. Saunders, 1958.
Webster's New Collegiate Dictionary, 9th ed.
Webster's New International Dictionary, 3d ed.

Journals

Achong, M. R., P. G. Fernandez, and P. J. McLeod. "Fatal Self-poisoning with Lithium Carbonate." *Canadian Medical Association Journal* 112 (1975): 868–70.

Aquanno, J. J., K. M. Chan, and D. N. Dietzler. "Accidental Poisoning of Two Laboratory Technologists with Sodium Nitrate." *Clinical Chemistry* 27 (1981): 1145–46.

Backer, R. C., R. V. Pisano, and I. M. Sopher. "Diphenhydramine Suicide — Case Report." *Journal of the Annals of Toxicology* 1 (1977): 227–28.

Baden, M. M., A. Blaustein, L. R. Ferraro, et al. "Sudden Death after Haloperidol." *Canadian Society of Forensic Science Journal* 14 (1981):70–72.

Bednarczyk, L. R. "A Death Due to Levorphanol." *Journal of the Annals of Toxicology* 3 (1979): 217–19.

Berger, R., G. Green, and A. Melnick. "Cardiac Arrest Caused by Oral Diazepam Intoxication." *Clinical Pediatrics* 14 (1975): 842–44.

Bickel, M. H., R. Brochon, B. Friolet, et al. "Clinical and Biochemical Results of a Fatal Case of Desipramine Intoxication." *Psychopharmicology* 10 (1967):431–36.

Bruce, A. M., and H. Smith. "The Investigation of Phenobarbitone, Phenytoin, and Primidone in the Death of Epileptics." *Medical Science Law* 17 (1977):195–99.

Caddy, B., and A. H. Stead. "Three Cases of Poisoning Involving the Drug Phenelzine." *Journal of Forensic Science Society* 18 (1978):207–8.

Christie, J. L. "Fatal Consequences of Local Anesthesia: Report of Five Cases and a Review of the Literature." *Journal of Forensic Science* 21 (1976):671–79.

De Beer, J., A. Heyndricks, and J. Timperman. "Suicidal Poisoning by Nitrite." *European Journal of Toxicology* 8 (1975): 247–51.

deGroot, G., R. A. A. Maes, C. N. Hodnett, et al. "Four Cases of Fatal Doxepin Poisoning." *Journal of the Annals of Toxicology* 2 (1978):18–20.

DiMaio, V. J. M., and J. C. Garriott. "Four Deaths Resulting from Abuse of Nitrous Oxide." *Journal of Forensic Science* 23 (1978): 169–72.

————. "A Fatal Overdose of Paraldehyde During Treatment of a Case of Delirium Tremens." *Journal of Forensic Science* 19 (1974):755–58.

Finkle, B. S., K. L. McCloskey, and L. S. Goodman. "Diazepam and Drug-Associated Deaths." *Journal of American Medical Association* 242 (1979):429–34.

Hansteen, V., D. Jacobsen, I. K. Knudsen, et al. "Acute Massive Poisoning with Digitoxin: Report of Seven Cases and Discussion of Treatment." *Clinical Toxicology* 18 (1981):679–92.

Ketai, R., J. Matthews, and J. J. Mozden, Jr. "Sudden Death in a Patient Taking Haloperidol." *American Journal of Psychiatry* 136 (1979):112–13.

Lee, K. Y., L. J. Beilin, and R. Vandongen. "Severe Hypertension after Ingestion of an Appetite Suppressant (Phenylpropanolamine) with Indomethacin." *Lancet* 1 (1979): 1110–11.

Rabinowtch, I. M. "Acute Nitroglycerine Poisoning." *Canadian Medical Association Journal* 50 (1944):199–202.

Raginsky, B. B., and W. Bourne. "Cyanosis in Nitrous Oxide Oxygen Anesthesia in Man." *Canadian Medical Association Journal* 30 (1934):518–22.

Reingold, I. M., and I. I. Lasky. "Acute Fatal Poisoning Following Ingestion of a Solution of DDT." *Annals of Internal Medicine* 26 (1947): 945-47.

Rives, H. F., B. B. Ward, and M. L. Hicks. "A Fatal Reaction to Methapyrilene." *Journal of American Medical Association* 140 (1949):1022–24.

Schou, M., A. Amdisen, and J. Trap-Jessen. "Lithium Poisoning." *American Journal of Psychiatry* 125 (1968): 520–27.

Smith, N. J. "Death Following Accidental Ingestion of DDT." *Journal of American Medical Association* 136 (1948):469–71.

Standefer, J. C., A. N. Jones, et al. "Death Associated with Nitrite Ingestion: Report of a Case." *Journal of Forensic Science* 24 (1979):768–71.

Stevens, H. M., and R. N. Fox. "A Method for Detecting Tubocurarine in Tissues." *Journal of Forensic Science Society* 11 (1971):177-82.

Usubiaga, J. E., J. Wikinski, R. Ferrero, et al. "Local Anesthetic-Induced Convulsions in Man." *Anesthesia Annals* 45 (1966):611-20.

Wikinski, A., J. E. Usubiaga, and R. W. Wikinski. "Cardiovascular and Neurological Effects of 4000 mg Procaine." *Journal of American Medical Association* 213 (1970):621-23.

Index

Other Great Books
in the Howdunit Series:

Missing Persons: A Writer's Guide to Finding the Lost, the Abducted and the Escaped—Now your characters can go beyond the phone book to search for missing relatives, old friends and vanishing villains! Professional PI, Fay Faron, shows you why people turn up missing and the search procedures used to find them.
#10511/$16.99/272 pages/paperback/available September 1997

Murder One: A Writer's Guide to Homicide—Build believable homicide scenarios—from accidental murders to crimes of passion. Prosecuting investigators Mauro Corvasce and Joseph Paglino take you step by step through motives, weapons and disposals of bodies—illustrated with scene-by-scene accounts from real life cases.
#10498/$16.99/240 pages/paperback/available September 1997

Amateur Detectives: A Writer's Guide to How Private Citizens Solve Criminal Cases—Make your amateur-crime-solver novels and stories accurate and convincing! You'll investigate what jobs work well with sleuthing, information-gathering methods, the law as it relates to amateur investigators and more!
#10487/$16.99/240 pages/paperback

Body Trauma: A Writer's Guide to Wounds and Injuries—Bring realism to your work using this detailed examination of serious bodily injury. You'll learn what happens to organs and bones maimed by accident or intent—from the 4 steps in trauma care to the "dirty dozen" dreadful—but survivable—chest injuries.
#10488/$16.99/240 pages/20 b&w illus./paperback

Malicious Intent: A Writer's Guide to How Criminals Think—Create unforgettable villains with the help of this guide to criminal psychology. You'll explore the fact and fiction of who these people are, why they commit their crimes, how they choose their victims and more!
#10413/$16.99/240 pages/paperback

Modus Operandi: A Writer's Guide to How Criminals Work—From murder to arson to prostitution, two seasoned detectives show you how to create masterful crimes while still dropping enough clues to let the good guys catch the bad guys.
#10414/$16.99/224 pages/paperback

Police Procedural: A Writer's Guide to the Police and How They Work—Learn how police officers work, when they work, what they wear, who they report to, and how they go about controlling and investigating crime. *#10374/$16.99/272 pages/paperback*

Private Eyes: A Writer's Guide to Private Investigators—How do people become investigators? What procedures do they use? What tricks/tactics do they use? This guide gives you the "inside scoop" on the world of private eyes!
#10373/$15.99/208 pages/paperback

SERITA DEBORAH STEVENS, RN, BSN: A registered nurse and graduate of University of Illinois Medical Center, Serita is an active member of Mystery Writers of America, Sisters In Crime, and International Crime Writers. She has sixteen published paperbacks to her credit, as well as numerous short stories and articles. Serita has also authored several produced video movies and radio plays. She is currently working on her third script for feature film.

Her young adult mystery, *Unholy Alliance* (Fawcett), was nominated Best Book for the Reluctant Reader by the American Library Association in 1989, and *Deadly Doses* was nominated for the Anthony Award and the Macavity Award. Her first hardcover mystery, *Red Sea, Dead Sea* (co-authored with Rayanne Moore), has been optioned for motion picture rights.

Serita's hobbies include reading, history, horseback riding, travel, and flying. Single, she lives in the north San Fernando Valley, California, with her three cats—Alexander the Great, Charlie Dickens, and Edgar Allen Poe—and her cocker spaniel, Ralph Waldo Emerson.

ANNE KLARNER: Living in Chino Hills, California, with her computer-expert husband, Gary, and daughter, Cory, Anne is an active member of Mystery Writers of America. She has penned many novels, but this is her first published work. Anne has a Master of Arts in Theatre from California State University, Fullerton. Anne's hobbies include racquetball, home sewing, and reading. In addition to studying poisons, Anne is an amateur historian and spends many hours in research.